THE THIRD FORCE IN MISSIONS

THE THIRD FORCE IN MISSIONS
A Pentecostal Contribution
to Contemporary Mission Theology

Paul A. Pomerville

HENDRICKSON PUBLISHERS
PEABODY, MASSACHUSETTS 01961-3473

14-939872

CONTENTS

FOREWORD

The appearance of this long-awaited volume on the distinct contribution of the Pentecostal movement to contemporary mission theology is an occasion for rejoicing. Dr. Paul A. Pomerville is uniquely qualified to produce this study. He has fruitfully served the American Church, has been an effective field missionary in Indonesia, and has through diligent study acquired a solid grasp of the complexity—in theory, praxis, and theology—of the cross-cultural communication of the Christian faith.

Pentecostals are often described as evangelicals with a plus. By the plus is meant a dynamic and joyful experience of God that is deep and ongoing and which heightens one's sense of Christ's Lordship and the Spirit's leading. Along with this is the claim that the Scriptures become Spirit-taught, that prayer attains new levels of edification, and that personal holiness is reinforced in every way. Moreover, one's witness to the living Christ becomes more spontaneous and it is tangibly confirmed in the minds of those who hear it.

All this is true. Many evangelicals have been challenged by the immediacy and reality of God that Pentecostals reflect along with their freedom and unabashed willingness to confess openly their allegiance to Christ. The achievements of their churches are equally impressive, reflecting their settled conviction that the full experience of the Holy Spirit will not only move the Church closer to Jesus at its center, but at the same time, press the Church to move out into the world in mission.

However, because this plus is almost totally in the realm of experiential religion there are those who would question whether the Pentecostal movement has any substantive contribution to make to the Church's understanding of the theology of her worldwide mission. They would contend that the basic building blocks of a trinitarian theology of mission existed long before Pentecostals appeared on the scene: the sovereign electing grace of God the Father, the universal sufficiency of the gospel of God the Son, and the calling into being and empowering of the church to make disciples of all peoples by God the Holy Spirit. And yet, when one places this study by Pomerville alongside the classical form of Protestant mission theology, it soon becomes apparent that concepts and themes have been supplied from the Pentecostal frame of reference that add both comprehensiveness and strength to the older framework.

As you peruse this study you will find yourself not only increasingly appreciating and respecting the Pentecostal movement worldwide for its devotion to Christ and its missionary obedience. You will also become increasingly grateful for its significant contribution to the evangelical understanding of the missionary calling and increasingly grateful to God for the provision of His Holy Spirit to enable the church to rise more fully to its demands.

I rejoice in the privilege of commending this book to the Christian public. My prayer is that it will help many to attain a deeper sense of the significance of the Pentecostal movement. God has truly raised up this "Third Force" in the 20th century to "hasten the coming" of His day through accelerating the missionary obedience of His Church.

Arthur F. Glasser
Dean Emeritus and Senior
Professor of Theology and
East Asian Studies
School of World Mission
Fuller Theological Seminary

FOREWORD

A conspicuous feature of the modern Pentecostal movement from its beginnings at the turn of the century has been a passion for evangelism and missions. Sensing the urgency of reaching the lost before the imminent return of Christ, Spirit-baptized believers scattered to remote places with the gospel. These pioneers, often lacking adequate academic preparation and material resources, regularly established strong national churches in areas that seemed to others to be almost impervious to significant Christian penetration. Particularly in animistic cultures that were deeply conscious of the world of spirits and demons, Pentecostals frequently secured unusual response. Has such church growth been the result of sheer expenditure of physical energy? Did these people stumble onto some particularly effective technique? Or, is it possible that underlying the experience and the practice of the Pentecostals there is a theology which merits exploration?

Paul Pomerville, Assemblies of God missiologist, has attempted to probe the theological implications underlying the unusual contribution of Pentecostal missions to the modern Christian Church. In this volume, the author has demonstrated convincingly that Pentecostals, although deeply-indebted to conservative, orthodox evangelicalism, nonetheless, have a distinctive theological contribution to make. Drawing upon his considerable knowledge of historical theology, Pomerville makes the point clear that from the age of the Enlightenment scholastic Protestantism has extended its influence on modern evangelicalism. This influence is disclosed in an uneasiness with the supernatural manifestations of God's power, in an eagerness to ascribe as "superstition" a serious belief in the demonic. Pentecostals, conscious of God's power to take authority over evil spirits and satanic power, at this point are not quite identical to their evangelical "cousins."

ix

This book is important for several reasons. First, it is a serious call to Pentecostals to articulate their theology, not just as an apologetic for parochial consumption, but as a contribution to evangelical missiology. What Pentecostals have sought to emphasize, perhaps almost intuitively, now needs to be expressed with clarity and skill. Pomerville points out, incidentally, that Pentecostals run the risk of missing this opportunity by default should they permit evangelicalism to dictate the hermeneutical and theological agenda for them.

Second, this study is a penetrating analysis of the development of evangelical theology. Pomerville is gently suggesting to his dear evangelical colleagues an important reason for the disparity in penetration of animistic cultures between rationalistic-oriented fundamentalism and Spirit-oriented Pentecostalism. The historical roots of fundamentalism may need to be examined afresh, so that new directions may be explored that will occasion a fresh breath from the Spirit of God.

When Paul Pomerville asked me to read his manuscript, I became aware that he was writing a volume of unusual significance. He has issued a useful challenge to Pentecostals, who should be articulating their theology with greater clarity, and a challenge to evangelicals to consider new ways to make room for the empowering of the Spirit. In this way, Pomerville places missiology in a new light, with a consequent bright impact on a dark world. This book should be read thoughtfully by every earnest Christian who is concerned about reaching his generation for Christ. I suspect that this study will become one of the most provocative essays to emerge in the field of mission theology in this decade.

William W. Menzies
Vice President of Academic Affairs
California Theological Seminary
Fresno, California

PREFACE

As the Third Force in Christendom, Pentecostalism has a significant contribution to make to contemporary missions. The purpose of this book is to state what that contribution is. Hopefully, others will be stimulated to further theological reflection in the pursuit of a Pentecostal theology of mission.

The phrase "Third Force" was coined midway through the century when the phenomenal vitality and growth of the Pentecostal Movement became evident. Perceptive churchmen saw that, along with Roman Catholicism and Protestantism, Pentecostalism made up a "third corner" or "Third Force" in contemporary Christianity. However, this phrase was not only used to refer to the Movement's statistics or size. It was applied to Pentecostalism because the Movement revived a dimension of the Christian faith which had almost been eclipsed in the western world—the experience of the Holy Spirit. The demise of the experiential dimension of Christianity, therefore, is the backdrop for Pentecostalism's contribution to contemporary missions. This theology and experience of the Spirit must be used to solve contemporary mission problems.

A chief value of my approach to Pentecostalism's contribution is that the methodology is not polemical in nature. The fact that the author is a missiologist within the Pentecostal Movement does have its advantages. However, both mainline Protestant and Roman Catholic theologians are the chief sources for affirming the neglected doctrine of pneumatology in the common Christian tradition and its bearing on the issues of contemporary mission theology. Our effort is to enrich a Pentecostal theology of mission from the common Christian tradition but at the same time to develop fresh Pentecostal insights into contemporary mission issues. This somewhat "ecumenical" focus in this approach also includes the Pentecostal Movement in the non-western world. A major context of contemporary mission issues concerns the African Independent Church Movement. The notion that the African Independent Churches, for the most part, represent indigenous Pentecostal movements highlights a major issue of mission theology—the contextualization of the gospel in non-western cultures. The inclusion of these "hidden Pentecostals" in the worldwide Pentecostal Movement gives the western church numerous case studies of the incarnation of the gospel in African culture.

I am indebted to Dr. Arthur F. Glasser of Fuller Theological Seminary's School of World Mission for direction and advice in researching Pentecostalism's contribution to contemporary mission theology. Special appreciation is also extended to Dr. William W. Menzies for reading the manuscript, offering invaluable advice, and encouraging me to publish my findings, and to Dr. Ben Aker for his editorial contribution.

THE THIRD FORCE IN MISSIONS

Introduction

Missions from a
Pentecostal Perspective

This book draws attention to the Pentecostal contribution to contemporary missions. The notion of a contribution involves not only a worldwide Pentecostal Movement representing phenomenal growth but also a deficiency in contemporary missions. An inordinate "silence on the Holy Spirit" is part of the Protestant mission heritage. The Pentecostal Movement addresses that silence in a significant way. The value of this book for contemporary missions concerns the degree to which that silence affects God's ongoing mission in the world today. From the Pentecostal perspective that pneumatological silence is critical for the church's response to God's mission today.

Contemporary theologies of mission neglect the role of the Holy Spirit.[1] Max Warren refers to the neglect of the Spirit when he speaks of Pentecostalism and the Charismatic Movement as "protest" movements. He states that the movements protest the neglect of the role of the Holy Spirit and that they are a healthy correction to the torpidity of church life (Warren 1976,126). Michael Green also speaks of the neglect as a "domestication" of the Spirit in the West (1975,12). The silence on the Holy Spirit, though, is not restricted to western mission theologies. William Menzies speaks of a "practical subordinationism" of the Spirit in Christian theology due to the contextual focus of eighteenth and nineteenth century theologies (1979.68,71). The creedal statements of the church in those periods testify to the low profile of the Holy Spirit in western theology. The root of the "silence" concerns the contextualization of the Christian faith in western culture.

While pneumatology often took the place of an appendage to theology in the above mentioned periods, its absence in contemporary mission theology is especially conspicuous. Early in the century Roland Allen stated, "Missionary work as an expression of the Holy Spirit has received such slight and casual

3

attention that it might almost escape the notice of the hasty reader" (1960,21). In the last quarter of the century Allen's observation, at least in terms of the missionary role of the Holy Spirit, still holds true. Relatively little has been written on the crucial significance of the Holy Spirit in connection with the missionary witness of the church, a subject which Allen spoke of as "one whole hemisphere of the Spirit" (1960,21).[2]

Pentecostals are quick to recognize the neglect of pneumatology but slow to articulate it. However, Melvin Hodges, a classical Pentecostal missiologist, is specific in describing the neglect. He describes the silence on the Holy Spirit as a neglect of an indispensable qualification for missions—the enduement of Pentecostal power (1977,149). He links the relative success of Pentecostal missions directly with the "place" that Pentecostals give to the Holy Spirit, a place similar to that which New Testament believers gave to Him (1977,35). The phenomenal growth of the Pentecostal Movement and its dynamic missionary thrust support Hodges's claim. Such evidence should be worthy of the attention of the evangelical world.

The value of this book for Pentecostals is that it is an effort to articulate the Pentecostal contribution to contemporary issues of mission theology. It will help to fill in the tremendous gap that exists with respect to Pentecostal-oriented missiological literature. The missiological information gap may be due to the tendency of Pentecostals toward activism; they are "task theologians" (their theological focus being on the specific encounters of mission). Or, it may be due to the want of academic training in the field of missiology (or the failure to appreciate its importance for mission in the modern world). Nevertheless, the articulation of a Pentecostal theology of mission *is* crucial for the Pentecostal Movement. Pentecostals are frequently not aware that mission theory lays the necessary theological foundation for guiding mission practice. But mission theology provides a biblical criterion for evaluating mission activity in the light of the contemporary problems of mission. In examining Pentecostal mission theology in this study the perspective is limited to the somewhat representative classical Pentecostal viewpoint and, of course, my own specific theological viewpoint.

An Evangelical-Pentecostal Perspective

I will attempt to define my own evangelical-Pentecostal perspective in this introduction. It may be surprising for some evangelicals to see that the Pentecostal perspective differs little from the rest of evangelicalism in matters of basic Christian belief. However, it will become clear that the Pentecostal perspective has an "edge" when it confronts the experiential dimension of the Christian faith. This perspective is also crucial for exposing a fundamental distortion that the western world view has brought to the Christian faith—its intellectualization, or rationalization. It is a definite asset when assessing the worldwide Pentecostal Movement. A sympathetic approach to Pentecostalism is crucial when non-western expressions of the phenomenon are evaluated (e.g., African Independent Churches).

I view my Pentecostal-evangelical perspective as an asset to the study of Pentecostalism and missions. My Pentecostal experience, education (in part), ordination, and ministry took place within the context of the Assemblies of God fellowship. As a participating Pentecostal I have been identified with classical Pentecostalism's missionary enterprise, its presuppositions, and its norms and values. In other words, I represent an insider's perspective with respect to the Pentecostal world view and the Movement's missions efforts. This intuitive understanding of the Movement affords the opportunity to make a critical evaluation from the perspective of a sympathetic participant. Often new religious movements like Pentecostalism are not described with objectivity by outside observers. Numerous illustrations of this are found throughout this study. Especially poignant are those which emerge from a discussion of Pentecostalism in non-western cultures. From the standpoint of critics, the movements often "serve as spiritual ink blots, reports of the movements tell us more about the observers than about the observed" (Needleman 1978,142). My inside perspective, therefore, is crucial for articulating the Pentecostal contribution to contemporary missions.

An awareness of the value of one's classical Pentecostal world view does not mean the study will be excessively biased or doctrinaire in nature. On the contrary, such awareness allows for the control of bias. Research is always an interpretation. Bias is inevitable; pure objectivity is an illusion. However, one's bias can be gauged when it is explicit. Rather than a supposed "presuppositionless" approach, objectivity involves the elimination of "unconscious" presuppositions, values, and desires. "Scientific" objectivity concerns the recognition of possible bias and the implementation of means to control it. This study is approached with a consciousness of the impact that my Pentecostal world view brings to the task. World view is recognized as a context which impinges on interpretation.

Who is an "Evangelical?"

The term "evangelical" is as problematic as the term "Pentecostal." What does the connection of the two terms with a hyphen (evangelical-Pentecostal) mean? In the first place, it intends to communicate that Pentecostals are part of contemporary evangelicalism. But this still needs clarification, for who is an evangelical? David Bosch notes that Pentecostal-charismatics make up one of six distinguishable evangelical groupings: the new evangelicals, the separatist fundamentalists, confessional evangelicals, the Pentecostal and Charismatic Movements, the radical evangelicals and ecumenical evangelicals (1980,30). This non-Pentecostal recognition of the Pentecostals as an evangelical group identifies my perspective as evangelical. However, my evangelical-Pentecostal perspective is closer to the "new evangelical" group listed above than the "separatist fundamentalist" group. The theological distance between these two groups represents, somewhat, my own theological pilgrimage. Such a pilgrimage involves a more informed understanding of Scripture, theology, and the contemporary Christian movement. But it also involves a holding on to and continued appreciation of what is basic to one's evangelical faith and experience. At least, Bosch's groupings above show evangelicalism to be anything but a monolithic block!

In an article entitled, "The Split-Up Evangelicals," Billy Graham says that he would have a hard time defining what evangelicalism is today (Woodward 1982,89). The "split" the article refers to concerns the fundamentalist evangelical group, whose leader the article states is Jerry Falwell, and the more moderate middle of evangelicalism (the new evangelicals), who "shook off the separatist tendencies inherent in fundamentalism" (Woodward 1982,89). The article attributes the leadership of the latter group, at least symbolically, to Billy Graham. However, the identification of evangelicalism with particular persons only confuses the issue. This article does attempt to define and identify "evangelical" when it states that a generation ago an evangelical was a Protestant who emphasized: 1) personal commitment to Jesus (usually a "born again" experience), 2) biblical authority, and 3) a "preoccupation" with making converts (Woodward 1982,89). Rather than what divides evangelicals, the key to their identification and definition is what they hold in common.

The definition of "evangelical" properly concerns an identification of principles which can be found in the central Christian tradition, principles which are impulses from the "evangel" in the New Testament. Some have called these principles the "evangelical impulse." According to the threefold Reformation emphasis the evangelical impulse concerned: 1) the authority of Scripture, 2) salvation by faith, and 3) the universal priesthood of believers (Webber and Bloesch 1978,46-47).

However, a description of the evangelical impulse by which we may approximate the meaning of evangelicalism must reach beyond the fundamentalist phenomenon and work of nineteenth century scholastic theologians!

Seven principles that have been identified with the evangelical impulse in history are: 1) the authority of the Word of God, 2) orthodoxy (correct belief), 3) personal salvation by grace, 4) dedication and commitment, 5) evangelism and missions, 6) ecumenism (koinōnia), and 7) social concern (Ramm 1973; Inch 1978; Quebedeaux 1974 and 1978; Webber and Bloesch 1978; Bloesch 1973; and Dayton 1976). An evangelical, therefore, is the Christian who identifies with this particular configuration of belief and practice. Evangelicalism represents this "impulse" which spans not only the history of the church from Pentecost to the present, but which also spans the full ecclesiastical spectrum of the Christian faith in the contemporary world. No particular group is in focus, therefore, when one speaks of "an evangelical," but principles of belief and practice are. They are drawn from the New Testament and are illustrated in the central tradition of the Christian church.

Pentecostalism's distinctive experience with the Holy Spirit brings a fresh sharpness to the term evangelical. This distinctive experience with the Spirit causes the Pentecostal to reach back beyond the nineteenth century fundamentalist phenomenon, and the Reformation itself, to the "evangel" as described by the early church in the New Testament. As a renewal movement, Pentecostalism represents a renewal of first century Christian experience. But it has more to contribute to contemporary evangelicalism than a specific New Testament reference point (Pentecost). It brings a dimension of the Christian faith to light which has all but been eclipsed in western Christianity—the experiential dimension.

Pentecostalism adds an "eighth principle" to the evangelical impulse described above—the principle of the dynamic nature of the Christian faith. Actually it is not an additional principle, but an inherent part of the whole evangelical impulse. It is spoken of as an additional principle here because of its demise in the history of western Christianity. Pentecostalism represents the restoration of the dynamic dimension to each of the seven principles of the evangelical impulse. The eighth principle involves the *activity of God* in contemporary Christian experience, in terms of the ministry of the Holy Spirit.

Each of the principles of the evangelical impulse could be, and often is, held in an intellectual and static way, not at all reflecting the activity of God in them. The principle of the authority of the

Word of God is static and devoid of the activity of the Holy Spirit. Its *locus* is held to be the text of Scripture rather than the witness of the Spirit in the believer's heart as the Reformers believed. The criterion of biblical scholarship is frequently confused with the ministry of the Holy Spirit in this matter. The principle of orthodoxy is likewise held in a static manner, referring to it as an unchangeable doctrinal deposit handed down from either the sixteenth or nineteenth century. · The rationalization of the Christian faith is especially evident here. The assumption is that the results of the contextualization of the Christian faith in a specific period of the history of the church are absolute, normative, and perennial. This view of orthodoxy presents problems for the contextualization of the faith in contemporary times. The chaos that this distortion brings to the Third World by means of western missionary efforts is illustrated both by the failure to contextualize the Christian faith and the resulting independent movements in that part of the world. The principle of salvation by grace has often been intellectualized until conversion is interpreted as intellectual acceptance of correct doctrine alone, and faith is considered to be an "evidenceless" affair (apart from Scripture, that is) in evangelicalism. An expectation of the activity of God beyond the conversion experience is considered a *lack* of faith! Further, the last two chapters of the book show how the principles of evangelism and missions are distorted when the mediated activity of the Holy Spirit through the church is eliminated in mission thinking. The terms are redefined until conversion, evangelism, and Great Commission mission disappear in the church's mission to the contemporary world. So it continues with each of the evangelical principles, each can be merely a static concept and can thereby be distorted when the dynamic dimension of pneumatology is neglected.

When the "eighth principle" of the evangelical impulse is taken into consideration, however, the Christian faith involves a dynamic, living experience with God the Holy Spirit. God the Holy Spirit is active in connection with His written Word (the principle of the authority of the Word of God). Its authority concerns the witness of the Spirit confirming the Word in the hearts of men and women. Also, God the Holy Spirit is active in the contextualization of the gospel, in fresh applications of the Word to the life of faith in society (the principle of orthodoxy). Theology is seen to be a dynamic, biblical, contemporary process, serving the church in its contemporary life of faith. The inordinate fear of syncretism so frequently shown by western theologians toward Third World theologies would be dissipated if the dynamic dimension of these first two principles were in focus. God the Holy Spirit is also active in conversion missions today; the dimensions of the salvation experience are central to mission theology (the principle of personal salvation by grace). Therefore, the motivation, nature, and execution of missions principally involve the evangelistic mandate under the active supervision of God the Holy Spirit (the principle of evangelism and missions). God the Holy Spirit is active, as He was in the first century, in the areas of piety and worship (the principle of dedication and commitment). In the Pentecostal-Charismatic Movement, God the Holy Spirit is active in bringing into being an ecumenism born of the Spirit (the principle of ecumenism). God the Holy Spirit is active both in and independent of the church in meeting the world's total need (the principle of social concern). By means of the mediated activity of the Holy Spirit, God works through the people of God in the world to bring about justice and righteousness. His immediate presence and activity in this cause is a reality.

These seven evangelical principles mentioned here, especially in the context of the "eighth Pentecostal principle"—the activity of God the Holy Spirit—make up the general agenda of contemporary mission theology. This in itself is an indication of the potential Pentecostal contribution to mission theology. Pentecostalism involves the assumption of God's continuing activity in the world today, and this assumption addresses a major dimension of contemporary mission theology.

The Pentecostal perspective brings fresh insights on how God is active by means of the inward and outward ministry of the Holy Spirit. It is concerned with the "ontic" principle of theology and Christian experience. This refers to a view of the faith in which the Christian is seen to confront not only Scripture but also the Holy Spirit. The theological process and Christian experience have the character of presence, the "thereness," the immediacy of God. This process and experience represent a confrontation with the reality of God the Holy Spirit and the Living Word. Because the neglect of the Spirit pervades the various areas of mission theology, it is beyond the scope of this book to articulate all of the various implications of such a common denominator as pneumatology. The Pentecostal contribution presented in this study is selective in that only the major implications of the Pentecostal perspective for contemporary mission theology are discussed.

The connection of "Pentecostal" with "evangelical" by means of a hyphen (evangelical-Pentecostal) also indicates that, from the Pentecostal's viewpoint, his or her distinctive experience with the Holy Spirit is part of the "evangelical impulse." The assumption of a valid, contemporary Pentecostal experience not unlike that recorded in the New Testament is based on both the contemporary, empirical Pentecostal Movement and the description of that experience in the New Testament. Its contemporaneity as a renewal of New Testament Christian experience rests on biblical theology. It concerns the interpretation of salvation history in which the contemporary period of the church is viewed as continuous with that of the New Testament. This interpretation is based on the kingdom of God motif in the New Testament and the ministry of the Holy Spirit in "the time between the times" (Ladd 1974,42,139,271; Blauw 1962,73,79; Bright 1953,197,216-219,232; Filson 1950,75-76; Bosch 1980,66,236; Cullmann 1964,144; Montague 1976,367). It is in this assumption of God's continuing activity in the world today that the Pentecostal contribution to contemporary mission theology emerges.

Who is a "Pentecostal?"
The question, who is a Pentecostal? is even more problematic than who is an evangelical? An attempt to define the modern Pentecostal Movement is beset with numerous difficulties. Some of the major ones are: 1) its origin and manifestation among diverse Christian traditions, 2) its penetration and expression in diverse cultural contexts around the world, 3) its very nature, involving a personal spiritual experience, 4) the historic controversy as to its biblical foundations, and 5) the great diversity of theological explanations concerning the nature of the Pentecostal experience and the Movement itself. The term "Pentecostal" is used in this study to designate the wider renewal of the charismatic work of the Holy Spirit in all forms of Christianity.[3] However, three major streams of Pentecostalism that are usually recognized are: 1) classical Pentecostalism, 2) neo-Pentecostalism, and 3) Catholic Charismatics (Sandidge 1976,6; Hummel 1978,39).
"Classical Pentecostalism" refers to those Pentecostal churches which broke away from the historic churches of Protestantism in the early part of this century. The issue which occasioned this break was the belief that the event on the day of Pentecost mentioned in Acts 2:4 refers to an experience available to Christians of all ages. The "baptism of the Holy Spirit" was believed to be evidenced by the accompanying sign of "speaking with other tongues as the Spirit gives utterance" (Menzies 1971,9). The issue of glossolalia caused the historic churches to ostracize the "tongues speakers." It also became the prime unifying factor among early Pentecostals who came from diverse Christian traditions.
The term "neo-Pentecostalism" refers to that movement of the Holy Spirit in the late 1950s in the historic Protestant churches which emphasized the baptism of the Holy Spirit and charismatic gifts and graces of the Spirit (Sandidge 1976,8). A difference

between classical Pentecostals and neo-Pentecostals (or Charismatics as they are often called) is that those who have had the Pentecostal experience have not left their own churches. Therefore, the "Charismatic Movement," or "Charismatic Renewal," refers to a manifestation of Pentecostal life *within* various traditions of Protestant Christianity. This is not to infer, however, that their theological explanation of the Pentecostal experience is identical to that of classical Pentecostalism.

The designation "Catholic Charismatics," or "Catholic Charismatic Renewal," refers to the Pentecostal Movement within the Roman Catholic Church. This movement also involves a "baptism of the Holy Spirit" and manifestations of the gifts of the Holy Spirit. However, Roman Catholics prefer the term "renewal" to "Movement." Such preference is connected with the view of the baptism of the Holy Spirit as an actualization of what was already received at baptism and confirmation. The baptism of the Holy Spirit is conceived, therefore, as a "release" of the Spirit rather than an "incoming" of the Spirit. The Catholic viewpoint emphasizes important characteristics of the Pentecostal experience in a personal and sacramental sense as "renewal" (an experience with the Holy Spirit who is "already there"). From an historical perspective, the Pentecostal Movement *is* a renewal (Sandidge 1976,11-12).

There is an advantage in speaking of the theological diversity represented by the above three classifications as a Pentecostal unity. It is found in the consideration of the Pentecostal-Charismatic Movement as a "renewal movement," a renewal of the experience of the Holy Spirit like that recorded in the history of the first century church. The common denominator among all the theological diversity in the Movement, of which there is considerable even among classical Pentecostals (not to mention Charismatics!), is an experience with the Holy Spirit not unlike that experienced by first century Christians. Such an experience of the Spirit has punctuated the entire history of the church. The "Pentecostal Movement" in the sense of a renewal movement, therefore, reaches back to the work of the Holy Spirit which began on the Day of Pentecost and continues throughout the "last days" until Jesus Christ returns for his church.[4]

We must add to this description of renewal the resurgence of the charismatic experience of the Holy Spirit among the Independent Churches of the Third World. This movement of the Holy Spirit, however, does not require further classification in terms of Pentecostalism.[5] The Pentecostal Movement among the African Independent Church Movement (AICM), for instance, involves both the classical Pentecostal type "come out" churches described above (e.g., the Aladura societies among the Yoruba churches) (Peel 1968,73,109). There are 5,000 separatist churches in the AICM, virtually all of which were at one time movements within the mission churches (Barrett 1979,63). A movement which in 1980 represented a Christian community of approximately thirty million, being largely Pentecostal in nature, must not be missed in describing the worldwide Pentecostal movement.

Since the Pentecostal contribution to contemporary mission theology given in this study is from the classical Pentecostal viewpoint, further distinction should be made within this somewhat diverse major stream of Pentecostalism. In *The American Pentecostal Movement: A Bibliographic Essay*, David Faupel suggests the following classifications of classical Pentecostalism:
1. Those denominations which hold a Keswick view of sanctification
2. Those denominations which hold a Holiness view of "entire sanctification"
3. Those denominations which hold a "Jesus Only" view of the God-head. (1972,12)[6]

For a period of some fifteen years the Pentecostal Movement in America had no distinctive doctrinal shape because its membership was drawn from various Protestant traditions. Only the Pentecostal experience held them together (Menzies 1975,83; Faupel 1972,13). However, the theological issues of sanctification and pneumatology became the primary issues causing the above threefold division.[7] That threefold division also reflects the varied theological traditions which influenced the Pentecostal Movement originally—Wesleyan-Holiness and Keswickian-Reformed.

In an article entitled, "The Non-Wesleyan Origins of the Pentecostal Movement," William Menzies discusses the strong influence of Keswickian and Baptistic theologies on the Assemblies of God in its formative years (1975,86,88,90-93). In his history of the Assemblies of God, *Anointed to Serve*, Menzies states:

> From the Keswick wing of the Holiness Movement, chiefly through the agency of the Christian and Missionary Alliance with its Missionary Training Institute at Nyack, New York, came the Bible Institute program, the ecclesiology of the Assemblies of God, the missionary vision, the emphasis on divine healing, much of its early hymnology, and even a significant portion of its early leadership (1971,27-28).

The very title of Menzies's history, *Anointed to Serve*, illustrates the Keswickian view that the second experience referred to as "the baptism of the Holy Spirit" was an "enduement of power" for service. This contrasted to the Wesleyan-Holiness view that it was a cleansing from sin (Wesleyan eradication-perfectionism) (Menzies 1971,26).

The Assemblies of God has been recognized as a representative model of classical Pentecostalism.[8] Such an observation concerning the denomination points to the representative value of my general viewpoint in describing the Pentecostal contribution to contemporary missions. Even though my perspective is that of Keswickian Pentecostalism, this particular Pentecostal viewpoint may be considered as somewhat representative for the whole of classical Pentecostalism in the West.

In the attempt to address the Pentecostal contribution to contemporary mission theology, the discussion enters areas of theological controversy for which there is no Assemblies of God or classical Pentecostal position. Therefore, the somewhat fresh theologizing in this study from the Pentecostal viewpoint is occasioned both by the underdeveloped nature of pneumatology in general and Pentecostal mission theology in particular. Of course, in these cases the viewpoint given is my own.[9] Also, it should be noted that theologizing in these new areas is not characterized by primarily quoting Pentecostal theologians. In fact, those quoted are relatively few throughout the book. Rather the fresh theologizing in such areas is supported by biblical exegesis and reference to mainline Protestant and Roman Catholic theologians. In other words, the attempt to develop pneumatology in connection with mission theology is done on the basis of Scripture and the central Christian tradition.

The reader should also be aware that, due to Pentecostalism's main contribution falling in the area of the experiential dimension of the Christian faith, an emphasis on the Christian "experience" does not necesarily involve existential theology. Christianity *is* an experience with God. Chapter 3, "A Correction of a Western Distortion," discusses the distortion the period of Protestant Scholasticism brought to the central Christian tradition. Pentecostalism provides a corrective balance to the intense intellectualization of the faith that took place in that period. That it is necessary to qualify an affirmation of the experiential dimension of the faith is a testimony to the distortion in contemporary evangelicalism. Existential theology, however, was also a reaction to that rationalization of the Christian faith. Therefore, those theologians *do* provide some insights into the scholastic distortion of the faith. But Pentecostalism's emphasis on Christian experience is dramatically different from that of existential theology. The crucial difference is that for Pentecostals the hermeneutical horizon (the authoritative starting point) for theologizing is not human experience or a philosophical position but *Scripture.*

The quoting of Karl Barth, for instance, does not make one a "Barthian." Barth's theology was a reaction to Liberalism, a reaction to theologians who started their theologizing at points other than Scripture. For instance, to use some of his insights into the primacy of Scripture in theology does not mean that one has "bought" his total view of revelation. The reluctance of some evangelicals to pursue the experiential dimension of the Christian faith, however, goes deeper than avoiding existential theology. It involves the excessive impact of the western world view and scholastic theology on evangelicalism.[10] Some evangelicals may be content with the unhappy combination of a warm conversion experience and a cold intellectual doctrine and apologetic, but the Pentecostal cannot afford that tension. The very center of his distinctive is jeopardized—the dynamic, charismatic experience of the Spirit in the Christian life. Therefore, he must probe the depths of the experiential dimension of the Christian faith within the bounds of biblical theology for a consistent Pentecostal theology. One could say that for this reason Pentecostalism represents an alternative to a Liberal subjectivism (existential theology) and a Conservative rationalistic-objectivism (scholastic-fundamentalist theology). The thesis of this book is that Pentecostalism represents a biblical, relevant contribution to contemporary Christendom.

The "evangelical-Pentecostal"perspective described here claims to be rooted in first century experience, that which was normative in the documents of the New Testament. The Christian faith is rooted in history, and biblical authority is a prominent evangelical principle in contemporary evangelicalism. The multiple evangelical groups Bosch mentioned previously, as well as the multiple Pentecostal groups, represent an ecclesiastical-theological entity which identifies their belief and experience with the "evangel" of the New Testament. These facts catapult the issue of hermeneutics to the center stage of evangelicalism. Billy Graham has stated, "the issue of the '80s is going to be hermeneutics, or how to interpret Scripture properly and apply it to personal and social life" (Woodward 1982,91).

A primary effort of this study is to face up to this key issue of hermeneutics and to do fresh theological reflection concerning the issue from a Pentecostal and Reformation perspective. Part Two of the book is concerned with this crucial issue. Chapter 5 is devoted to the hermeneutical task as the idea of mission strategy is examined. The hermeneutical issue is central in a discussion of contemporary mission theology. Not only do the various approaches to contemporary mission issues reflect different hermeneutical methods, but the idea of contextualizing the Christian faith in non-western cultures and ethnotheology makes its discussion imperative.

Part One, "Pentecostalism: Distortion or Correction?"

introduces the phenomenon of the Pentecostal Movement by outlining its worldwide scope, examining its historical origins, and describing its theological nature. Part Two, "Pentecostalism: A Missions Contribution" continues the examination of Pentecostal theology focusing on its theological contribution in terms of the Pentecostal experience and the nature of mission strategy. The Movement's contribution to western Christendom is viewed as a correction of a fundamental distortion which has significantly impaired contemporary mission theology and practice. Contemporary mission issues are addressed from a Pentecostal-biblical viewpoint, using the much neglected biblical theme of the kingdom of God.

PART ONE:
Pentecostalism: Distortion or Correction?

1

An Emerging "Third Force"

The international Pentecostal Movement is a modern missionary phenomenon. Pentecostal historian Vinson Synan writes that the Movement in 1980 consisted of "over 50,000,000 classical pentecostals in uncounted churches and missions in practically every nation of the world" (1980,ix). While referring to the impact of the Los Angeles Azusa Street revival, Synan wrote in 1980:

> By this year, there are estimates of the number of pentecostals and charismatics in the world that approach the 75,000,000 mark. That would mean that roughly 1,000,000 persons per year have accepted the premises of the Los Angeles Pentecost in the years since 1906 (1980,xxiv).

Therefore, the Pentecostal Movement may be spoken of as a modern missionary phenomenon due to its rapid growth in a relatively short period of the Christian Church's history, and due to its international and ecclesiastical scope. The Movement has reached across a multitude of cultural frontiers in its missionary ventures. It has also penetrated all of the traditional expressions of the Christian faith.

The phenomenal growth of the Movement has been cited as a major cause for a change in the attitude of Christendom toward Pentecostalism. Generally speaking, an attitude of passive toleration in the early 1920s gave way to one of acceptance midway through the century. This acceptance was due to many factors. Among them was the appearance of the neo-Pentecostal Movement in the denominational churches, and the classical Pentecostal Movement's move into what has been called the "maximum efficiency stage" of organization (Synan 1971,223-224). Another way of referring to the latter factor would be to say that many Pentecostal "fellowships" began to be recognized as permanent

19

Christian denominations. In comparing the modern Pentecostal Movement with previous "abortive" charismatic revivals in the history of the church, Menzies states:

> It would not be until the modern, 20th-century Pentecostal revival that such a charismatic movement would enjoy the uniqueness of *survival*. The outstanding characteristic of the modern revival is that it has endured sufficiently long to be more or less accepted within the broader confines of orthodox evangelical Christianity. This has not happened since the first century (1971,28-29)!

With regard to the Assemblies of God, such acceptance was marked by their acceptance and participation in the National Association of Evangelicals. This was to the dismay, however, of separatist fundamentalist groups (Menzies 1971,183-184).

However, the phenomenal growth of the Movement, especially on the mission fields of the world, has generally attracted the attention of non-Pentecostal Christianity. Even those in disagreement with Pentecostal theology began to praise the Movement's missionary success. In terms of numbers, growth, and influence, the Movement was recognized to be at the heart of the international missionary movement. It was noted that "Pentecostalism and mission are almost synonymous" (Bruner 1970,32).

The factor of Pentecostalism's rapid growth and worldwide scope began to gain the attention of Christendom in a new way midway through the century. One of the earlier prophetic statements about Pentecostalism was Henry P. Van Dusen's coining of the phrase, "The Third Force," when referring to the scope and potential of the Movement (1958,113). Van Dusen spoke of the modern Pentecostal Movement as a new "Reformation," the emergence of a new, third major type and branch of Christendom alongside Roman Catholicism and historic Protestantism (1955,946). Van Dusen's statement referring to Pentecostalism as "The Third Force in Christendom" marked a change from an attitude of mere acceptance of a Movement, which caused some embarrassment to the Protestant world, to a patent acknowledgement that Pentecostals had a *contribution* to make to modern Christendom. Van Dusen stated concerning that contribution:

> The tendency to dismiss its Christian message as inadequate is being replaced by a chastened readiness to investigate the secrets of its mighty sweep, especially to learn if it may not have important neglected elements in a full and true Christian witness (1958,124).

Bishop Lesslie Newbigin in his book, *The Household of God* (1954), identified another potential contribution by the Movement. The idea of the "Third Force" was also inherent in Newbigin's evaluation of the Movement. He suggested that the Pentecostals may contribute to a Catholic and Protestant understanding of the church in terms of its dynamic dimension in the reception of and abiding in the Holy Spirit (1954,xi,24,82-83). This "three cornered" understanding of the church—Catholic, Protestant, and Pentecostal—echoes Van Dusen's idea of Pentecostalism as a Third Force in Christendom, only in terms of a specific contribution.

Various other non-Pentecostal theologians who examined Pentecostal theology also began to speak of the Movement's contribution to Christendom. While challenging the Pentecostal doctrine of the Baptism of the Holy Spirit, James D. G. Dunn began his analysis of Pentecostal theology by noting:

> The Pentecostal contribution should cause Christians in the "mainline" denominations to look afresh with critical eyes at the place they give to the Holy Spirit in doctrine and experience and in their various theologies of conversion, initiation and baptism (1970,viii).

In 1976 Kilian McDonnell, A Roman Catholic charismatic, stated:

> It does however seem both unrealistic and wanting in theological discernment for the non-Pentecostal world to write off the deep commitment, profound prayer life, and exceptional growth of Classical Pentecostals, from fifteen to thirty-five million people (1976,264).

With the increased attention paid to the Pentecostal Movement, due to its vitality and phenomenal growth, was a growing realization that the Movement may represent a renewal of neglected elements of the Christian faith.

The rapid growth of Pentecostalism on various mission fields was somewhat indirectly publicized in missiological circles through church growth studies designed to scientifically gauge the growth of the various Protestant churches. Such scientifically prepared materials helped greatly in drawing the Christian world's attention to the Pentecostal Movement as a "missionary" phenomenon. Several studies directed specifically to examine Pentecostal church growth, especially in the areas such as Brazil where Pentecostalism was flourishing, gave direct, reliable knowledge of the dynamics of Pentecostal growth and the extent of the Movement (Read 1965; Read, Monterosso and Johnson 1969; McGavran, Huegel and Tayler 1963; Montgomery 1967; Palmer 1974; Gaxiola 1970; and Smith 1970).

C. Peter Wagner in *Look Out! The Pentecostals Are Coming* (1973) centered attention on why Pentecostalism was experiencing phenomenal growth in Latin America. Wagner's sympathetic treatment and "church growth" analysis of Pentecostalism uncovered numerous causes for Pentecostal church growth. At the same time his work pointed to the basic dynamic behind such growth factors—the Pentecostal experience of the Holy Spirit

(1973,29,39,79-80). That Wagner also believed that the Pentecostal Movement provided a valuable contribution to contemporary missions is indicated by the new title of the 1978 edition of his book. It was changed from *Look Out! The Pentecostals Are Coming* to *What Are We Missing?*

Therefore, in the 1960s and 1970s it became known that the Pentecostal Movement was worldwide in scope and that Pentecostal communities were the fastest growing in the world (Synan 1971,223). It was predicted that Pentecostalism was to become the major form of Christianity in the developing nations (Marty 1975,196). However, some may question whether there is sufficient evidence to speak of the Pentecostal Movement in such hyperbolic terms as the Third Force in Christendom. These doubts may exist even in the light of the growing awareness of the impact of Pentecostalism around the world, its phenomenal growth, and its apparent potential for a contribution.

An Information Gap

It is a gross understatement to say that there is an information gap in evangelical Christianity's perception of the Pentecostal Movement. It is somewhat paradoxical that a Movement of such worldwide scope should have such a paucity of documentation (that is, in the English language). However, Pentecostals themselves are part of the reason for the information gap. They are not known for documenting their growth nor for articulating their theology. Traditionally their whole experiential-pragmatic orientation has tended to make them neglect such endeavors. Of course, the nature of the information gap referred to here is a lack of information about the nature and scope of the Movement. What is especially wanting is the type of information which the non-Pentecostal Christian world would deem reliable, such as works written under scientific discipline (histories, theologies, church growth studies, etc.). On the other hand, the lack of scientific materials may also be due to the lack of conviction on the part of some Pentecostals and evangelicals as to the usefulness of such materials. This is especially true with church growth studies; even the theological ground for such studies is often questioned (McQuilkin 1973,12-13,39-40).

Recent histories on the Pentecostal Movement in the United States, written by both Pentecostal and non-Pentecostal historians, have helped to clarify the nature and distinctives of the Movement. But when the challange of the *worldwide* Pentecostal Movement's existence is addressed, in non-western cultures especially, the proportions of the information gap are overwhelming.

Walter Hollenweger, author of the history and worldwide survey of the Pentecostal Movement, *The Pentecostals* (1972), is one of the most knowledgeable historians about the extent of the worldwide Movement. Unfortunately, due to the rapid growth of the Pentecostal Movement in some countries, the statistics as old as those found in Hollenweger's work are no longer adequate. In a subsequent article Hollenweger states that there is no reliable overview of the charismatic renewal in the Third World (1980,68). [1]

Hollenweger's observation that among the Pentecostals themselves there is an ignorance of the worldwide scope of the Movement is instructive. In addition to the experiential-pragmatic orientation of the Pentecostal, the general lack of appreciation for history and an active sectarianism among Pentecostals may be reasons for the information gap (Hollenweger 1972,413). Often numerous Pentecostal groups in relatively close geographical proximity know little about each other, not to mention their ignorance of the larger Pentecostal Movement in the world. This fragmentation of local Pentecostal movements, as well as the loss of perspective of a worldwide movement, must be counter-productive with regard to the effectiveness of their missionary thrust in the world. Apart from the benefits of a unified missionary thrust, such fragmentation must be apprehended by the non-Christian world as particularly unappealing.

The reason why a worldwide phenomenon like the Pentecostal Movement has existed relatively unknown in Christendom, however, cannot be explained merely by focusing on the Pentecostal's value orientation, neglect, or shortcomings. An examination of western Protestantism's complicity in regard to the information gap is also necessary. There are tendencies and factors in western theology and world view which shed light on the information gap. Some of the more influential are a latent ethnocentrism, a heritage of scholasticism, and the influence of dispensationalism. To varying degrees each of these tendencies can be attributed to the impact of the Enlightenment on western culture. They represent distinct liabilities for assessing the validity of Pentecostal movements, especially those in non-western cultures.

A Latent Ethnocentrism

First, the Pentecostal Movement's existence in a variety of non-western cultures presents a special problem with regard to the acceptance of such movements for western Protestant Christianity in general. This is especially true for indigenous Christian movements which exist with no formal ties with western mission churches, such as the "independency movements" in Africa. This aversion to other forms and expressions of the Christian faith is rooted in a traditional, latent ethnocentrism in western Christianity. Such a cultural-oriented expression of the Christian faith is well documented in the histories of western Christian missions. It is often characterized as the "colonial era" of missions. Oosthuizen cites the cultural development of western Christianity as the reason for the "western approach" in African missions. He explains:

> Hemmed in by Islam, the gospel had been accommodated to the social and personal life of European peoples to such a degree that the false idea developed that a nation can be conceived of as *corpus Christianum*. This fallacy is alive in the concept of Christian civilization. The synthesis that has taken place between gospel and culture in the west has not only affected the expansion of Christianity but distorted its very depth and vitality (1968,3).

Prior to the period of Protestant missions, Protestant Christianity became "contextualized" in western European culture due to isolation. Islam bracketed western Europe in the south and east, and Roman Catholic Spain and Portugal ruled the seas. It was contextualized to the point, according to Oosthuizen, where the gospel was severely impacted by western culture, even to the point of distortion.

The particular "distortion" inherent in the idea of *corpus Christianum* was that the western political-economic-sociological structure, religiously founded, was to be expanded throughout the world. Of course this idea of bringing western civilization to the peoples of Asia and Africa was supported by the belief that western culture and its expression of Christianity were superior. With the establishment of thriving, indigenous churches outside of western civilization, the concept of *corpus Christianum* died (Margull 1960,147). However, the death of *corpus Christianum* did not mean that western ethnocentrism died. The Christian faith was still "contextualized" in western culture in the missions sending countries. The idea of a propagation of western Christian civilization died, and perhaps the idea that western culture was superior diminished somewhat. But the idea that the western expression of the gospel was somehow normative did not die in western missions, nor did it die in *western theology*. The latent ethnocentrism in the western expression of Christianity remains as a potential liability for recognizing the validity of indigenous Christian movements.

Western Scholastic Theology

There is a growing awareness today that the gospel is supracultural in nature and that all cultures are valid for the expression of the Christian faith (granting the gospel is always intrusive in that all cultures must be transformed and redeemed by it). But the recent history of Christian missions still shows a latent ethnocentrism in the missionary endeavor. Although the distortion of western Christianity that Oosthuizen cites—*corpus Christianum*—is no longer a living concept in western missions, western theology is still highly impacted by the historical circumstances and influence of the Enlightenment. This introduces the second difficulty with respect to identifying valid Pentecostal movements in non-western cultures: Scholasticism, or scholastic theology.

Protestant Scholasticism in the post-Reformation period produced a theology which was greatly influenced by western culture. In the later post-Reformation period a rationalistic, static theology was influenced further by Common Sense philosophy—a highly ethnocentric view of reality (Pomerville 1980,73-75,78-80, 94). It is difficult, therefore, to separate the influence of scholastic theology from the discussion of a latent ethnocentrism in western missions. The discussion of the two must blend together at this point. The notion that theology developed in the West is somehow normative (often it is held to be absolute and perennial) is shown by the attitude of some western theologians and missiologists toward African, Asian, and Latin American theologies. Such endeavors are often under a cloud of suspicion in the minds of western theologians. Generally speaking, however, they only represent efforts of non-western peoples in theologizing from their *own* perspective of biblical revelation in the light of problems and questions in their *own* cultural context. Syncretism and heresies, both present and past, in western Christianity are forgotten by the western critics. Or, they do not seem as sinister as those alleged to emerge from non-western cultural contexts. The same attitude often prevails when considering indigenous Christian movements in non-western contexts.

Before the western theologian can attempt to remove the "mote" in the expression of African or Asian Christianity, he must first recognize the "beam" in his own expression of the faith. The problem in focus is not one that merely involves a fidelity to the gospel in non-western cultures and its distortion there. But it also involves a fidelity to the gospel in western culture and its distortion *there*. What distortions have resulted due to the impact of *western* culture on the gospel? The erosion of the sense of the supernatural has to be at the top of the list of distortions, as well as the eclipse of the experiential dimension of the Christian faith. The dynamic, biblical theologizing represented by the notion of ethnic theologies is in stark contrast with a static, rationalistic, scholastically-oriented systematic theology of westerners. The dynamic experiential nature of independency movements contrasts with the western cerebral expression of the faith. The nature and shape of western theology itself is often at the bottom of the western aversion to both indigenous Christian theologies and indigenous Christian movements—especially those of the Pentecostal type. A latent ethnocentrism influencing western theology and world view has been a major factor that has contributed to the information gap on Pentecostal movements in non-western cultures.

Dispensationalism

The third difficulty in assessing the worldwide scope of the Movement, dispensationalism, is combined with the two previous ones in a case study. The following study on the African Independent Church Movement (AICM) focuses on all of the major difficulties in the western approach and evaluation of such movements. One of the clearest evidences of a latent ethnocentrism in the history of modern missions is the phenomenon of independent church movements in the Third World. Add to the previously mentioned latent ethnocentrism the factor of Pentecostal phenomena, which are prominent in the movements, and a major potential difficulty emerges in evaluating the worldwide Pentecostal Movement. The Pentecostal nature of many of the indigenous Christian movements not only presents a problem for objective evaluation, but it has been the occasion for the rejection of the movements in the history of missions. Therefore, the bias against Pentecostal phenomena has largely contributed to the information gap on such movements.

Whether the westerner's difficulty with Pentecostal phenomena in the non-western indigenous movements is due to pure bias, sectarianism, or one's theological stance, such as dispensationalism (often a combination of these is the case), all of these have contributed to the information gap on the movements. Such theological attitudes and positions have created a parallel to what missiologists call "hidden peoples." "Hidden peoples" are those groups (whether geographically near or far) which are isolated from being reached by the gospel because of their cultural differences. These cultural differences act as an invisible cultural barrier which "hide" them, especially from those who bring the gospel to them from a diverse cultural background (Wagner and Dayton 1978:47). In a real sense, the above affective and theological biases against Pentecostal phenomena have created the "hidden Pentecostals."

The Hidden Pentecostals
Two representative works on the African Independent Church Movements (AICMs) are examined here. This case study illustrates

the impact of western ethnocentrism in relation to Christianity in non-western contexts. Another reason for the examination of the movements is to illustrate how the same "root causation" factor of the movements—the impact of western culture—is the same factor which tends to prevent objective evaluation of the movements today in the west. First the cause and nature of the movements are briefly discussed, using both the viewpoint of a recognized authority on the AICM and the viewpoint of an African participant. Then the two western evaluations of the movements are discussed, one a classic evaluation from South Africa, and another concerning Africa in general. An authority on the AICM, D.B. Barrett, views the phenomenon as

> representing a genuinely African response to the Christian faith. All center around the basic African concept of the people of God as a community and the legitimacy of Christianizing African traditional concepts and practices. They represent a creative response on the part of African Christianity to the turmoil and disruption that followed the breakdown of traditional patterns of life as a result of contact with the western world (1979,63).

Barrett underlines the necessity of accepting the "contextualization phenomenon" in understanding the movements. In other words, it is necessary to recognize the imperative of the gospel being "incarnated" in African culture, even though it is impacted by that milieu. Also it is necessary in order to recognize the inevitability of the impact of western culture upon that expression of Christianity and theology. The contextualization phenomenon, in accord with an "incarnational" concept of divine revelation, deals with a *twofold fidelity*.

First, contextualization involves a fidelity to the gospel as it is incarnated in culture. But it also involves a fidelity to the cultural context to which it comes. The Incarnation is the theological model for this view of the contextualization phenomenon. Barrett states concerning the former fidelity:

> Granted the spectrum of types, ranging from the ultraorthodox to the definitely syncretistic, almost all these bodies are nevertheless characterized by a clear acceptance, often under new and original African forms, of the centrality of the historical Jesus as Lord (1979,65).

Barrett views the AICMs as a single phenomenon with regard to their causation. He states that often local causes are emphasized, but in his analysis of the movements all over Africa there is a correlation between separatism and 1) a strong traditional African society, 2) a strong colonial impact, and 3) a strong missionary impact (1979,65). He states, "The correlation suggests that the underlying cause of the whole AICM is the clash of African culture with colonial and missionary cultures" (1979,65).

In an article entitled, "Identity Crisis in the African Church," Ngoni Sengwe views the origin of the AICM as a reaction of African Christians to a western cerebral-oriented expression of the Christian faith. Sengwe, once a member of an AICM, sees the movements as efforts of the African church to meet the felt-needs of Christians in their African cultural milieu (1981,93,95). Sengwe's theory of causation is supported by some of the best authorities on the AICM (D.B. Barrett, H.W. Turner, V.E. Hayward and others who are both western and non-western in origin). The theory chiefly has to do with the neglect, and at times, the direct destruction of the African world view and society due to its contact with western missions (Sengwe 1981,95).

The missionary neglect involved with this particular theory of causation is not only a "passive-avoidance" neglect of African society, perhaps due to ignorance of it or prejudice against it, but it also involves the western failure to respond *positively and biblically* to the vacuum created in African society after the western form of Christianity displaced so much of its traditional customs. Western missions not only failed to understand the African milieu sufficiently, but they also failed to articulate the biblical view of the supernatural so the African could apply it in his Christian life. That life concerned a sociocultural milieu dominated by the spirit world. The African lacked the necessary biblical models for living and coping with his environment "as a Christian." Sengwe speaks of the effort of the AICMs in restoring the "place of the supernatural" in African Christianity by providing such a biblical model (1981,95).

Both of the failures of western missions noted here are rooted in the western development and expression of the Christian faith. Due to the impact of the Enlightenment in western culture, with its emphasis on a rational, word-oriented faith, this faith was ill prepared to understand and empathize with African culture. It was also ill prepared to respond to African culture biblically in presenting the supernatural as represented by New Testament theology and pneumatology. Those areas of theology were seriously underdeveloped in western culture, due to the impact of the Enlightenment. Sengwe is correct when he notes that the AICM arose out of a clash between western culture and African culture, and *not* out of a clash between the *gospel* and African culture (1981,94). A primary factor in the contemporary rejection of indigenous Christian movements, therefore, is often a recurrence of the factor which caused them—a latent ethnocentrism.

Sengwe gives three reasons why missions and mainline denominations have ignored the AICMs:

1. The AICMs are not in "the camp"; they have no connection

with the mainline denominations
2. Their structures and worship patterns are "foreign": they may not be in line with western Protestant tradition
3. Dangers of syncretism (1981,92)

The same reasons, however, could be cited for avoiding and rejecting the early Pentecostal Movement in the United States. Also, the characteristics of the Zionist and Aladura-type churches that Sengwe points out in his article are essentially the same as those that historians of the Pentecostal Movement in the United States have discovered about their movement.[2] As early as 1963 H.W. Turner suggested that movements such as the Zionist and Aladura in Africa are non-western varieties of the worldwide Pentecostal Movement (1963,116). Both the indigenous garb and Pentecostal nature of the movements have been reasons why they have been neglected and rejected by western observers. In the western treatment of the AICMs often a combination of ethnocentrism, rigid scholastic oriented theology and dispensationalism are mixed together with an explicit bias against Pentecostal phenomena. Such treatments reveal the necessity of evaluations from a "native" perspective, both African and Pentecostal.[3]

One of the most quoted works on the AICM, which also is considered a classic on the movements, is Bengt Sundkler's *Bantu Prophets in South Africa* (1948). It should be noted that Sundkler's first edition represents a relatively early evaluation of Pentecostal-type independent churches (Zionist) in the problematic racial context of South Africa. The first edition of the work is a classic example of biased reporting of Pentecostal phenomena by a non-Pentecostal. It encompasses all of the above cited western prejudices.[4] The "ink blot" principle is especially evident in Sundkler's work. His account of the Zionist church movement reveals more about his presuppositions than it does about the phenomena taking place among the Bantu movement. Perhaps one of the chief contemporary contributions of the work is the lesson it illustrates concerning the contextualization phenomenon in this regard. Sundkler's world view and presuppositions were a *context* which impacted on his theology and perception of the target culture.

Sundkler's basic premise was that Zionist Christianity was a bridge leading Zulu Christians back to traditional African religion, to paganism (1961,17,196,240,259-260,262-263). He speaks of efforts of indigenization as "Bantu syncretism in the independent churches" (1961,196), and describes the movement as a "syncretistic movement of baptizers" (1961,201). The similarity of religious institutional forms and functions between Zulu traditional religion and Zulu Zionism (the African-Pentecostal expression of the Christian faith) is, for Sundkler, clear evidence of syncretism. In his estimation, this supports his "bridge to paganism" theory concerning the movements. He states, "The basic pattern from which Zulu Zionism is copied is that of diviner and witch-finder activities rather than that of the historic Christian church" (1961,242). However, the prophet-exorcist role Sundkler refers to is *also* represented in the New Testament and in contemporary Pentecostalism.

Basic to Sundkler's "bridge to paganism" theory is the out-of-hand rejection of apostolic-Pentecostal theology and a Pentecostal expression of the Christian faith (1961,259-260,262-263). Sundkler's theological presupposition, therefore, ruled out a Christian alternative which, if valid, brings his "bridge" theory into serious question. A Pentecostal expression of the Christian faith would allow for a "Christianizing" of the religious and social forms and functions that were so crucial to African society. It would also provide New Testament models and meanings with which to reinterpret their old customs and world view.

Pentecostal missionaries had been in South Africa since 1908. The "separatistic church movement," as Sundkler calls it, was dated as early as 1890 to 1910. The main secessions took place about 1917-1920 (Sundkler 1961, 48-49). Perhaps an indication of Sundkler's being a product of his time, especially in regard to paternalism, is his statement that the African Zionist leaders emerged due to the churches being "left in the hands of the Africans" by Pentecostal missionaries. Again, the difference in views of mission supervision of indigenous churches is evident, but the Pentecostal indigenous view here is in a pejorative context.[5] Sundkler *is* aware of Pentecostalism, at least from America (classical Pentecostalism) and England (Apostolic Faith, Irvingite Pentecostal tradition). Yet, Pentecostal phenomena are consistently equated with Zulu practice and only occasionally to western Pentecostalism, and then in a pejorative sense (Sundkler 1961,221). We do not deny here the possibility of non-Christian Pentecostal-like phenomena in the Africa context. We merely draw attention to the direction of Sundkler's bias with regard to Pentecostal phenomena.

Another classic example of a treatment of the AICMs, which exemplifies the combined factors of ethnocentrism, rigid scholastic theology, and a rejection of Pentecostalism, is G.C. Oosthuizen's *Post-Christianity in Africa: A Theological and Anthropological Study* (1968). This work also illustrates the use of Sundkler's book as a main source (27 references alone in a chapter on "The Holy Spirit Misunderstood"), with no mention of his repudiation of the "bridge to paganism" theory (Oosthuizen 1968,128-129). It is evident that Oosthuizen espouses this theory throughout his work, with the difference that he speaks of it as a "bridge to *nativism*." Oosthuizen's statement that *some* of the African Independent Movements develop into "post-Christianity" is eclipsed by the book's title (1968,xi). The title, *Post-Christianity in Africa*, accords with his "bridge to nativism" idea that is borrowed from Sundkler, and his nearly consistent reference to the movements as "nativistic movements."

Oosthuizen deals with the "independent movement" as a sociological phenomenon apart from the church. In his view, rapid social change causes African society to turn back upon its traditional world view—prophetism (1968,30). Oosthuizen believes the factors that give rise to independent movements are disappointment with white civilization and western Christianity, reactions against missionary paternalism, and an injunction of "the Spirit" (1968,60-61). He then summarizes:

> Basically, it is this: the misunderstanding by White-dominated
> non-indigenous Churches of the psychology, philosophy,
> languages, culture and traditions of the African, resulting in
> very little communication in depth and leading, via frustration,
> to *fanaticism* (1968,61, italics mine).

While pointing to the traumatic, in-depth impact of western culture on African Christianity, Oosthuizen still does not allow for truly "Christian" secessions from mission churches. He identifies the same dynamics in the origin of nativistic movements as that in the independent movements in Africa and, therefore, assumes that the presence of the same dynamics makes the AICMs also nativistic in nature! The context in which the AICMs take place is Christian, however. The movements represent secessions from Protestant mission churches (some of them even remaining in the mission churches, e.g., the Aladura societies). The same dynamics of deprivation and revitalization also take place in *Christian* movements (Wallace 1979,423). For Oosthuizen, an effort to contextualize the gospel in African culture is equivalent to the syncretization of the gospel with traditional African religion (1968,xiv). Therefore, in his view the movements are understood as nativistic movements, not valid Christian movements.

The dimensions of ethnocentrism and influence of a rigid scholastic theology emerge in Oosthuizen's discussion of the doctrine of the church. He does not call the movements "churches," due to their efforts to attain African identity! Indigeneity appears as a dilemma which a rigid western-oriented ecclesiology is unable to resolve.[6] Oosthuizen's presupposition is that churches cannot be "ethno-centric" like nativistic movements. His reasoning is that, "being ethno-centric, they are not churches; because the church can only be defined as the Body of Christ"

(1968,xiv). Oosthuizen uses the term "ethno-centric" as synonymous with "ethnic identity," which to him has the same pejorative connotation as does "ethnocentrism." He does not admit that the western church is an expression of the Christian faith contextualized in western culture, having ethnic identity, and in turn is not the "pure" Body of Christ devoid of cultural identity.

Oosthuizen states concerning the contextualization of the Christian faith in non-western cultures:

> Although some of the movements referred to in the analysis are *not* nativistic, they have nevertheless non-Christian elements in their bosom, as in the case of many Churches in Africa, which are easy bridges to nativism. All this shows how dangerous an emphasis on indigenisation or relevance for its own sake is for the Church, because it is easily misunderstood (1968,79).

Oosthuizen seems little aware that western churches also have non-Christian, western elements in their bosom, and this fact does not necessarily lead to a defection from the Christian faith. Furthermore, missiologically speaking, "relevancy" is never merely for "its own sake," but it has to do with a people's understanding of the gospel and its vitality in society in terms of its power and spontaneous expansion. While risk is present in indigenization, it evolves into a syncretism phobia, or a syndrome, when the factor of the Holy Spirit is omitted in the venture.

Reflecting the typical western "syncretism syndrome," Oosthuizen states, "Indigenisation or relevance of the church in Africa is most important, but this is a dangerous task, which should be based on sound theological judgment" (1968,xiv). Of course, by sound theological judgment he means sound "western" theological judgment. The subjective criterion which Oosthuizen uses to judge whether a movement is a "church" or not is the traditional "where the Word is rightly preached and the sacraments rightly administered" (1968,xiv). The western theological criteria used to determine what "rightly" means are: 1) the position on the Trinity held, 2) the position of the prophet in the movement, and 3) the function of the Holy Spirit (a vital force, numinous power, or the Holy Spirit glorifying Jesus Christ in men) (Oosthuizen 1968, xiii). If applied to classical Pentecostals in the United States by someone prejudiced against Pentecostal phenomena, this theological criteria would also rule out the Christian validity of the majority of Pentecostalism (e.g., the Jesus Only groups, and those emphasizing the gifts of healing and prophecy)!

The most important factor to observe here, however, is not subjective criteria applied by one prejudiced against Pentecostalism. Such a "syncretism syndrome" view of indigenization and "bridges back to nativism" view of independent movements reveals a serious deficiency in pneumatology. The domination of fear with respect to indigenization shows a serious undervaluing of the ministry of the Holy Spirit among a people in the venture. Indeed, the Spirit's ministry is entirely missing from the discussion. This "silence on the Holy Spirit" by western theologians reveals the pneumatological bankruptcy of such scholastic-oriented western theology.

In Oosthuizen's explanation of the rise of Messianic Movements in the context of Christian missions he says:

> In the Gospels the main theme is: "Fear Not!" The power of evil spirits is broken, and this makes an immense impression on the converts from the animistic world. But this relief creates a vacuum which is later filled again in times of crisis either with the old or with all kinds of utopian expectations (1968,87).[7]

While Oosthuizen is correct to mention the vacuum left in African society, the failure to mention the New Testament alternative for filling the vacuum—the Christian doctrine concerning the ministry of the Holy Spirit—is very conspicuous. In the power-encounter that Oosthuizen refers to in the above statement, pneumatology is ignored. He repeatedly refers to the missionary's message reacting against African tradition, creating a "vacuum" in society, and rightly so (1968,87). But he always speaks of the people filling the vacuum by a return to traditional African religion. Is it true that the gospel is inadequate in filling a spiritual vacuum left in an animistic African society after it turns to Christ? Is there no source of immediate contact with the presence and power of God? Or is it specifically the "western" expression of the gospel which was found to be wanting?[8]

Surely a people coming out of mainline Protestant mission churches, possessing the Scriptures in their vernacular, and particularly oriented to the spirit world would be aware of the New Testament alternative in filling the vacuum. Also, would not the Holy Spirit among them reveal His power in their situation? True, a western radically reduced expression of the Christian faith could not fill the vacuum, but a Pentecostal expression *could and did* in numerous cases. Also it is important to remember here that the Pentecostal expression of Christianity under discussion, as well as the majority of the AICMs, began in a *Christian context,* not African nativism.[9]

Oosthuizen's "bridge to nativism" theory is as lacking as Sundkler's early "bridge to paganism" theory. The theory fails when the *a priori* rejection of the Holy Spirit's apostolic ministry is considered in the light of the contemporary Pentecostal Movement. That expression of the faith is a valid Christian alternative for filling the vacuum in African society. The possibility that the AICMs may represent *a bridge to New Testament Christianity in the African context* rather than a bridge to paganism is not considered. As previously mentioned, this alternative of a Pentecostal-type ministry manifesting itself in the African context is supported by some of the leading authorities of the AICMs. Oosthuizen's silence on New Testament pneumatology in this respect points to a theological bias against Pentecostalism.[10]

Oosthuizen states that the great theological problem in Africa is the confusion that exists with regard to the Holy Spirit and ancestral spirits (1968,122). Recounting some of the charges leveled on the mission churches by the African Independent Churches he states:

> Their hostility against the missions was summed up in the accusation that they had no spirit in the congregations and they maintained that, with rare exceptions, none of the missionary evangelists had it either (1968,124).

He explains further that these missionaries did not fall in line with the ancestral cult like their (the AICM) prophets did (1968,124). Oosthuizen moves from a description of traditional African Animism to a description of worship in the AICMs without any discrimination whatsoever. For him, there is no difference, "The functions of the ancestor spirits have been transferred to the Holy Spirit, or simply 'the Spirit' so that in the independent post-Christian movements their 'holy spirit' is no longer the Holy Spirit of whom we learn in Scripture" (Oosthuizen 1968,129). Yet Oosthuizen rejects clear references to the operation of the spiritual gifts, such as those listed in 1 Corinthians 12 (1968,125). He not only fails to admit the insufficiency of pneumatology in western theology in the face of the needs of the African context, but he assumes that any spiritual manifestations on the part of the African are "ancestral spirits" and not the Holy Spirit. The question that emerges is, who misunderstands the biblical meaning of the Holy Spirit in this case, the African or the western theologian? Or does this situation under discussion reveal a deficiency on the part of both parties, at opposite ends of the theological continuum?

Furthermore, it is insufficient to merely point out a parallel between spirit-possession in traditional African religion and the Pentecostal phenomena in the AICM. The presence of oracles and ecstatic religion in New Testament times and its parallel with the New Testament experience with the Holy Spirit was no proof that the early New Testament experience was pagan. In the context of the discussion here we could ask, "Could it be that the parallel between pagan spiritism and Pentecostal phenomena is frequently pointed out because pneumatology in the minds of western theologians is such an esoteric subject?"[11] Of course, the problem could be merely a prejudice against a Pentecostal expression of the Christian faith.

The generalizations Oosthuizen makes concerning the Holy

Spirit and the AICM are reminiscent of the prejudicial charges made against early Pentecostalism in the United States. The validity of the activity of the Holy Spirit, in terms of apostolic-charismatic type ministry today, is problematic for many. It is relatively easy to attribute such activity in the African context to paganism, especially for the ethnocentric theologian. For in doing so, this frees him from the possibility of further Christian response. It also agrees with his western theological dichotomy of the religious "upper world" and the naturalistic "lower world." It preserves the western elimination of the "middle spirit world" and its deistic concept of the Providence of God. It will become evident in later chapters that such a view of the activity of God is at the bottom of major missiological issues. Also a dispensational theology is preserved which reserves charismatic phenomena to another period of salvation history. In other words, it is easier to fault the African world view than it is to fault one's own western world view and theology when considering contemporary Pentecostal phenomena.

A Reliable Estimate of Pentecostalism

The difficulties enumerated previously about the definition of the worldwide Pentecostal Movement also represent the problems involved with gathering statistics on it. The elusive nature of a definition, however, is nothing in comparison to the elusive statistical picture of the worldwide movement. The penetration of the Pentecostal phenomenon across the ecclesiastical spectrum presents a problem. This is the case with charismatic groups who do not want to leave the impression that they are a schismatic group within their own Christian tradition. Phenomenal rates of growth also add to the difficulty of obtaining current statistics; they are almost an impossibility on a worldwide scale. The presence of the Pentecostal phenomenon among a diversity of cultural contexts has also presented difficulties with its identification. This diversity has also impeded the statistical enumeration of the groups. The question, Who is Christian? becomes problematic with non-western Pentecostal movements.

Frequently, legalistic Pentecostal groups have a large number of affiliated persons who, although they are Pentecostal in experience, are not included in the membership statistics. Often the reason for this is their non-conformity to a particular practice which is required for membership. This factor in itself renders Pentecostal statistics to be less reliable. Often adherents number as many as the membership of a church. The Assemblies of God statistics for El Salvador show 43,000 baptized members and 95,000 "other believers." The Statistics for Guatemala show 43,000 baptized

members and 78,015 "others believers." Brazil shows 3,350,000
baptized believers with 2,750,000 "other believers" (Division of
Foreign Missions 1981,7). The fact that the Pentecostal
phenomenon involves a spiritual experience which can be
interpreted differently according to one's particular theological
tradition and perspective also complicates the statistical task. The
question, who is Pentecostal? then becomes problematic. Add to
the above difficulties an incipient ethnocentrism toward non-
western expressions of Pentecostalism and a prejudice against that
expression of the faith, and you have a picture of the difficulty in
gaining a reliable estimate of the worldwide Pentecostal
Movement.

Various figures concerning the scope of the Movement have
already been suggested by various persons quoted in the chapter.
The figures: thirty-five million, fifty million and seventy-five
million have already been mentioned. Are these Pentecostal claims
about the Movement exaggerated? Is the assessment of non-
Pentecostal churchmen, theologians and missiologists about the
significance of the Movement hyperbolic in nature? Does
Pentecostalism deserve the accolade, "The Third Force in
Christendom?" A survey of available statistics on the worldwide
Movement, growth rates of Pentecostal-charismatic communities,
and reports of Pentecostal leaders indicate that the commonly
reported statistical picture of the Movement's scope is too
conservative. Rather, the typical view of its scope is something like
the "tip of the iceberg," or to use a more appropriate metaphor,
like "a wisp of smoke from a rapidly spreading flame."

The section title, "A Reliable Estimate of Pentecostalism," was
chosen due to these difficulties involved with gathering statistics on
the worldwide Movement. A proper statistical survey would
consume a book in itself if it were comprehensive, accurate, and
up-to-date. The term "reliable" refers to the effort to base the
estimate on the best information available. D.B. Barrett's *World
Christian Encyclopedia* (1982) represents a monumental survey of
the Christian faith worldwide. This comprehensive volume presents
data from which a reliable estimate can be made. Many of the
problems mentioned previously are overcome in Barrett's work.
The work surveys 150 major ecclesiastical traditions, 20,800
distinct Christian denominations, and the status of Christianity in
223 countries.

Barrett's information concerning Pentecostalism is significant
due to his sympathtic and knowledgeable grasp of the Pentecostal
Movement in the non-western world. Although some of his
statistics are based on the years 1970-72 (1982,46), projections of
growth are given based on growth rates up to 1985. Of course, the

significance of Barrett's statistics must be measured by his methodology.[12]

In this book Pentecostals are classified in three major streams: 1) classical Pentecostals, 2) neo-Pentecostals, and 3) Catholic Charismatics. However, there are many tributaries within these three main streams that Barrett mentions in his *World Christian Encyclopedia*. His "Global Tables" show the following charismatic classifications: Roman Catholic Pentecostals, neo-Pentecostals, and Catholic Pentecostals (non-Roman, apostolic-type, Irvingites) (Barrett 1982, 782-783). Barrett explains that the statistics on charismatics serve merely to aid in understanding the scope of charismatic renewal, because of their tendency to avoid the image of schism in the church.[13] Also the statistics given for charismatics are often limited to the "practicing Christian" category.

A significant statistic that Barrett gives for charismatic groups, however, is their phenomenal *rate of growth*. For instance, in Africa, Catholic Pentecostals are growing at an unbelievable rate of forty-five percent per year, neo-Pentecostals at twenty-seven percent per year, and Anglican Pentecostals at twenty-five percent per year. Other Christian groups are reported at two to five percent growth per year. The same phenomenal rate of growth for Pentecostals holds for the other continents as well (Barrett 1982, 782-783). Barrett states:

> Our Tables 1 [country by country survey] envisage phenomenal growth in the number of Catholic charismatics (pentecostals) in South America, rising by AD 2000 to 7 million in Brazil alone....This projection is based on present trends; but many observers hold it to be distinctly probable that within the next decade or two the trends may be accelerated and the leadership or even the bulk of the laity in Latin American Catholicism may become predominantly charismatic (1982,69).[14]

Barrett gives the total number of charismatic Christians in the above classifications worldwide to be 14,444,830 in 1985 (1982,6).

Barrett divides classical Pentecostalism into two basic, separate ecclesiastical traditions: 1) White classical Pentecostalism, and 2) Non-White or Black/Third World pentecostalism ("Pentecostal" with a capital *P* always refers to classical White Pentecostalism in Barrett's work). He states concerning this classification:

> This distinction between Pentecostal and pentecostal is made here to make it clear that these are 2 separate ecclesiastical traditions. Non-White or Black/Third-World pentecostalism has arisen, outside the USA, quite independently of Classical Pentecostalism; and within the USA itself, Black pentecostalism has some claim to have preceded White Pentecostalism in time, to be a phenomenon distinct and separate from it, and to itself be regarded as the classical tradition (1982,81).

But Barrett's subtypes within each of these main Pentecostal traditions are the same. Barrett's principle of determining distinct classifications within the main traditions is both ecclesiastical and theological. The nature and number of subsequent experiences with the Holy Spirit in post-conversion experience are the main discrimination factor.[15]

The significance of Barrett's classification is that it recognizes non-western Pentecostal expressions of the Christian faith. His classification tends to present the worldwide Movement as a unity, although the separate traditions are affirmed. This is so because the focus is on the common Pentecostal experience of the Spirit; it is this that is set forth as the Pentecostal distinctive. Barrett's use of the same subtypes in the indigenous Pentecostal Movements shows that he considers them to be parallel Pentecostal expressions of the Christian faith, only in diverse cultural contexts. Also with regard to the origins of the worldwide Movement, the common experience of the Spirit in the diversity of cultural contexts suggests a unity in the Movement and the probability of a spontaneous worldwide outpouring of the Spirit. There is evidence of historical-causal linkage between some of the various ecclesiastical traditions, but with others there is no such historical-causal connection. This phenomenon is discussed in detail in chapter 2.

Barrett gives the figure of 21,909,778 for the White classical Pentecostals worldwide, and 29,257,409 for the Non-White indigenous Pentecostals for 1980 (1982,14). Adding to these 29,257,409 indigenous Pentecostals Barrett's combined figure for all classical Pentecostals and all Charismatics—49,235,400—and a total of Pentecostal-charismatics worldwide of 78,492,800 emerges. However, in the "Dictionary" section under the heading, *Pentecostal-charismatic,* the Encyclopedia states:

> A blanket term [is Pentecostal-charismatic] for all Pentecostals, pentecostals, neo-Pentecostals, and charismatics (qv). Global totals (1980) [include]: (a) active regularly-involved persons, 62,200,000; (b) all persons professing or claiming to be Pentecostal-charismatics, over 100 million worldwide (Barrett 1982,838).

There is every reason to believe that Barrett's figure of "over 100 million worldwide" for Pentecostal-charismatics is a "reliable estimate."

There is even reason to believe that the actual number of Pentecostal-charismatics worldwide exceeds the 100 million figure. The phenomenal growth rates of Charismatics and neo-Pentecostals on all continents makes one expect a greater global figure for this category. But in view of the identity problem mentioned previously, it is not surprising that the statistics are as low as they are. A statistical picture emerges, however, which is smaller than it should be. The large adherent communities, or "other believers," that are not always reported in Pentecostal membership statistics tend to make those figures low also,[16] and not represent the true scope of this segment of the worldwide Movement. The problem with regard to the identification and acceptance of the largest and most rapidly growing Pentecostal group, the non-western indigenous Pentecostals, is a reason for the probable underestimation of that group. The problem of obtaining *current* statistics is also another factor which tends to make the 100 million figure too conservative.[17]

The purpose of the discussion here has been to bring into focus a reliable estimate of the worldwide Pentecostal Movement so that its scope and, therefore, its significance could be considered. Both its scope and rate of growth are phenomenal; the designation, "Third Force," in Christendom is appropriate. In fact, it may approach a literal truth. In Barrett's "Definitions of types of Christians" graph, he shows three categories of Christians from the standpoint of "belief:" 1) uncommitted Christians—350 million, 2) partially committed Christians—303 million, and 3) Committed Christians —780 million. The last category is broken down further into 420 million Christians who attend church weekly and confess to be "born again" (Barrett 1982,49). Of course, Barrett's definitions and qualifications must be read in order to appreciate his categories. However, when the estimates of Pentecostal-charismatics worldwide are placed against this figure of "committed-born again" Christians, Pentecostalism may not only represent a significant group of Christians and may, therefore, be called a "Third Force," but may in reality come close to representing nearly a third of this group of committed Christians.

2

A Renewal Movement

A discussion of the origins of the Pentecostal Movement is crucial
and instructive in discovering its true nature. The matter of origins
concerns more than an interest in the historical roots of the
Movement simply for the purposes of nostalgia or identifying
founders and the various streams of Pentecostalism today. A
theory of origins sheds light on the very nature of the Pentecostal
Movement itself. In the last analysis, the matter of origins concerns
a theological issue—salvation history. Therefore, the methodology
one uses in attempting to understand a movement whose origins are
universal and spontaneous, a renewal of the Spirit in salvation
history, must be appropriate to the phenomenon under
investigation.

The Necessity of a Holistic Approach
A holistic approach is necessary for an examination of the
Pentecostal Movement. We must approach the task recognizing the
Movement as not only a phenomenon taking place in a human,
sociocultural milieu, but one which takes place as a divinely
initiated phenomenon. The importance of a balanced approach,
giving each dimension (divine and human) its appropriate
emphasis, is illustrated here by two contemporary European
accounts of the American Pentecostal Movement. Both the account
of W.J. Hollenweger and that of Nils Bloch-Hoell represent
imbalanced treatments with regard to the divine and human
dimensions of causation and, therefore, represent distortions of the
true nature of the Movement. Also theories about the origins of the
Pentecostal Movement are examined, comparing historical-causal
theories with a theory emphasizing the universal and spontaneous
origins of the worldwide movement. Giving a priority role to the

divine dimension of the Movement is also necessary in formulating a theory of origins.

What is the nature of this Movement which in less than a century has become a "Third Force" in Christendom? Should the various worldwide Pentecostal "outpourings" be perceived as one movement because it began with a particular Christian group in a particular geographical location? Did it then spread outward from its site of origin to other groups in other parts of the world? Can such historical-casual linkage between the various Pentecostal revivals in the world be established? Or is the Movement "one" because its origins, for the most part, were universal and spontaneous? A more fundamental question in this regard is, What is a movement? Or more specifically, When does the Pentecostal phenomenon become a Movement?

Some historians focus their treatment on the sociocultural contexts in which the movements emerge, citing various socioeconomic theories of causation. Others emphasize the divine element in the movement, pointing to the factor of the sovereign act of God in connection with their origins. Others, emphasizing the divine element, view the movements as renewals or restorations of certain neglected characteristics or potentials of the Christian faith in contemporary times. Earlier critics of the Pentecostal Movement in America, and more recent critics in Europe, emphasized the influence of demonic activity with regard to the question of origins (Hollenweger 1972,226,228). However, most of the recent critics of the Movement emphasize its human dimensions by citing psychological, social and cultural theories of causation.

Due to the incarnational nature of divine revelation, *Christian* movements involve both a divine and a human dimension.[1] The divine Word is enlivened by the Holy Spirit *in* human sociocultural contexts. Men and women respond in faith in a variety of human circumstances, and some of those circumstances are highly productive in heightening "expectant" faith. A fidelity must be shown toward both the divine and human dimensions in the effort to understand the movements. A holistic, multidisciplinary approach to the subject of origins is needed, with an emphasis on the theological dimension.

A prime example of the failure to hold in tension the two major dimensions of a movement is the case of the African Independent Church Movement (AICM). The AICMs are commonly viewed as "reaction movements." Observers usually focus on the socioeconomic and cultural dimensions of the movements, the human context. The theological dimension of causation—the deficiency of western theology in meeting the needs of African society—has had a very low profile in discussions of causation.

Focus on the theological dimension reveals a positive response of African Christianity to biblical revelation, appropriating a Pentecostal expression of Christianity. Such an expression of the Christian faith addressed the problems, questions, and needs of African society. The nature of the Movement as an indication of God pouring out his Spirit on African Christians who were responding to the New Testament is overlooked. It is overlooked due to the overemphasis on the human dimensions of the movements' origins to the point of excluding the divine.

All the approaches to origins are important in comprehending the complexities of the phenomenon, especially in its non-western context. In discussing the various contributions of the social sciences and religious phenomenology, Oosterwal qualifies in the following way the meaning of a holistic approach to messianic movements:

> A *holistic understanding* is more than the sum of these different contributions. It is an insight gained only by an approach that considers the social *and* the cultural-historical *and* the psychological *and* the religious aspects as parts of one total whole of which the *theological* (ideology) is the creative center, and the cement that binds them together in one integrated whole (1973,30).

Emphasis on any one of the approaches to the exclusion of the others can distort one's perception of the nature of religious movements. Often an observer's world view or presuppositions tend to make him emphasize only one dimension of the movements. This is especially the case in western culture with the scientific approach. Often an overemphasis is given to the human dimensions of Pentecostal movements. It should be noted, however, that Oosterwal gives a special integrative role to the religious or theological dimension. The reason for this is that divine revelation is involved.

One of the major factors which militates against a holistic approach to religious movements, especially Pentecostal movements, is the prominence of the anthropological concept of "nativistic movements" and its corresponding theory of causation—"deprivation." Linton states that a nativistic movement is "any conscious organized attempt on the part of society's members to revive or perpetuate selected aspects of its culture" (1979,415). This definition focuses on the *human* dynamics and context of the movement. A.F.C. Wallace views the nativistic movement as a subclass of a larger class of phenomena called "revitalization movements."[2] He describes revitalization movements as "the deliberate, conscious, organized efforts of the members of society to create a more satisfying culture" (1979,429). High stress on the members of society often results in a distortion of their cultural *Gestalt* (Wallace 1979,429). Wallace, however, does not confine "deprivation" to the human-empirical dimension, as does Linton.

Linton notes that inherent in "deprivation theory" is the assumption that religious change, or a movement's origination, is the result of psychological, social, economic, or political deprivation.[3] The theory focuses clearly on the human dimension and context of religious movements. While deprivation theory is useful for the insights it brings concerning the human-cultural context and background of religious movements, it must be used with care. One must disassociate its reductionistic tendencies about the supernatural from its otherwise valid insights. Both of the concepts discussed above view religious movements as reactionary movements. The members of a society attempt to reduce stress on their culture. That stress is usually due to a society's contact with another culture (Wallace 1979,422-423). While the idea of reaction is important for the origins of religious movements, the reaction should not be limited to phenomena originating in the human context (socioeconomic, political, cultural, etc.). However, this is often the case. Deprivation can also refer to "spiritual deprivation," or deprivation of the supernatural. This appears to be the case with the origins of both the classical Pentecostal Movement and also the African Independent Church Movements.

"Religious" movements to a non-Christian anthropologist, on the basis of his presuppositions, may not include special revelation or the supernatural intervention of God. A "Christian" movement, however, would necessarily involve the dimension of special revelation. A definition of "movement" would necessarily include both the human-cultural dimension and the supernatural-revelational dimension. Both dimensions would be considered in the question of a movement's origins. But even the inclusion of both dimensions in one's approach to the origins of the Pentecostal Movement, for instance, is no guarantee of a balanced approach. If one's presuppositions do not allow for supernatural "break-throughs" in contemporary times, then his view of the origins of the movement will reflect this bias. The tendency would be to emphasize the human factors of causation. The case of the AICMs, of which many are clearly Pentecostal expressions of the Christian faith in African society, is an illustration of this tendency or bias. Often socioeconomic, sociocultural, and "religious" factors (pagan) are the predominant factors used to explain causation. The factor of an eschatological Pentecostal outpouring of the Spirit is seldom considered when dealing with causation.

The whole discussion of origins, therefore, calls attention to the nature of Pentecostalism. W.J. Hollenweger's description of the American classical Pentecostal Movement's origins illustrates the above reductionistic tendency. He emphasizes the human dimensions of the Movement to the extent that its divine nature is called into question. His analysis of the precipitating factors of the Movement eclipses the fact of divine visitation. Speaking of the origins of the American Movement Hollenweger states, "The origins of the Pentecostal Movement go back to a revival amongst the negroes of North America at the beginning of the present century" (1972,xvii). He states further concerning the Azusa Street revival:

> The "Pentecostal experience of Los Angeles" was neither the leading astray of the church by demons (as the German Evangelical Movement claimed), *nor the eschatological pouring out of the Holy Spirit* (as the Pentecostal Movement itself claims) but an outburst of enthusiastic religion of a kind well-known and frequent in the history of Negro churches in America which derived its specifically Pentecostal features from Parham's theory that speaking with tongues is a necessary concomitant of the baptism of the Spirit (1972,23-24; italics mine).

This "origins" statement, linking causation with the American "Negro enthusiasm" is followed by the lame qualifier: "I do not wish to assert here that the Holy Spirit was not at work in the Los Angeles revival" (Hollenweger 1972,24)! Apparently Hollenweger sees the operation of the Holy Spirit limited to an ecumenical effort in bringing together American White and Black Christians in the Azusa revival.

Hollenweger's denial of the eschatological outpouring of the Spirit in Pentecostal fashion (the theological issue) is crucial. The central role of Black "holiness" Christians in the early American Pentecostal Movement cannot be disputed, nor can we doubt that their world view and West African cultural heritage were reasons for their being open to the Pentecostal expression of Christianity. However, Hollenweger misuses this information about the context of the revival. He appears to want to give the impression that the Pentecostal Movement in the United States was a Negro "enthusiast" expression of Christianity rather than a renewal of New Testament Christianity. A precipitating factor of readiness, or the Black's orientation to the spirit world, is used to explain away the eschatological phenomenon of glossolalia. Of course, Hollenweger denies that speaking in tongues is the initial evidence of the Pentecostal experience. This is in spite of the fact that tongues speaking is widely held to be the identifying mark of the Movement (Atter 1962,7). This bias leads Hollenweger to attribute the religious phenomena of Azusa Street to Black enthusiast religion.[4]

The divine-vertical dimension of God's eschatological act in pouring out the Holy Spirit upon his people is lost in the human-horizontal analysis. Such reductionistic, imbalanced explanations which ignore the creative center of the Movement—the renewal of the Spirit in salvation history—seriously distorts its true nature.

Nils Bloch-Hoell's view of the Pentecostal Movement is similarly imbalanced with regard to the divine dimension. While he notes that the Pentecostal Movement is regarded as a revival movement even by non-Pentecostal observers, he chooses to disregard the spiritual dynamics of the Movement. He states, "the dynamic character of the movement, then, is connected with a primitive emotionalism" (1964,49) and "is ecstatic in nature" (1964,173). His description of those participants in the Pentecostal Movement in North America strongly reflects his biases about the nature of the Pentecostal phenomena. He states that Parham was mentally unstable, a homosexual, and "probably was a neurotic" (1964,19-21,193). Miss Ozman, the first to speak in tongues in Topeka, Bloch-Hoell states, "must have been of a nervous constitution" (1964,23). He notes concerning Frank Bartleman, chief chronicler of the Azusa revival, that he "had ecstatic experiences and was undoubtedly a neurotic" (1964,32). Bloch-Hoell, therefore, sees the early Pentecostal manifestation of tongues as psychological-pathological in nature (1964,23-24). That view dominates in his treatment of Pentecostal phenomena (Bloch-Hoell 1964,26,28,42,199).[5]

A presupposition of empirical scientism controls Bloch-Hoell's evaluation of the Pentecostal Movement. Rather than a presupposition of "faith," in which biblical authority is the basis for evaluation, the science of religion is used as an authoritative base. The Pentecostal experience is described as "rapturous ecstasy and mysticism" and explained wholly in psychological terms (Bloch-Hoell 1964,174). If there is no rational-scientific explanation for ecstasy, then no explanation exists for Bloch-Hoell. He represents a rationalistic-scholastic response to supernatural phenomena; faith is totally subordinated to reason in the discussion of the Pentecostal experience. Of course, his treatment of the origins and nature of the Pentecostal Movement is greatly distorted.

Both of the above approaches to the Pentecostal Movement are reductionistic. Behind Hollenweger's reductionism is a theological presupposition concerning the issue of tongues in the Movement. His imbalanced treatment about the origins of the American Pentecostal Movement violates the "theological center" of the Pentecostal phenomenon itself—that it is an eschatological renewal of Pentecostal Christianity. Methodologically, he shifts from that theological center to one emphasizing peripheral, precipitating factors.

Bloch-Hoell's reductionism is more severe due to the limits set by the methodologies and presuppositions of the disciplines he uses exclusively. Oosterwal states in this regard:

> The sciences of anthropology, psychology, and phenomenology, which have contributed so much to our understanding of messianic movements, are not able to cope with this aspect of the issue [the relationship between revelation and the crisis context] since it is beyond the limits set by their own disciplines (1973,13).

Bloch-Hoell's approach to origins rules out that crucial theological center of the Movement *a priori* by his scientific empiricism. Presuppositions contrary to those of New Testament Christianity control his analysis. His approach is like that of a truncated biblical theology; historical critical methodology is present, but biblical theological presuppositions and interpretation are missing. Such methodology is insufficient for probing the depths of a Christian movement, and it is certainly inappropriate for examining the origins of a *Pentecostal* Movement.

The "Jerusalem-Centrifugal" Theory

Perhaps the extensive documentation of the Pentecostal Movement in the United States, with the corresponding paucity of information on the worldwide Movement and the catalytic nature of the Azusa Street revival, contributes to why the United States is often cited as the origin of the worldwide Pentecostal Movement. Another possible source for this viewpoint is the feelings of those who participated in the Azusa Street revival. In the eyes of Frank Bartleman, Chronicler of the revival, the Pentecostal outpouring in Los Angeles was the world's second "Pentecost." He states:

> I wrote further in "Way of Faith" August 1, 1906: "Pentecost" has come to Los Angeles, the American Jerusalem. Every sect, creed and doctrine under heaven is found in Los Angeles, as well as every nation represented (1980,63).

Bartleman's account of the Azusa Street revival clearly shows that he saw what was happening there to be of eschatological significance for the whole church in the whole world.[6] Bartleman's foresight or "vision" concerning the significance of the revival cannot be denied in terms of the revival's influence and the special role it played in the development of the worldwide Pentecostal Movement.

The parallel between the Los Angeles "Pentecost" and the first century Jerusalem Pentecost is accurate in terms of the emphasis on the Pentecostal baptism of the Spirit, evidenced by speaking in other tongues. This experience in itself was catalytic for the identity and spread of the Movement. Historical evidence shows that the influence of the Azusa Street revival was central to the formation of the Pentecostal Movement in the United States, and there is no question that its influence went beyond the borders of the nation. The beginnings of the Pentecostal Movement in Scandinavia were the direct result of the Azusa revival, and Scandinavia's influence aided in the subsequent spread of the Movement through Europe and South America. However, the claim that the worldwide Pentecostal Movement started in Los Angeles and from there spread to the rest of the world is problematic. It puts too much weight on the centrifugal activities of those who were present or who visited Azusa Street. The claim also detracts from the actual historical development of the worldwide Movement, in terms of its universal and spontaneous origins.

As Hollenweger's approach has already illustrated, those treating the Pentecostal Movement's history often leave the erroneous impression that the phenomenon is characteristically American. Bruner states:

> Pentecostalism, which we shall see was born in America and appears to have been exported there from around the world, may now perhaps be listed as the most recent contribution to the world's religious groups (1970,39).

In the introduction to Frank Bartleman's *Azusa Street,* Vinson Synan leaves the same impression. He states that the Azusa revival "ushered into being the worldwide twentieth-century pentecostal renewal" (1980,ix). It is Synan's opinion that Bartleman's journalistic reporting of the revival "informed the world about the Pentecostal Movement but in a large measure also helped to form it" (1980,xii). In his own history of the Pentecostal Movement, *The Holiness-Pentecostal Movement in the United States,* Synan clearly subscribes to what we have called the "Jerusalem-Centrifugal" theory of the origins of the *worldwide* Movement, citing the United States as its "Jerusalem" (Synan 1971,37,109,114,215,217). He states further, "It is also clear that the Pentecostal Movement is one of the few major religious movements to originate in America and subsequently become a major force beyond the borders of the nation" (Synan 1971,215). But are the origins of the worldwide Pentecostal Movement to be thought of as a centrifugal Movement arising from America's "Jerusalem," Azusa Street?

Synan's description of the Azusa Street revival as a catalyst for bringing into being scores of Pentecostal denominations in the United States is true. However, the statement that "directly or indirectly, practically all of the pentecostal groups in existence can trace their lineage to the Azusa Mission" (Synan 1971,114), is inaccurate concerning the worldwide Movement. Even if confined to classical Pentecostal groups, such statements are problematic. They overlook other significant, previous and simultaneous, Pentecostal outpourings around the world which have no historical-causal linkage to the American revival. They also tend to portray the Pentecostal Movement as an American expression of the Christian faith. They detract not only from the universal origins of the Movement, but they also provide the opportunity for the *nature* of the Movement to be misunderstood. The Movement appears to some, therefore, as an American contextualization of the Christian faith (Bruner 1970,39). Or it appears as a mere psychosociological phenomenon due to economic and social deprivation (Bloch-Hoell 1964,144,173-174; Hollenweger 1972,23-24), rather than a divine renewal of the church in the context of salvation history.

Walter Hollenweger appears at first glance to agree with the "Jerusalem-Centrifugal" theory when he states, "The origins of the Pentecostal Movement go back to a revival amongst the negroes of North America at the beginning of the present century" (1972,xvii). Also Hollenweger states that T.B. Barratt, a participant in the Azusa Street revival, brought the Pentecostal Movement to Norway and the other Scandinavian countries, and also to Germany, Great Britain, and Switzerland (Hollenweger 1972,63). Hollenweger, however, mentions prior Pentecostal outpourings of the Spirit in Germany, Wales and India, *before* the 1906 Azusa Street revival. The apparent contradiction about historical origins and historical-causal linkage between the various movements is resolved when it is understood that Hollenweger does not see the Pentecostal Movement in America and the Charismatic Movement in the denominational churches in Europe as "one Movement."[7]

Evidence of Universal Origins

In a balanced and careful statement concerning the role of the Azusa Street revival in relation to other Pentecostal Movements, Assemblies of God historian William Menzies states:

> From 1905 to 1910, Pentecostal revivals erupted in widely scattered parts of the world: the United States and Canada, Great Britain, Holland, Germany, Norway, Sweden, Chile, and India. Some of these occurred without visible links with one another; others were the result of revival reports falling on fertile soil....It would not be accurate to ascribe the entire story of the spread of the Pentecostal message to the Great Revival at Azusa Mission in Los Angeles, but without question it was that center that was the most significant instrument in the proliferation of the Latter Rain (1971,60).

Similar care is taken in Menzies's article, "The Non-Wesleyan Origins of the Pentecostal Movement" (1975). He thinks it is necessary to include a fifteen-year span when speaking of Pentecostal origins and states by way of limitation that only the American Pentecostal Movement is in focus (1975,83). It is clear that the origins of the Movement are somewhat "fluid," pointing to a spontaneous, universal outpouring of the Spirit.

While noting the impact of the Azusa Street revival, its centrifugal activities, and its influence in bringing the revival to other parts of the world, Larry Christenson observes:

> Yet during this same period, charismatic manifestations were a
> common place occurrence in a body of churches outside pentecostal-
> ism. In congregations scattered around the world, but predominantly
> in Europe and North America, members of the Catholic Apostolic
> church recorded their experience of tongues, prophecy, and
> healings—as they had quietly been doing for more than half a century
> previous (1975,17).

Christenson's documentation of a charismatic awakening in Great
Britain in the 1830s and a resulting "come out" Pentecostal church
led by Edward Irving, suggests that perhaps a similar, but
somewhat longer, time-span is also necessary when speaking of the
origins of the worldwide Pentecostal Movement. Christenson
speaks of Irving as a forerunner of the Catholic Apostolic church
and the entire Pentecostal phenomenon of the twentieth century
(1975,20). But at the same time he makes it clear that there is no
historical connection between the Catholic Apostolic church and
classical Pentecostalism (1975,22-23).

By Christenson's use of the term "forerunner" it appears that he
views the movements somehow as a unity. How is it that Irving and
the Catholic Apostolic church are in some way a "forerunner"of
classical Pentecostalism in the twentieth century, if there is no
historical relationship between the movements? Christenson
explains:

> One is faced, at last, with the mystery of two movements existing side
> by side in history, sharing in considerable measure a unique religious
> outlook and experience, yet historically unrelated to one
> another....No serious study of the beginnings of the Pentecostal
> Movement will want to ignore the Catholic Apostolic church. For the
> story of the Catholic Apostolic church, *precisely because* of the
> absence of any historical connection between the two movements,
> sheds a particular light on the origins of Pentecostalism
> (1975,23; italics mine).

Christenson sees a difference between a "historical-causal
relationship," and an "existential-independent relationship," or
an independent encounter with the same essential reality—God the
Holy Spirit (1975,23-25).

In Christenson's view similarities in the particular expression of
Christianity may point to a historical-causal relationship between
revivals. But they may also point *beyond* any such influence to a
sovereign, divine influence, or independent encounters with God
the Holy Spirit which are unrelated historically-causally (1975,25).
Christenson, therefore, points out the similarity of the movements,
yet the lack of historical-causal linkage as evidence for the *divine
origin* of the movements. The "particular light" that the absence of
historical-causal linkage sheds on the origins of the Pentecostal
Movement is that it represents a renewal of Pentecostal Christianity
in salvation history. The similarity of pre-Azusa Street revivals in

Europe and Asia and the Los Angeles revival, therefore, does not necessarily mean that a historical-causal relationship between those Movements exists, as Synan infers (1971,114-115). Rather, the similarity may point to independent encounters with the same renewing work of the Holy Spirit.

In terms of centrifugal direction and origins of influence, it is much more probable that the original impetus for the Pentecostal Movement came from the European continent to the United States, and not vice versa. The influence of the Welsh revival on the Azusa Street revival is well documented (Synan 1980,xi,xvi; Synan 1971,97; Hollenweger 1972,22; Menzies 1971,49). Furthermore, Atter states that Russia experienced a Pentecostal revival in approximately 1862, and that the Russians took the Pentecostal message to Armenia in approximately 1880. He states that Pentecostal Armenians migrated to the United States in 1900 and were present when the Pentecostal revival broke out in Los Angeles in 1906 (1962,21). Other early Pentecostal outpourings of the Spirit in Northern Europe and Asia at the turn of the century are evidence of the universal origins of Pentecostalism.

Attempts to assign a "starting point" for the worldwide Pentecostal Movement in terms of a geographical location, founder, or group detracts from its universal and spontaneous origins. Donald Gee states in this regard, "The Pentecostal Movement does not owe its origin to any outstanding personality or religious leader; but was a spontaneous revival, appearing almost simultaneously in various parts of the world" (1949,3). Such a view of the Movement's origins is held by other historians of the Pentecostal Movement (Menzies 1971,60; Atter 1962,43; Frodsham 1946,9,53). Concerning the matter of origins, it must be realized that the centrifugal spread of the Pentecostal Movement took place not only "horizontally" in terms of historical-causal expansion, but also "vertically" by means of the sovereign activity of God. In numerous places in the world where Christians were expectantly awaiting a divine renewal, Pentecostal phenomena were expressions of the God-given renewal.

The discussion of the origins of the Pentecostal Movement raises the question, What makes the worldwide Pentecostal phenomenon a movement? Certainly, a combination of factors make the phenomenon a movement: the political, organizational, psychological, social, economic, and the historical-causal linkage between revivals. But as previously noted, if the Movement is *Christian,* the factor of the sovereign move of God the Holy Spirit must be added. It was seen that a focus on the human factors alone contributes some confusion to the issue of the Movement's origins. When did the Pentecostal "Movement" start? In the 1830s with the

Irvingites? In 1862 among the Russians, who in turn brought the
revival to the Armenians, who were present at Azusa Street? Or
were its origins found in Topeka, when the evidence of speaking in
tongues was connected doctrinally with the baptism of the Holy
Spirit? Or was the "Jerusalem" of the centrifugal worldwide
Movement at Los Angeles in 1906? Or was it in one of the previous
holiness revivals?

All of these factors, the historical-causal linkage of the revivals,
human efforts at organization, doctrinal formulations, the
catalytic impetus of Azusa Street and its centrifugal influence, shed
important light on the matter of the Pentecostal Movement's
origins and development. However, in the last analysis the
universal and spontaneous origins of the Movement point to the
divine dimension of the Movement as the crucial dimension in
understanding causation. A statement often heard among
Pentecostals is, " 'Pentecost' is not a denomination but an
experience." Clearly this statement is intended to put the emphasis
on the divine dimension of the Movement's origin and nature. The
statement refers to the Movement as a renewal of the Pentecostal
experience in contemporary Christian experience.

A Pentecostal world view and theological presuppositions allow
for a view of origins which emphasizes *God's* action. The
Pentecostal's emphasis is on the theological "creative center" of
the Movement. The Movement is a renewal of the Holy Spirit *first*
and *foremost*. Only secondly is it an effort of men to reinstitute a
neglected apostolic orientation to the contemporary church. This
effort, however, is preceded by and accompanied with the divine
dynamic. The Movement represents a cooperation with the
eschatological, renewing Spirit of God in the context of salvation
history. Whether this emphasis on the divine dimension—the
theological creative center—is appropriate in defining the origins
and nature of the Pentecostal Movement is discussed now. What
are the grounds for this emphasis and presupposition? Is it valid to
view the Pentecostal Movement as an eschatological renewal of the
Spirit in salvation history? These questions lead to a discussion of
biblical theology, and in turn, an analysis of the theological
creative center of the Pentecostal Movement.

The Salvation History Nature of the Movement

The discussion of the origins of the Pentecostal Movement
naturally, and eventually, lead to the question of its nature. In a
sense, the approach in studying the Movement so far has been
deductive, moving from a discussion of its historical origins to a
consideration of its nature. Here the theological question is in
focus. The assumption up to this point is that the Pentecostal

Movement is a "Christian" phenomenon. However, before the Christian nature of the Movement is addressed, it must be realized that substantiation of the Movement's Christian validity is a theological matter. It concerns one's world view and theological presuppositions. The discussion of origins showed that from one ideological viewpoint the Movement may appear to be primarily a psychosociological response of men to a crisis situation. From another, the Movement may appear as a visitation of God to renew His church in salvation history. Of course, no clean dichotomy (in terms of either/or) is possible in assessing the nature of the Movement.

Formerly, we saw that a holistic approach to the complex phenomenon of the Pentecostal Movement was necessary for understanding its various dimensions. "Christian" movements necessarily have two major dimensions, the divine and the human. This is due to the incarnational nature of divine revelation. God reveals himself in human cultures and he works through them, as the Incarnation and the doctrine of Scripture itself illustrates. In dealing with Christian movements one must encounter not only the social, psychological, and phenomenological, but also the revelational—the dynamics of the divine Word and Spirit. The idea of salvation history (*Heilsgeschichte*) also comes to the fore.[8] These matters not only reveal the limitations of the sciences that must be used in order to understand the full dimension of Christian movements, but they also determine the controlling ideological context from which the movements must be examined. The character of the movements determine the appropriate orientation and methodology for their examination.

The modifier "Christian" in regard to a movement determines that one's orientation be theological, and from the evangelical standpoint that theological orientation must be conditioned and controlled by *biblical authority*. This evangelical orientation does not exclude the various orientations, presuppositions, and insights of the social sciences. But it holds biblical content to be the norm for judging their validity and use. Previous erroneous views concerning the nature of the Pentecostal Movement emerged from a perspective of origins in which anti-Christian presuppositions were controlling the evaluation of the Movement. Biblical authority determines the attitude and presuppositions with which the Movement must be evaluated. It calls "faith" into the arena of study. It also determines that the Movement be evaluated in the light of biblical theology.

A prior question when approaching the nature of the Pentecostal Movement is, How does it fare under the scrutiny of biblical theology? Is the claim that it represents an eschatological renewal of New Testament, Pentecostal Christianity in accord with a sound biblical theology? Are there biblical grounds for considering the worldwide Pentecostal Movement as "one" Movement, an eschatological outpouring of the Holy Spirit in salvation history?

An Eschatological Renewal

In attempting to identify the "creative theological center" of the Pentecostal Movement, the various definitions of the Movement and its common claims are instructive. Menzies's definition of the Movement is clearly eschatological in the salvation history sense when he states:

> The Pentecostal Movement is that group of sects within the Christian church which is characterized by the belief that the occurrence mentioned in Acts 2 on the Day of Pentecost not only signalled a birth of the church, but described an experience available to believers in all ages (1971,9).

Numerous other definitions of the Movement emphasize the same central thought, that God is visiting His people in contemporary times as He visited them in the first century. Atter defines the Pentecostal Movement as "that section of the Christian church which constantly maintains that the church today *should enjoy the same blessings, believe the same doctrines, and receive the same power as did the early church*" (1962,6). Bloch-Hoell notes that "Pentecostal" is an appropriate term for describing the classical Pentecostal Movement due to its implication that the first Pentecost (Acts 2:4) was to be repeated in the experience of the Christian (1964,1).[9]

The Pentecostal claims and definitions of the Movement characterize it as a *renewal movement*. They believe renewal takes place in an eschatological period described as the "last days," a period in which contemporary Christians are now living. Even those outside the Movement agree that it represents a renewal. Clark H. Pinnock, a sympathetic evangelical observer of the Movement, states, "The new Pentecostalism seems to this observer to be a genuine movement of the Spirit of God renewing His church" (1976,183). Furthermore, Menzies observes that the Pentecostal Movement did not add new doctrines, but rather it was a "reactionary" movement, calling the church back to historic truth. He states, "The Pentecostal Movement has stood within the framework of Orthodox Christianity" (1971,17). The renewal, therefore, has taken place within traditional Protestantism. It is not only a product of the Protestant tradition, but it has also subsequently adopted the traditional beliefs of Protestantism, such as those affirmed by the Apostle's Creed (Gause 1976,108).

Some would say that the doctrine of the baptism of the Holy Spirit, connected with the initial evidence of speaking with other tongues, would be a "new" doctrine. Generally Pentecostals hold that the distinctive characteristic of the classical Pentecostal Movement is the linking together of speaking with other tongues and the baptism of the Holy Spirit. This, of course, addresses a central issue of classical Pentecostalism. But the issue of "new," in the sense of true orthodoxy, rests upon whether there is a basis for the doctrine in the New Testament or not. It does not rest on the historic formulation of the doctrine by a particular group which has experienced a renewing of the Pentecostal experience and therefore theologizes about that experience. Such fresh theologizing often takes place in the history of the Church. Theologizing concerning the doctrine of the Trinity in church history is a case in point. The formulation of the "new" doctrine was not outside of orthodox Christian truth, it was firmly rooted in Scripture.

Bruner also characterizes the Movement in terms of renewal when he states:

> In terms of the church's theology and mission Pentecostalism's significance may be that it incarnates a neglected reality of the New Testament Church: the Holy Spirit in the experience of believers. What to some may seem an overemphasis of the Spirit and especially of the Spirit's more noticeable operations may, perhaps, be intended to startle the church into an awareness of its little emphasis on the same Spirit. Perhaps in the divine perspective a church that gives too much attention to the Spirit is no more culpable—perhaps less—than a church that gives him too little. Perhaps the Pentecostal Movement is a voice—albeit an ecstatic and at times a harsh voice—calling the people to hear what the Spirit is capable of saying to and doing with a church that listens (1970,33).

A renewal movement emphasizing neglected charismatic ministries of the Holy Spirit would, perhaps, appear overemphasized to those outside of the Movement. However, those *within* the Pentecostal Movement, in both Protestant and Roman Catholic Christendom, do not view the Movement as representing an overemphasis. They view the Movement as a renewal of normative Christian experience (McDonnell 1980,180-181).

It is important at this point to discriminate between the concepts of "reaction" and "renewal." The Pentecostal Movement is not merely a reaction to an overly rationalistic expression of the Christian faith. It involves a neglected dimension of New Testament Christianity which God is renewing. The view of the Movement as a "reaction" is helpful in emphasizing the human causative factors in it. In this way it may be viewed in an "historical" perspective but not in a *salvation history* perspective. As pointed out previously, the Pentecostal Movement is more than the contextualization of the Christian faith in reaction to certain circumstances of its particular historical moment. It is not merely a phenomenon in history with no necessary connections with the past. It is a renewal of the Holy Spirit in the context of salvation history, in accord with the particular character of the Age of the Holy Spirit. While "reaction" indicates causation, by itself it is an inadequate term in addressing the nature of the Movement. "Renewal" points to the Movement as a phenomenon of the Holy Spirit in the course of salvation history, a *New Testament* phenomenon.

While theological interpretations of the doctrine of the baptism of the Holy Spirit differ among Pentecostal-charismatics, the belief that God is restoring a charismatic dimension of the Christian experience is commonly held. For Roman Catholics especially, the idea of "renewal" is in accord with their sacramental framework for interpreting the charismatic experience. The baptism of the Holy Spirit is viewed as an actualization of what was already received at baptism and confirmation. Although Catholic theologians say that charismatic manifestations were always present in the history of the church, they also see the charismatic experience today as an historical renewal of the church (McDonnell 1980,1-6,51; Grassi 1978,7-8). The Pentecostal Movement in general views itself as representing a renewal of the charismatic ministry of the Holy Spirit in salvation history (Sandidge 1976,11).

A Missionary Renewal

Bruner's characterization of the Pentecostal Movement as a missionary phenomenon is also in accord with how classical Pentecostals view the Movement. This view of the Movement as a missionary phenomenon explains, somewhat, their eschatological orientation. Due to the representative nature of the Assemblies of God in classical Pentecostalism, this group is used here in order to illustrate the eschatologically-oriented world view of classical Pentecostalism.

From the beginnings of the Assemblies of God the fellowship was considered to be a missionary movement. Unlike the creedal affirmations of many Protestant denominations, the "Fundamental Truths" of the Assemblies of God contain a clear statement on mission:

> Since God's purpose concerning man is to seek and to save that which is lost, to be worshiped by man, and to build a body of believers in the image of His Son, the priority reason-for-being of the Assemblies of God as part of the Church is:
> a. To be an agency of God for evangelizing the world (Acts 1:8, Matthew 28:19,20; Mark 16:15,16) (Menzies 1971,389).

Menzies states further, "Significant is the fact that out of a concern for effective missionary enterprise a semblance of inter-church structure was created" (1971,86). The fellowship's early intense aversion to "organization" was overcome due to the realization that it was necessary in order to fulfill its "missionary calling" (Menzies 1971,106,131). The view of the Assemblies of God fellowship as a "missionary" movement, however, was connected with the idea that it was a missionary movement in an eschatological period of salvation history—the "last days." The outpouring of the Spirit in the twentieth century was seen as an outpouring for the express purpose of accomplishing the church's mission in the world.

Pentecostals view the time context of contemporary mission as an eschatological time characterized by both supernatural blessing and opposition, of Spirit-outpourings and spiritual decline and opposition. Generally speaking, Pentecostals view these times clearly as days of power-encounter where the forces of God clash with the forces of evil in cosmic struggle in the "last days." Therefore, the realities of the spirit world are predominant in Pentecostal thinking concerning the church and its worldwide mission. Emphasis varies among Pentecostals between the poles of pessimism and optimism. The position one occupies on the pessimism-optimism continuum is largely a matter of his view of eschatology. When speaking of evangelicals in general, David Bosch says concerning the pessimism end of the continuum:

> In the more pronouncedly adventist and dispensational circles all emphasis lies on the *coming* Kingdom of God. The believer looks forward with longing to Christ's return. The present is empty. All that really matters is the glorious future (1980,32).

Assemblies of God missiologist Melvin Hodges, however, gives a representative, optimistic Pentecostal view of mission. It is a view in which mission is a task which "fills" the present-eschatological "time between the times." Hodges's optimism in regard to the task of mission is clearly linked with his view of the ministry of the Holy Spirit in the church today. For Hodges, the present is *not empty* , it is filled with mission. Supernatural intervention is expected as the church engages in mission. This expectancy is specifically related to his view that contemporary mission takes place in an *eschatological context*. Hodges, as well as the majority of classical Pentecostals, believe contemporary times to be the biblical "last days," in which God abundantly pours out his Spirit. Present day activity of the Holy Spirit in the world is seen to be the fulfillment of the biblical promise found in Joel 2:28-32 (Hodges 1970,3).[11]

Hodges specifically connects twentieth century movements of the Spirit, at the beginning and midway through the century, with the movement of the Spirit on the Day of Pentecost. The connection is made because of his view that the unusual activity of the Spirit marks the Church Age, or, in the Apostle Peter's words, "the last days" (Acts 2:17). There is expectancy for the Spirit's ministry in mission today because the church is perceived to live and minister in the *same salvation history time context* as the New Testament church. On the basis of a biblical promise Pentecostals look for a supernatural enablement and ministry in their own contemporary times like the apostles and disciples experienced at the beginning of the missionary task. This enablement is deemed necessary to finish the same missionary task that was started in the "beginning" of the "last days." The theological basis for such expectancy is the belief that they occupy the same time context in their engagement in Christ's mission as the early church occupied—"the last days."

A Manifestation of the Kingdom of God
What is the theological basis for conceiving of an age as the "last days," extending from the time of the apostles until now? Of course, this question has great importance for viewing the Pentecostal Movement as an eschatological renewal in contemporary times. The theological basis for this view is the biblical motif of the kingdom of God. Both the assumption that mission takes place in an eschatological context and the emphasis on the extraordinary working of the Holy Spirit in contemporary mission are fundamental to the New Testament concept of the kingdom of God. The Kingdom motif is understood to be a part of a larger theological context—salvation history. In that context the Pentecostal Movement may be considered a manifestation of the kingdom of God, for it witnesses to the dynamic redemptive activity of God in contemporary times.

The Kingdom: Fulfillment Without Consummation
Johannes Blauw notes that the eschatological character of the parables reveals that the meaning of "eschatological" is not exhausted in its reference to the future. For in the parables the coming of Jesus does not mean *"the absolute end*, but rather that it ushers in *a new period* in the history of Israel and of the world" (1962,73). In a discussion concerning the continuity of the testaments Blauw states emphatically: *"The progression of Heilsgeschichte which is here found continues, in that the 'last of the days' does not mean the end of the days, but a great turning of the days toward a new future"* (1962,79). Blauw describes the last stages of history (Jesus' times and the times following his death and resurrection) as one last phase of salvation history; the "last of days" becomes a new beginning. The time of eschatological expectation is past (1962,82). Of course, according to Blauw the "last of the days" would have begun with the ministry of Jesus and would have continued into contemporary times.

John Bright states that the present aspect of the kingdom of God was an integral part of the New Testament *kerygma* (Mark 1:14-15) and that the proclamation of that message is the binding element in New Testament theology (1953,190). Bright also believes that the kingdom of God, the dynamic concept of the rule of God, is the bond that binds the testaments together. But in distinction from the Old Testament he states concerning the New:

> In the New Testament we encounter a change: the tense is a resounding present indicative—the Kingdom is *here!* And that is a very "new thing" indeed: *it is gospel*—the good news that God has acted! . . . Nowhere is it better put than in the word of Jesus which Mark begins the story of his ministry, and which sum up . . . the very essence of his teaching: "The time has come," he said. "The kingdom of God is near. Repent and believe the good news" (Mark 1:15)! What all the ages have desired to see now is here—in this Jesus (Luke 10:23-24). In him has the old order ended and a new order begun (1953,197).

For Bright, the Kingdom invades the world in the person and work of Jesus. His miracles were understood eschatologically in New Testament times; they illustrated the fact that a new age was intruding upon the present evil age; the cosmic end-struggle had begun (Bright 1953,216-217).

George Eldon Ladd addresses the key issue in relation to the eschatological context of mission when he states:

> One of the most important tasks of modern biblical theology has been the search for the key to this problem of how the Kingdom can be both future and present so that both sets of sayings—those of present fulfillment and those of future consummation—can be preserved. We believe the solution to this problem [of hermeneutics] is to be found in the dynamic meaning of the Kingdom of God (1974,120-121).

Ladd notes that both the above sets of sayings in Scripture, present fulfillment and future eschatological consummation, are two central emphases of Jesus' message (1974,33). He finds that the kingdom of God is the reign of God not merely in the heart of the Christian, but that it is dynamically active in the person of Jesus and in human history. This view of the Kingdom allows for present and future, inward and outward, and spiritual and apocalyptic aspects (Ladd 1974,42). Ladd's central thesis is, "Before the eschatological appearing of God's Kingdom at the end of the age, God's Kingdom has become dynamically active among men in Jesus' person and mission" (1974,139). When the church engages in mission, the kingdom of God is a dynamic power at work among men in this age *before* the appearing of the future, outward, apocalyptic Kingdom.

Ladd states that the early church claimed the presence of the eschatological blessings of the age to come. The resurrection of Jesus was the beginning of the final resurrection (1 Cor 15:23); the coming of the Holy Spirit was the fulfillment of the Old Testament promise for the eschatological Kingdom (Joel 2:28-32). Paul speaks of the Gift of the Holy Spirit as a "down payment" (2 Cor 1:22; 5:5; Eph 1:14) of the eschatological inheritance (Ladd 1974,271). Furthermore, Ladd states that another way of looking at this experience of the eschatological blessing is that the kingdom of God is *present* (1974,271). When discussing the Kingdom parables Ladd notes, "The mystery of the Kingdom is the coming of the Kingdom into history in advance of its apocalyptic manifestation" (1974,222). He states that the "mystery" of the Kingdom "is in short, 'fulfillment without consummation' " (Ladd 1974,222).

The view that the contemporary mission is a continuation of the Age of the Spirit, which broke through at the Day of Pentecost and continues to break through today as men engage in mission, is consistent with the kingdom of God motif. The view of the Pentecostal Movement as a missionary phenomenon is, in a sense, a manifestation of the very present and powerful kingdom of God. For it is evidence of the dynamic, redemptive activity of God the Holy Spirit in contemporary times.

The Kingdom: The New Age of the Spirit
What is missing from Ladd's explanation of the Kingdom motif is the specific mention of the *manner* of God's active rule and working in the contemporary world. According to Bright, the kingdom of God is dynamic; it is a power already released in the world (1953,218-219). He speaks of the Kingdom as a present power in this age by means of the ministry of the Holy Spirit. Bright, along with Hodges, refers to the church's Pentecostal experience of the Holy Spirit as a demonstration of the beginning of the "last days," based on Joel's prophecy.

Floyd Filson also connects the present age of the kingdom with the coming of the Holy Spirit.[12] He states that the promise in the synoptic Gospels that Christ will give the Spirit must be read in the light of the preaching of the Baptist and of Jesus. They proclaimed that the Kingdom was at the threshold.[13] The term "last days," therefore, represents an age which is characteristically an age of the Spirit. Pentecost was the crucial turning point of those "eschatological days." Filson states, "Pentecost therefore has an eschatological quality which modern interpretation of Acts frequently fails to mention" (1950,76). Blauw likewise speaks of the presence of the Kingdom in terms of the coming of the Holy Spirit, "In the New Testament, 'the last days' can mean the days which have broken forth with Christ (Heb. 1:1) and the Holy Spirit (Acts 2:17), but also the time of the Last Judgment and the Second Coming (e.g. [*sic*] John 11:24, 12:48; 1 Pet. 1:5)" (1962,111). Blauw shows that the evidence of the presence of the Kingdom is the power of the Holy Spirit.

The view that mission takes place in an eschatological context is firmly rooted in the New Testament concept of the present kingdom of God. That eschatological context in salvation history represents a new era—an era of the Holy Spirit. The Pentecostal view that the contemporary church engages in mission in the *same period* as well as the *same power* as the early church finds theological support in the biblical motif of the kingdom of God. Bosch states that mission is an eschatological event due to the certainty that the kingdom of God is not only a future reality but is present in contemporary times.[14] He states that Israel expected salvation exclusively from the future, but Christ divided that future into two; in Him the forces of the coming age have flowed into the present (Bosch 1980,236).

The Kingdom: God's Working in Salvation History

It is important to recognize the dynamic nature of the kingdom of God, that it represents God's working in salvation history. Often the term is used in the Bible in a way that emphasizes that the Kingdom is a realm to be entered, or a sphere in which God rules. But the dynamic nature of the Kingdom needs to be emphasized too. The crucial point is that the manner of God's working in contemporary times is by means of the ministry of the third person of the Godhead—the Holy Spirit. Significant mission issues are decided on this pivotal theological point. This specific identification of the manner of God's working in the church age introduces the necessity for a full-blown trinitarian view of mission.

The kingdom of God is God's dynamic power at work among men and His power at work in history itself. The presence of the Kingdom is characterized by the activity of God the Holy Spirit. The miracles of Jesus illustrated that the new age had come, and the cosmic end-struggle had begun. The Kingdom's presence means that a power was already released in the world; the powers of the coming age are visible in the power of the Holy Spirit, in the present working of *God Himself* (Ladd 1974,144).

The nature of the Kingdom cannot be determined if it separates God from His Kingdom.[15] The kingdom of God is an expression of the ontic presence of God, God's present rule, God's action, God encountering men and women in history. In Jesus, therefore, God has become present among mankind; the Kingdom is God himself actively at work among men and women (Ladd 1974,145). The kingdom of God is not the ideal good to be realized in a spiritual universal kingdom, or inevitable progress, or an abstract principle of divine rule, but God's redemptive working in history. Nor can the Kingdom be identified merely as God's working in and through historical events in general; it is God's supernatural breaking into history in the person of Jesus (Ladd 1974,188-189). "The coming of the Kingdom into history . . . is [a] miracle—God's deed" (Ladd 1974,189).

Joseph Grassi, a Roman Catholic theologian, also identifies the Spirit as the "manner" of God's working among men:

> The new age would be an age when all of God's power and Spirit would be evident in the world. In the Bible, the Spirit was the name given to God as manifest in the activity and life of people. It was first of all the source of all life, as when God breathed into the first human being to give life (Gen. 2:7). But the Spirit was also the source of all that showed God's presence in people in quite an extraordinary or unusual way. The coming of the new age would be accompanied by the discovery of a *new full dimension and depth of the Spirit of God* that would result in exciting *new manifestations of God's power and presence* (1978,7-8; italics mine).

Grassi goes on to quote Joel 3:1-2 in connection with the above description of the extraordinary experience that the people of God would have in the new age. Grassi identifies *two dimensions* of the working of the Spirit, a life-source dimension and what could be called an outward, charismatic dimension.

In summarizing his study of the growth of a biblical tradition of the Spirit, George T. Montague likewise views the Spirit as another way of referring to the work of God himself. Then he states, "This Spirit was not really other than a way of saying that God himself was moving those whom he touched" (1976,366). In the Deuteronomist tradition Montague identifies the Spirit which at times comes upon the recipient in an ecstatic way (1976,32). The nature of the Kingdom, therefore, involves the people of God experiencing the full dimension and depth of the Spirit of God. God is present and actively working by means of the Holy Spirit, both inwardly as the source of spiritual life and outwardly in charismatic power. He also works immediately in the world apart from the church.

In summary, the Pentecostal-charismatic claim is that the Pentecostal Movement represents an eschatological renewal of the Holy Spirit in salvation history. The theological creative center of the Movement is the charismatic working of the Holy Spirit in contemporary times. The experience that the apostles had with the Holy Spirit is also available in this present age. This claim is not founded on a naive biblicism. It is founded on New Testament theology. The hermeneutical horizon for Pentecostal theology is the biblical concept of salvation history; its hermeneutical key is the already-present kingdom of God. The "new age," according to New Testament theology, is an age of the Spirit, one characterized by His rule and the manifestation of His power. The nature of the dynamic, present kingdom of God is such that it provides the people of God an experience of the full dimension and depth of the Holy Spirit's ministry as they engage in their mission in the world.

3

A Correction of
a Western Distortion

How does Pentecostalism represent a potential correction for a distortion in twentieth century missions? The answer to this question is found in Pentecostalism's focus on the experiential dimension of the Christian faith. In terms of the dynamic and evidential experience of the Holy Spirit, Pentecostalism contrasts with the static intellectual-oriented expression of Christianity inherited from the post-Reformation period. The impact of Protestant Scholasticism on western theology and the imbalanced nature of its theological orientation are well documented in contemporary theology (Berkouwer 1952, 1975, 1977; Dunn 1970; Green 1975; Kraft 1979; Ramm 1959, 1977; Rogers 1966, 1977; Rogers and McKim 1979; Webber and Bloesch 1978). Pentecostalism represents a restoration of the experiential dimension of the Christian faith in the wake of its scholastic reduction. In view of the excessive impact of western culture on the Christian faith as it was contextualized in the West, Pentecostalism may be seen as a renewal movement which restores the significance of its experiential dimension. It brings a needed correction to a western distortion of the faith.

Therefore, the Pentecostal's orientation corresponds to a theological hiatus in western theological tradition, specifically a *pneumatological hiatus, a silence on the Holy Spirit.* This chapter identifies that theological hiatus in western theology and in the Protestant missionary heritage. The demise of pneumatology in western tradition is outlined, as well as the evidence of that demise in recent missions history. General areas of missions which are impacted by the "silence on the Holy Spirit" in western Christianity are mentioned. The full discussion of the results of this

silence on contemporary mission issues is the subject of chapters 6
and 7. In this chapter the orientation of Pentecostalism addresses
the theological hiatus in a significant way. It restores balance to
western theology and opens up new vistas for solutions to
contemporary issues in mission theology.

Evidence of Distortion in Western Theology

The correction that the Pentecostal orientation provides for
twentieth century mission is clarified when the theological and
historical context of its origin is in focus. To speak of the
Pentecostal Movement as restoring a crucial orientation of the
Christian faith infers a demise or a loss of that orientation in the
course of the history of the church. An opposite theological
orientation to that of Pentecostalism is that the intellectual
dimension of the faith is emphasized to the point where the
dynamic and experiential are eclipsed. This is the very dimension
which Pentecostalism epitomizes. Historical, theological, and
missiological evidence follows which points to a theological hiatus
in western theology—a pneumatological hiatus. This hiatus has
impacted western missions and contemporary mission theology,
bringing considerable distortion and confusion.

A Pneumatological Hiatus: Historical Evidence

In an article surveying the development of pneumatology in the
history of the western church, William Menzies outlines the areas in
which it is underdeveloped. He also suggests reasons why the
doctrine was neglected. Menzies shows that until the Reformation
the doctrine developed only in terms of the essential being of the
third person of the Trinity (Menzies 1979,69). The historic creeds
of the church, as well as some western systematic theologies, testify
to this underdevelopment (Menzies 1979,71,74). Little is said about
the function or mission of the Holy Spirit in the theology during
this period. Menzies suggests two possible reasons for the lack of
development: 1) a practical or ontological subordinationism of the
third person of the Trinity, and 2) the contextualization of
theology in the period; the fact that theology focuses on the issues
and questions of the historical moment, and therefore theological
development reflects this narrow focus (1979,71).

A possible third reason is implicit in the second reason cited
above. Not only does theology naturally narrow its response to
certain issues, due to the questions that need theological attention,
but also there is often a reaction against certain questions and
issues. "Selectivity" is an active principle in theological
development, both positively as response to issues and *negatively in
terms of avoidance* of other issues. The subjective dimension of the

Spirit in Christian experience was one issue that was avoided. Such avoidance was due to excesses that occurred regarding the experiential-subjective dimension of the faith, both at the beginning of the period (due to Montanism) and at its end (the *Schwarmerei*) (Menzies 1979,73).

Also, due to the contextual focus of Reformation theology, the theology of the Spirit was mostly developed along the lines of the Spirit's relationship and function with the Scriptures (Menzies 1979,74). What was not developed in the period was the mission of the Spirit and His outward expressive ministry. There was an almost immediate move into a scholastic period following the Reformation. Because of the effort to systematize the "theological deposit" of the Reformers, this contributed to the underdevelopment of pneumatology and the eclipse of the Spirit in His missionary role. Menzies notes that this neglected dimension began to receive attention in the theological traditions which represent the roots of modern Pentecostalism—Wesleyan holiness and Keswickian theology of the eighteenth and nineteenth centuries (1979,74-75).

Under the title "The Reticent Spirit," Harry Boer discusses the question as to why the church is so unaware of the Spirit's ministry as the source of its witness. He notes that that question could be asked concerning *all* of the Spirit's work. He suggests reasons why the doctrine of the Spirit tends to be neglected, especially in an age strongly influenced by empiricism and rationalism.

First, Boer states that, in relation to the other persons of the Trinity, the Spirit has remained in the background, and has been overshadowed by the more concrete figures of the Father and Son in theological reflection. The very name "Holy Spirit" contributes to the obscurity of the third person of the Trinity in our thinking. Boer suggests, "Perhaps it is because of the hidden role which the Spirit plays in redemption that He has been given a name which, as contrasted with that of the Father and the Son, allows of no concrete representation or association in our minds"—*Holy Spirit* (1961,134). Such a factor would be influential in a scholastic-apologetic period where the objective dimension of Christianity received primary attention. While the church has produced developed theologies and Christologies, there has been no unified and clearly circumscribed pneumatology developed (Boer 1961,130-131). Perhaps the very systematic and controversial theological context in which pneumatology has developed has contributed to the "silence on the Holy Spirit." In that context the Holy Spirit has been chiefly viewed in terms of his subordination and representation with respect to the other persons of the Trinity.

Second, as the "Spirit of *God*," the qualitative or representative aspects of the Holy Spirit stand on the foreground rather than His own personality and personhood (Boer 1961,131). Furthermore, He is the "Spirit of *Christ*"; His ministry of bearing witness to Jesus is emphasized in the New Testament (John 15:26; 16:13-15). In the synoptic Gospels, Christ is prominent in that this Spirit anoints and empowers Christ for His mission (Luke 4:1,14,18-19). Also in this sense of the Spirit's "anointing" in His relationship with the church, the Holy Spirit recedes into the background. For He is the power of witness; the church is the organ of the Spirit's expression (Boer 1961,133).

Boer observes that the Holy Spirit as *loving* Spirit, *life-giving* Spirit, and *witnessing* Spirit in each case directs attention away from himself to the object of His ministry, the object of love, the expressions of life, and the content of the witness—Christ. The Spirit does not press himself on the attention of the church; He is a *reticent Spirit*; He remains in the background (Boer 1961,133). For several reasons, therefore, it is not surprising that pneumatology was neglected, especially in an age of controversy and rationalism: 1) the historical circumstances in which theological reflection took place, as well as the scholastic methodology of theologians; 2) the difficulties the subject matter itself presented in an age of reason and controversy; and 3) the representative and reticent nature of the Spirit. Scholastic theologians were also reticent in dealing with the "subjective" dimension of the Christian faith.

The Scholastic Roots: Theological Evidence

Historical and theological perspectives which find their source in western culture contribute toward this "silence on the Holy Spirit." They have fostered the development of negative attitudes toward the Holy Spirit which range from a passive neglect to studied repression of His outward charismatic ministry. Considerable theologizing has taken place to justify the absence of the Spirit's charismatic activity in segments of the church. Scholasticism and dispensationalism have been frequent sources for this. This theologizing has eroded "expectancy" and has contributed to the inability of many to enter into the full potential of the present kingdom of God. Without question, this constricting of the activity of the Spirit in mission theology has weakened the missionary thrust of the western church in the Third World.

In discussing the question, Should we expect to see the charismatic gifts in the church today? Michael Green suggests a western cultural reason for the frequent negative response, "Both Catholic and Protestant camps have been heavily infected by the rationalism of the Enlightenment, and our Christianity has been unduly cerebral . . ."(1975,197). This statement refers to the word-oriented nature of the faith we have inherited from the post-Reformation period. Green's statement about the impact of scholastic thought on western Christianity equally applies to the western missionary heritage. The historic moment in which William Carey made his appearance to appeal for foreign missions was the Enlightenment. Protestant missions had their beginning in the post-Reformation period, a truly scholastic, Cartesian age.

In an age of rationalism, empiricism, and scientific and philosophical breakthroughs, as well as under the pressure of the Roman Catholic Counter Reformation, the Protestant church became involved in defending the Reformation "theological deposit." Attention moved away from the functional nature of Scripture and the experiential dimension of the faith to the form of Scripture—the text—and rationalistic apologetics.

In the immediate post-Reformation period, therefore, theologians began systematizing the writings of the Reformers. McClintock and Strong state concerning this phenomenon:

> Whenever the Church begins to let the writings of any of its eminent ministers stand between it and a free and direct interpretation of the Scriptures in the light of intuition and experience, that moment it enters into its scholastic stage (1970,422).

Under the impact of the Enlightenment the post-Reformation period produced a scholastic theology. Theology was a theoretical discipline, an abstract-technical science, a logical system of belief cast in an Aristotelian mold. It was static in nature, with an emphasis on a rational defense of a settled deposit of doctrine (Pomerville 1980,94). The view of scholastic theologians was that they were working with a "finished" theological deposit. In its systematic form, theology consisted of propositional statements rather than an ongoing, dynamic process where biblical revelation was constantly interacting with historical and cultural contexts. Rationality and system were characteristic of the methodology of scholastic theologians. Theology, therefore, was viewed as a scholastic science rather than a practical discipline.

The primary role of reason in eighteenth century theological work was the result of a philosophical shift. Augustine's "I believe that I may understand," which emphasized reason's subordination to faith, shifted under the impact of the Enlightenment to Protestant Scholasticism's "I know that I may believe." Such a confidence in reason led to a naive realism, which in turn led theologians to believe that there was a direct correspondence between their western perception and reality. Human reason was elevated to such a point in Reformed Scholasticism, under the influence of Scottish Common Sense philosophy, that theologians assumed that they were thinking the thoughts of God after him. That is, they assumed that they saw objectively as God saw things

(Pomerville 1980,79-81). This perception of theology tended toward a view that theological speculation was *absolute.*

In this age of controversy the noetic principle of theology (reflection, reason, epistemology, propositional statements on the confrontation of being) eclipsed the ontic principle (immediacy, presence, "thereness" of God, confrontation with reality). The apologetic tools of the "Age of reason" did not involve the subjective dimension of the Holy Spirit. Rather the church's apologetic stance manifested itself in Reformed Scholasticism. The church implemented a Medieval scholastic methodology. However, the Reformation principle *sola scriptura* now eliminated church tradition as an apologetic means *and as an arbiter* functioning to withstand the impact of the Enlightenment on theology. Also the church made an effort to objectify religious authority by limiting the concept of revelation to Scripture alone (Pomerville 1980,66,73-75).

This effort to objectify revelation in order to defend it against Roman Catholic claims and the claims of science resulted in a reduction of Reformation theology. As Reformed Scholasticism developed, the reduction chiefly took the form of *limiting the activity of the Holy Spirit at the contemporary end of biblical revelation.* Rogers and McKim state, "By the nineteenth century, the Princeton theologians would allow the work of the Holy Spirit only in inspiring the original authors of Scripture, and not at all in enabling modern readers to understand their Bibles" (1979,176). Therefore, due the apologetic nature of theology in the period, and the value placed in empirical and "objective" truth, theology was inflexible and static in nature. A correlative to this was a de-emphasis on the subjective dimension of theology, and a reductionism with regard to the Holy Spirit's ministry at "this end" of biblical revelation.

These scholastic historical roots influence greatly the continuing tendency in western missions to neglect the subjective dimension of the Holy Spirit in both theory and practice. The limiting of the activity of the Spirit to the author-end of Scripture and the prominence of the noetic principle of theology both tend to militate against, and in their extreme application, deny the Pentecostal's fundamental belief, that God is dynamically present today in Christian experience and ministry in the person of the Holy Spirit.

In *I Believe in the Holy Spirit*, Michael Green speaks of the contemporary neglect of the Holy Spirit under the provocative title, "The Spirit: Unknown—or Domesticated?" He speaks of one group of Christians to whom the Holy Spirit is virtually unknown, due to their lack of expectancy with regard to His intervention in their everyday lives. Green suggests that the neglect of the Spirit among another group may be characterized by efforts to circumscribe His activities and hem Him in with respect to His charismatic workings. These groups attempt to "domesticate" the Spirit, for they say He is a disturbing influence. Green represents these Christians as saying:

> Let him [the Holy Spirit] therefore be paid lip service, but for all practical purposes be shut up in the Bible where he can do no harm. Let his presence attend the confessional statement of our particular brand of Protestantism. Let the bizarre and miraculous elements which the New Testament documents narrate about his activity be relegated to those far-off apostolic days: it would be very embarrassing and doctrinally untidy if the Holy Spirit were to speak to men today, or to enable miracles to be performed and men to speak in tongues not their own. The Bible, accordingly, is the safest place for the Spirit. That is where he belongs; not in the hurly-burly of real life (1975,12).

Although a caricature, Green's description of the modern response to the Holy Spirit captures the influence of the Enlightenment's prejudice against the supernatural. It also expresses the truth that some Christians are *affectively closed* to the notion of the outward charismatic working of the Holy Spirit today. That "closed" attitude of some results in a studied repression of the Holy Spirit and represents the antithesis of the Pentecostal's theological and practical orientation to the Spirit.

Green also rejects the theological position which restricts the work of the Spirit to His inward work, claiming the ebb of the charismatic dimension of His ministry on the basis of dispensationalism. He states, "It is simply not the case that healing, prophecy, exorcism and speaking in tongues died out with the last apostle" (1975,198).[1] Green goes on to state that there is plenty of evidence that in sub-apostolic days, and periodically throughout church history, this charismatic ministry of the Spirit did not die out. He also elaborates on the place of such ministry in the church today (1975,198-204).

While evangelical missiologists readily confess the neglect of the Holy Spirit in mission theology and practice, they may not express that neglect in terms of the charismatic dimension of the Spirit's ministry. However, Geradus van der Leeuw suggest that *any* neglect of the Spirit's ministry should be avoided. He states:

> Mission is a vital expression of the Holy Spirit whom we may never hem in. For this very reason every constricting of the activities of the Holy Spirit to the individual or the Church or orthodox doctrine drains the vital force of missions (Bosch 1980,199).

Protestant Scholasticism represents the theological roots of the silence on the Spirit in western missions. The neglect and hemming in of the Spirit is part and parcel of that theological tradition. This weakness is due to the influence of western world view in the period and the apologetic methodology used. Central in the tradition is the prominence of abstract reason; its precedence over faith and the experiential dimension of Christianity. The residual effect of that imbalance is evident in evangelical theology today.

Pneumatological Neglect in Mission Theory and Practice

Neglect in Mission Theory: The Western World

There is evidence in Protestant mission history and theology that the neglect of pneumatology has impacted adversely on the western missionary heritage. It is not surprising that Lindsell (1949), Allen (1960), Boer (1961), Kane (1974), and Hodges (1977) all see the role of the Holy Spirit in modern missions to be greatly neglected. Allen emphasizes that the revelation of the Holy Spirit as a missionary Spirit in the Acts of the Apostles causes that portion of the New Testament to stand alone. He states the missionary role of the Holy Spirit is crucial for any true understanding of the Holy Spirit and his work:

> This revelation embraces one whole hemisphere of the Spirit. If we ignore it, or treat it less seriously than the revelation of truth or righteousness, we lose sight of the perfection of the Spirit. Our view is necessarily one-sided, our understanding of the past is robbed of its true foundation, our conception of our present duty is incomplete, and our hope for the future is rendered doubtful and indistinct (1960,21).

Allen discusses the neglect of the Spirit in terms of limiting his ministry to only certain areas: the revelation of truth, of holiness, and of church government and order (1960,21). He thinks the missionary role of the Spirit, found in Acts, is largely neglected. This "whole hemisphere of the Spirit" in Acts involves largely the outward-expressive dimension of the Spirit's ministry. Allen says the neglect of this dimension destroys the "perfection" or completeness of the Holy Spirit, rendering a "one-sided" view of the Spirit. The development of pneumatology in the area that Allen spoke of still remains largely undeveloped, even toward the end of the century. Such a neglect could only adversely affect one's concept of mission theory and practice.

In *Pentecost and Missions* (1961), Harry Boer shows how the eclipse of the missionary role of the Spirit was partly due to the emergence of the Protestant missionary movement in the post-Reformation period. Boer concentrates on explaining why the Protestant missionary movement emphasized the Great Commission as its motivation for missions, the *written* command, over the New Testament's emphasis on the inner motivation of the Holy Spirit. The influence of scholastic thought in the post-Reformation period is illustrated by the role the Great Commission played as the motivation for missions in the history of Protestant missions. Boer notes a striking contrast between the bases that have undergirded the missionary witness of the church in the early period and the recent period of the church. The first contrast he notes is that since the post-Reformation period there has been a heavy emphasis on the Great Commission as motivation for missions, but in the early church there is a complete absence of this motivation as a conscious factor. The second contrast Boer notes is the lack of attention paid to Pentecost in relation to missions through the history of Protestantism, and the major emphasis Acts gives to Pentecost in terms of initiating and "wholly conditioning the missionary witness and expansion of the early church" (1961,15). This apparent misunderstanding of the role of the Great Commission has contributed to the eclipse of the Holy Spirit's missionary role.

The reason why the Great Commission played such a major role was that it was connected with a theological misconception of the Reformation period and the circumstances of the post-Reformation period. The Reformers and the majority of seventeenth century theologians believed the Great Commission was binding only on the apostles. They believed that when the apostles died Christ's command died with them. They held that since the apostles were extraordinary officers with no successors, that which was binding on them was no longer binding on the church (Boer 1961,17,20). The Reformers (Calvin, Luther, Melanchthon, Zwingli) saw the expansion of the church in terms of witness in the immediate community, or an extended witness as a result of scattering due to persecution. The Reformers believed another occasion for an extended witness was the non-Christian areas of the colonies. They believed that it was the duty of Christian governments to bring the gospel to them. The church, however, was believed to have had no mandate to preach the gospel and plant churches in distant lands by means of a program of missions. They believed the gospel was *in principle* declared to the whole world by the apostles (Boer 1961,18-20).[2]

Even though some voices were raised in opposition to this misconception about the Great Commission, the view held until it was assailed by the Pietists in the post-Reformation period. William Carey's *An Enquiry into the Obligations of Christians to use Means for the Conversion of the Heathen* argued that the Great Commission given by the Lord was still binding on the church (Boer 1961,16). Due to the success of Carey's argument in proving the continuing missionary obligation of the church on the basis of the Great Commission, it became the basis on which the missionary witness of the church was built (Boer 1961,24-25). The emphasis on the command of Christ for mission's motivation has prevailed until today. But the theological context and historical circumstances out of which this emphasis came have been largely forgotten. It is clear that the appeal to the Great Commission, among other factors, was powerful during an age when emphasis was placed on the written Word of God and obedience. The appeal to the command continued to revive missions for about 150 years.

Boer questions "whether an emphasis whose origins lie embedded so strongly in reaction to a long held theological misconception is also a *scriptural* emphasis" (1961,27). The fact that Jesus actually gave the command is not in doubt. Neither is there any doubt that the Scriptures are authoritative. An examination of the role of the Great Commission in initiating mission in Protestant history shows it to function in the biblical sense. It acts as a corrective, a reminder, and objective command to return the church to a task which is in accord with its purpose and its very nature—mission. However, the historical circumstances of the mobilization of the Protestant church in centrifugal mission does not provide the original biblical basis for mission. Nor do those circumstances reflect the church's true motivation for mission. Rather, the emphasis on the Commission represents the historical mobilization of the Protestant church, its return to an activity which was in accord with its purpose for being, and its inner nature. Furthermore, as Boer shows, an examination of the Acts reveals a complete absence of the Great Commission as the motivating impetus for mission. Instead, the Holy Spirit predominates the scene of mission.

Allen captures the significance of the absence of command for mission in Acts and the emphasis of the Spirit as an inward dynamic for witness. He believes that Acts stands alone in the New Testament in its revelation of the Holy Spirit as a *missionary Spirit* (1960,21). In the new age, the new people of God are by *nature* a witnessing community, because they have received a witnessing Spirit (John 15:26).[3] The primary motivation, therefore, is not an outward command, but an inward Spirit. The Acts is governed by one dominant, overriding and all-controlling theme, the expansion of the church through missionary witness in the power of the Holy Spirit (Acts 1:8).

It is interesting to note that in his book, *I Believe in the Great Commission*, Max Warren personifies the Great Commission as the Spirit of Christ within the believer. He states that Jesus himself is the Great Commission (1976,13). In the New Covenant we are not confronted by an ethical demand, we are confronted with a person. The claim of the New Testament is that the message is Jesus and Jesus is the Great Commission—the revealer of God. "To have received that revelation is to have entered into a particular relationship with the Great Commission. It is to know oneself commissioned" (Warren 1976,23-24).[4] This emphasis on the inward motivation and dynamic of mission agrees with Allen's statement and is in accord with the theology of the Holy Spirit and mission in Acts.

Warren is correct when he speaks of the Great Commission as personified, Christ dwelling within the believer by the Holy Spirit. However, this is only evident when the Holy Spirit's relation to Christ is clarified, when Christology is properly related to pneumatology. St. Luke begins volume two of his work (Acts) by referring to volume one where he says he wrote about all that Jesus *began* to do and teach (Acts 1:1). Then he immediately speaks of the promised Holy Spirit. The implication is that now through the inward presence of the Spirit in His people, Jesus would *continue* His mission (Mark 16:20; John 14:18; 17:26). For Luke, it is the Holy Spirit that gives the continuity to the period of the church and the period of Jesus, the same Spirit is operative in both. This is shown by the many parallels of the early community with the experience of Jesus (Montague 1976,268).

Both Warren and Allen captured Luke's thrust in Acts; the impetus for mission is internal—the Word of command is internalized. The commission is no longer merely an outward command, an ethical demand. It is now personified by the missionary Spirit's indwelling presence. Therefore, the Great Commission derives its meaning from this internalizing event. The Pentecostal event then is decisive for an understanding of the Spirit's role in initiating and universalizing mission. Of course, this does not take away from the function of the objective command in Scripture. It is a constant reminder of the missionary nature and purpose of the people of God. Nor does it take away from its value in providing the church with a strategy for mission.

Warren's work appears to be an effort to correct the misconception inherent in the western missionary heritage concerning the church's motivation for mission. In this way he addresses the demise of the experiential dimension of the faith. The Great Commission is honored in its function as a reminder of the church's missionary purpose in the world. But the emphasis is on the experiential dimension, the inward impetus of the Spirit of Christ in initiating and universalizing mission.

A result of the emergence of the Protestant missionary movement during the Enlightenment, therefore, was that the Holy Spirit's missionary role was neglected. The beginnings of the movement were characterized by an emphasis on the written command to the point where the outward-expressive dimension of the Spirit's missionary ministry was severely limited. This neglect by western theologians compelled Roland Allen to stress it (Branner 1975,18). Boer's study on the role of the Pentecost event and the Holy Spirit's role in the missionary expansion of the church illustrates the extent of the scholastic distortion in the post-Reformation period. It shows the impact of that theological tradition on the western missionary heritage.

Neglect in Mission Practice: The Non-Western World

Further evidence of the pneumatological hiatus in the western Protestant missionary heritage, perhaps the greatest evidence of all, concerns the impact of the western expression of Christianity and its theology on non-western cultures. The phenomenon of "independency" movements in the wake of the impact of western missions in the Third World is a chief contemporary evidence of the neglect of the Spirit. These movements have already been noted in chapters 1 and 2. How are these movements in the non-western world *evidence* of the silence on the Holy Spirit in western Christianity? How has western Christianity helped to provoke, or inspire, such movements?

There is no doubt that western Christianity has been chiefly instrumental in the causation of independency movements. Peel is representative in his somewhat general statement with regard to Christianity's role:

> Christianity has been both cause and catalyst of social change in Africa; and one of the most prominent features of modern Africa has been the emergence of independent churches, founded by Africans in protest at some feature of the Christianity of the missionary societies (1968,1).

Previously, Ngoni Sengwe clarified the issue of causation when he stated that the movements were the result of the clash of western culture and African culture, not the clash of the gospel and African culture (1981,94). Contrary to popular belief, in terms of cultural clash the roots of causation lie not in African culture but in *western* culture. The loss of value for, and perception of, the supernatural in western culture is an all-important antecedent factor in the study of independency movements.[5] Western Christianity's "practical anti-supernaturalism" (i.e. neglect of the Spirit) in supernaturalis-tic-oriented societies forms the conceptual framework for the study of their causation.

The excessive impact of western culture on the theology brought by the missionary to non-western cultures resulted in an extremely naturalistic, rationalistic, and abstract-oriented theological product being introduced into supernaturalistic, intuitive, and concrete-oriented societies. The contextualization of the Christian faith in such cultural situations should have involved both a fidelity to cultural context and a fidelity to biblical revelation. Where independency movements occurred, there appears to have been a failure on the part of western missionaries at *both* points of fidelity.

The more obvious failure, often noted, is the failure to consider the non-western cultural context with sufficient sensitivity. The less frequently observed failure concerns *the lack of articulation and application of the very supernaturalistic-oriented New Testament view of life* by the western missionary in African society. The lack of fidelity to the African cultural milieu was directly related to the lack of fidelity to divine revelation in the missionary's own culture first. The area of non-western culture that was consistently neglected by the western missionary in African society was the transempirical "middle world" of spirits. This area permeated every aspect of native culture. The neglect of this area represented a neglect of the life supporting matrix of those cultures and, therefore, was the increasing point of stress in them.

The failure to provide a biblical world view regarding the spirit world and the role of the Holy Spirit for the church is a western lack of fidelity to biblical revelation. Neglect, therefore, is to be perceived not only in a passive-avoidance of, or aggressive reaction against, the needs of African society. But it also should be perceived a *a failure to respond positively and biblically to those needs*. The failure concerns not only the cultural insensitivity of the western missionary, but it also involves his failure to respond biblically to needs which biblical revelation *amply provided for*.

In a real sense, explaining the causation of the African Independent churches as a reactionary movement in the African cultural milieu alone is inconclusive. The reaction in African society is the "fruit," not the "root" of causation. The "root" concerns the missionary neglect in articulating the biblical view of the supernatural in connection with the African view of reality (Sengwe 1981,95). The failure at fidelity to biblical revelation, because of the obtuse nature of the supernatural-experiential dimension of Christianity for the westerner, directs the discussion of causation away from the reactions of African society to the "root-cause"—*a western world view*.

Further evidence of the obscurity of the spirit world for the western missionary is found in his denial of that dimension in traditional societies and in his studied attack of traditional institutions which dealt with that dimension in non-western cultures. Oosterwal addresses this "blind spot" in the western missionary and its effects in the Third World in the following manner:

> For, it is precisely the absence or the lack of the power of God as a reality people can live by that has been a precipitating factor to these movements. In the African, Asian or Melanesian traditional religious

setting, *power* was at the center of their thinking, life and experience. And the *spirit*—of God, the gods or the ancestor—was a tangible reality. How remote, how intellectual, how powerless seems to be the God and the Spirit missionaries preach about or we [Western] Christians show in our lives. As one leader once expressed it in a conversation with a missionary: "you have held back the Spirit." The movements challenge our understanding of God, and our pneumatology . . . (1973,36).[6]

In his thesis on "African Independency," Avery states that in evaluating independency movements some western missionaries demanded that a "clean break" with paganism be a qualification before the movements could be considered Christian. However, the "clean break" was defined as the total repudiation of other supernatural forces, all forms of magic, benevolent or malevolent, and traditional medicine (1969,31). It appears that often missionaries took a God-against-culture position in African societies.[7]

In an article entitled, "Missions Churches, Independent Churches, and Felt Needs in Africa," Jacob Loewen gives several case studies where mission churches were found to have no way of dealing with phenomena of the transempirical dimension of spirit. He states the mission churches had no way of dealing effectively with dewitching processes and with witchcraft itself. But he points out that both traditional African society and the Independent African Churches did (1976,406-407). Loewen outlines the felt needs of African Christians which were met by the shaman in traditional societies: protection against witchcraft, the need for physical and psychical health, the need for supernatural sanction for confession, and the need for protection against evil spirits (1976,409-410). Concerning the avoidance of these areas by western mission churches Loewen states:

> Verbally missionaries tend to confess a belief in spirits, especially the Spirit of God. But it seems to be more lip service than anything else, because most of them have never seen or experienced an evil spirit. Their knowledge is entirely conceptual, rather than experiential. In fact, their whole educational system in the western scientific world has taught them that there is a deep cleavage between the material and the spiritual, and whether they want to or not, they tend to accept the material as much more real than the spiritual (1976,414-415).

Loewen's mention of the "deep cleavage between the material and the spiritual" is another way of saying the "middle" transempirical dimension of spirit is obscure in western culture.

The missionary assault on African traditional society was comprehensive. Barrett lists the following ten major areas which were attacked from tribe to tribe in varying degrees: community structure, land and property, laws and taboos, religious concepts, religious leadership, religious symbolism, magical concepts, rituals, worship, and the vernacular languages (1968,266-267). A period of stress and cultural distortion is described by Barrett:

Africans now realized with some *bitterness* that the hopes aroused by the early days of Christian preaching would not materialize. They had not anticipated the consequences in the severe strain being put on their traditional institutions. They had failed to obtain the *force vitale,* the mysterious power of the whites—either material, financial, cultural, religious, spiritual or ecclesiastical. Their societies were not being fulfilled by the new religion, but were being demolished. In the place of the secure religion they thought they had of old, there was now a religious void (1968,267).

An emasculated, western gospel could not possibly have filled that social and spiritual void. The neglect of the dynamic dimension of the Christian faith and the failure to articulate the biblical view about the spirit world in African society was disastrous.

On the other hand, the discovery of a dynamic, power-oriented expression of the Christian faith was like a *resurrection* for African Christians. This took place increasingly when the Scriptures were translated into the vernacular. The discovery of a Pentecostal expression of the faith did not result in a resurrection of traditional religion, nor in a bridge to paganism. But the discovery of an expression of Christianity which spoke to the needs of the African in his cultural context and provided Christian means for dealing with the spirit world, became the impetus for the African independency movements.

Barrett's investigation into the causation of independency movements in Africa emphasized the sociological and ecclesiastical dimensions in the clash between the western mission and the African traditional societies. His thesis concerning the root cause of the movements reflects the social level of his investigation:

The root cause common to the entire movement of independency, therefore, may be seen in this one aspect of culture clash: *a failure in sensitivity, the failure of missions at one small point to demonstrate consistently the fulness of the biblical concept of love as sensitive understanding towards others as equals, the failure to study or understand African society, religion and psychology in any depth, together with a dawning African perception from the vernacular scriptures of the catastrophic nature of this failure and of the urgent necessity to remedy it in order that Christianity might survive on African soil* (1968,156).[8]

However, Barrett's thesis concerns the "fruit" of causation, not the "root." He emphasizes the African response to the neglect of his culture and the resulting ecclesiastical problems. The attack on traditional institutions *in toto*, not differentiating the good elements from the bad, is only the surface manifestation of the inadequacy. The comprehensive attack of the western missionary on society is evidence of a deeper level of causation—at *world view level.*

Barrett's "lack of love" theory appears to be imposed on the evidence of his investigation. Perhaps this is due to the centrality of "love" in the Christian gospel and its application on the level of Barrett's investigation—church/missions tensions. Certainly more than a "lack of love" was behind the ethnocentrism which kept missionaries from learning African culture. Often the missionary failure is excessively characterized as "intentional." This intentional charge is especially prominent in the African viewpoint; that western missionaries were deliberately withholding "the fulness of the biblical welcome" (Barrett 1968,154). But the failure to teach the full benefits of the Holy Spirit was more due to the *deficiency of that dimension in western Christianity* than deliberate withholding of the truth. Rather than a discovery of divine love when the Scriptures were translated, it was the discovery of New Testament pneumatology that was so revolutionary for the African. The catastrophic nature of the missionary failure concerned the power of the Holy Spirit in the Christian life. This failure arose from an ethnocentrism rooted in a world view that caused the western missionary to neglect the same dimension of the Spirit in his own culture. The investigation of causation must probe deeper than the socioecclesiastical level. It must focus on the deficiency of a western world view with its aversion toward the spirit world. Such a deficiency in the Christian message in African society provided the catalyst for the independency movements. Therefore, the deprivation in African society goes beyond the social and economic. It primarily concerns a "spiritual" deprivation.

The western doubt as to the authenticity of these movements, as to their "Christianness," appears to be rooted in western Christianity's awkwardness with the subjective and experiential dimensions of the Spirit, and in a latent ethnocentrism. What appears to be problematic to the western missionary is the movements indigenous expression and their orientation to the dynamic-experiential dimension of Christianity. Establishing the validity of independency movements, therefore, must be done against the backdrop of a western ethnocentrism, its inadequate grasp of the experiential dimension of the faith, and a deficient pneumatology. The ease with which westerners reject New Testament models in evaluating Pentecostal phenomena in the movements speaks of the inadequacy of the western theological apparatus. The rejection takes place in spite of the lack of any biblical or Reformation principle that would preclude the manifestation of contemporary Pentecostal phenomena. The same pneumatological deficiency which precipitated independency movements, therefore, is also a liability in their contemporary evaluation.

4

An Experience with the Spirit

The purpose of this chapter is to outline the distinctives of
Pentecostalism. Basic to the whole study is the question, Who are
the Pentecostals? A concise definition is elusive when we view the
worldwide phenomenon. In a sense, the answer to this question is
only found in the context of the whole study. This chapter
examines the common denominator of the Pentecostal Movement,
the Pentecostal experience of the Spirit. The issues of a
"subsequent" and "evidential" experience with the Spirit are
analyzed. These issues are most frequently questioned by non-
Pentecostals. The primary motive for this focus is not to present an
apologetic for Pentecostal doctrine. Rather, it is to promote an
understanding of the Movement and thereby "open the door" for
Pentecostalism to make its maximum contribution to
contemporary missions.

The notion that Pentecostalism provides direction for
contemporary missions is based on its emphasis on the experiential
dimension of the Christian faith, the dynamic experience of the
Spirit. As a renewal movement, emphasizing a neglected dimension
of the Holy Spirit's ministry, Pentecostalism sets the subtle
influence of post-Reformation Protestant Scholasticism in bold
relief. It is at this point that Pentecostalism functions as a
"corrective" in contemporary missions. Criticisms of Pentecostalism often emerge from the above theological context, showing the
influence of scholastic tradition in modern evangelicalism. It is at
this point that Pentecostalism's "God with us" experience makes
its major contribution to contemporary missions. Paradoxically,
the chief criticism of the Movement, the distinct, dynamic
experience of the Spirit, reveals its chief contribution for
contemporary missions.

Who Are the Pentecostals? A Common Denominator

The historical study of the phenomenon of the Pentecostal Movement has pointed to common Pentecostal distinctives among a Movement with diverse denominational and cultural traditions. The possiblility of a common denominator in Pentecostalism is indicated by the spontaneous origins of the Movement and its distinct nature as a divine eschatological renewal. A common denominator is suggested by the belief among the three streams of Pentecostalism that God is renewing the church by restoring the full spectrum of the Holy Spirit's ministry today. Any common denominator having to do with Pentecostal distinctives, therefore, will concern the outward charismatic work of the Holy Spirit among classical Pentecostals, neo-Pentecostals, and Catholic Charismatics. The initial stage of this ministry of the Spirit after conversion is commonly called the "baptism of the Holy Spirit."

There are several evangelical criticisms that arise when one speaks of the "Pentecostal experience." Perhaps the chief objection is that charismatic manifestations of the Spirit belong to a past period of the church, the apostolic period. However, this objection to Pentecostalism has been largely abandoned since the Charismatic Movement began midway through the century. Those holding what some would call an "extreme" dispensational theology still object to believing that charismatic phenomena are normative today. It appears, however, that this objection is influenced by western culture under the impact of the Enlightenment as much as it is by biblical theology. In chapter 2, New Testament theology was seen to support the present-day occurrence of charismatic phenomena. The biblical evidence and theological underpinnings for contemporary charismatic phenomena rest in the New Testament concept of the dynamic, present kingdom of God. Pentecostalism was viewed as an *eschatological* phenomenon, a Movement consistent with the biblical meaning of the term. The dispensational objection to Pentecostalism is, therefore, the weakest criticism in terms of biblical theology.

Another criticism concerns the Pentecostal belief that the Pentecostal experience is normative for contemporary Christian experience. While some non-Pentecostal traditions hold to an experience with the Spirit subsequent to conversion, they object to the Pentecostal's emphasis on speaking in tongues in connection with the experience.

The Pentecostal's answer to these criticisms of his doctrine and experience can be formulated by the question, Is not Scripture normative? Of course, this is not a simple question, for it involves the matter of hermeneutics. While that question is discussed here, especially in connection with the Acts of the Apostles, chapters 5 and 6 also treat Pentecostal hermeneutics. There the question arises, What is the Pentecostal's view of biblical revelation, and how does he use Scripture to support the Pentecostal experience? In this chapter the focus is on the dynamic nature of Christianity itself. In addition to the question on the normative nature of Scripture, the Pentecostal would ask, is not Christianity the demonstration of God's power? This last question brings into focus a chief contribution of Pentecostalism for contemporary missions—the very nature of the Christian faith.

A Renewal Experience

In order to understand and evaluate Pentecostal pneumatology fairly, it must be viewed within the context of renewal. It concerns a neglected dimension of the Holy Spirit's ministry. It is a response to, and restoration of, New Testament Christian experience. "Renewal," therefore, explains the Pentecostal's emphasis on the outward-charismatic dimension of the Spirit's ministry. Pentecostalism's emphasis on the baptism of the Spirit and His charismatic gifts does not indicate a truncated, narrow pneumatology. Rather in dealing with a *restoration* of the Holy Spirit's outward charismatic ministry of power, it represents a return to a New Testament pneumatology. Pentecostal pneumatology is no different from that of Protestantism in general, except for this emphasis on the Holy Spirit's subsequent baptizing and charismatic work. It also includes the inward work of the Spirit in Christian initiation (initiation and growth in Christ, and in the fruit of the Spirit). However, as a *renewal* movement it emphasizes the charismatic-power dimension of the Spirit's ministry. The Pentecostal distinctives *do* concern this dimension of pneumatology, but this does not indicate the full spectrum of even classical Pentecostal pneumatology, contrary to Bruner's assertion (1970,57-59). The evangelical criticism that Pentecostals overemphasize the Holy Spirit in the Godhead must also be seen in this context. Michael Green observes that the charge of overemphasizing a particular person of the Godhead could also be leveled against Roman Catholicism and evangelicalism, and that only a fully trinitarian Christianity can stand the test of orthodoxy (1975,53).

A common denominator among all of the streams of Pentecostalism is the belief in a further experience with the Holy Spirit in addition to that of conversion. This experience is believed to be related to the experience of the early Christian community in the New Testament. All view their Pentecostal-charismatic experience as *normative*, in the sense that it follows the pattern or experience of the early church. "Renewal" indicates that Pentecostals believe a *neglected dimension* of the Holy Spirit's ministry is restored in contemporary times. In addition to the Holy Spirit's ministry as the principle of life in regeneration and sanctification, the outward-charismatic ministry of the Spirit is the dimension which is being renewed.

The discussion of the contemporary Pentecostal-charismatic experience as "subsequent" is especially fitting under the title of this section, "A Renewal Experience." When seen in an historical renewal framework some difficulties to the acceptance of "subsequence" are dispelled. Difficulties in accepting this "other" experience with the Holy Spirit are due to the long periods of church history where the full experience of the Spirit was lost. This "ebb and flow" phenomenon with regard to the charismatic experience in church history is addressed in greater detail in chapter 7.

The recognition of two dimensions of the Holy Spirit's work, even in terms of His initial and subsequent work in Christian experience, is found in Wesleyan holiness theology, Keswickian Reformed theology (Menzies 1975,86), and Roman Catholic theology (Grassi 1978,7-8; Montague 1976,32). The Wesleyan stream of Pentecostalism made a distinction of subsequent experience to conversion in connection with the holiness view of sanctification and perfectionism. That tradition in Pentecostalism holds to a three stage view of the Christian's experience with the Holy Spirit. However, the Keswickian tradition views a subsequent experience as an enduement of power for service (Menzies 1975,86-88; Dunn 1970,2,32). These two theological traditions in Pentecostalism represent the subsequent experience as "necessary," or "normative," and may be classified as *subsequence theologies*. Subsequence theologies hold to two or three crisis experiences with the Holy Spirit in Christian experience. Other Protestant neo-Pentecostal groups also fit within this theological classification, in terms of their view of a subsequent experience with the Holy Spirit (Menzies 1978,1).

When Bruner treats this subsequent experience in Pentecostalism entirely in terms of Wesleyan eradication theology (1970,94,117), he is mistaken. He emphasizes a "doctrine of conditions" as though this was an accepted norm in the Movement instead of a matter where there is a wide diversity, even a plethora of opinion in classical Pentecostalism alone. Actually, Bruner only speaks of one theological tradition when he says:

> The doctrine of conditions, then, is actually a corollary of the doctrine of subsequence and a premise for the doctrine of evidence and as such occupies a cornerstone position in the edifice of the distinctive Pentecostal doctrine (1970,88).

The Keswickian wing of Pentecostalism, however, does not view the Spirit's work in the subsequent stage as eradication of sin with the above mentioned corresponding "condition." Rather it is viewed as an enduement of power received by *faith*.

Bruner's fixation on a "doctrine of conditions" (1970,87-116) appears to be due to his distaste for the Arminian theology of the Wesleyan holiness doctrine, which emphasizes the will of man in connection with faith. However, Roman Catholic theology stresses, and rightly so, the importance of "subjective dispositions": awareness, expectancy and openness with regard to the faith-appropriation of the charismatic experience (McDonnell 1980,27-29). This point is dealt with in detail in chapter 7 from the standpoint of Scripture. Bruner appears to be strongly influenced by Protestant Scholasticism in his denial of the dynamic, continuing nature of faith. This is evident in his extremely static-punctilliar view of faith. This contrast to that which sees faith as a principle by which the believer is justified in the forensic sense and as a continuing principle by which he lives (Rom. 1:17).

The Roman Catholic theological tradition also includes two distinct experiences with the Holy Spirit in the Christian life. But the emphasis is on the *growth process* in the Christian experience (McDonnell 1980,38-39). The subsequent experience of the Spirit is viewed more in terms of the Spirit, who was given at water baptism, coming to conscious experience at a particular point in the Christian life. They consider this experience as a "new relationship to the Holy Spirit." However, it is sometimes seen as a new imparting of the Spirit in connection with a particular ministry in the Christian community (McDonnell 1980,38-39). The Protestant neo-Pentecostal traditions which view the subsequent experience with the Holy Spirit in the sacramental sense as described here, as well as Roman Catholic tradition, may be classified as *actualization theologies*. Menzies states concerning these theologies, "The normal expectation of the believer is to bring to conscious experience what is incipient from baptism or new birth" (1978,1).

There is no doubt that the impact of the Enlightenment on western Christianity in the post-Reformation period has much to do with the difficulty of accepting the restoration of the Pentecostal-charismatic experience in contemporary western Christianity. A western difficulty in evaluating subsequent Pentecostal experiences is the theological paradigm inherited from the scholastic theology of the post-Reformation period. In this paradigm the role of the Spirit is reduced to His work in connection with Scripture (almost exclusively with His work at the author-end). This in turn has eliminated the "witness of the Spirit" in verifying Christian experience. Biblical authority was, therefore, reduced to the "objective" written Word. Its locus was wrongly conceived as the text of Scripture rather than the *witness of the Spirit* in conjunction with that written Word *in the heart of the Christian*. This deficiency in pneumatology leaves the impression that biblical authority is primarily *noetic* in nature (having to do with reflection, thinking, propositional statements on the confrontation of being) rather than *ontic* (having to do with immediacy, presence, "thereness," confrontation with reality). Biblical authority is ontic in nature in that it deals primarily with the witness of the Spirit to the Word in the heart of the believer. Therefore, the tendency is to limit the Spirit's work to New Testament times, or at least, to his inward work of regeneration and sanctification today.

In the conclusion to James Dunn's study, *Baptism in the Holy Spirit*, he sees the Pentecostal emphasis on "experience" as an attempt to correct the above western distortion of pneumatology. He states:

> Against the mechanical sacramentalism of extreme Catholicism and the dead biblicist orthodoxy of extreme Protestantism they [the Pentecostals] have shifted the focus of attention to the *experience* of the Spirit. Our examination of the NT evidence has shown that they were wholly justified in this (1970,225).

The counterpart of the Pentecostal experience of the Spirit is the scholastic theological articulation of the Spirit, which Dunn calls the "biblicist orthodoxy of extreme Protestantism."[1]

The notion of a subsequent experience with the Spirit collides with the Protestant orthodoxy represented by the post-Reformation period. The relatively new and sustained restoration of the full experience of the Holy Spirit in the history of the church via Pentecostalism is both a reaction to scholastic orthodoxy and a challenge to it. The above western aversion to the subjective dimension of the Spirit in Protestantism (and evangelicalism) has a direct bearing on the evangelical criticisms of the Pentecostal claim to a subsequent experience with the Holy Spirit. Discussion of a "subsequent" charismatic experience of the Spirit uncovers a *western disposition* which militates against renewal of this neglected dimension of the Spirit.

As mentioned previously, "renewal" reveals that "subsequence" is in one sense "necessary," due to the *historical* restoration of the charismatic dimension of the Spirit's ministry in the contemporary church. A.J. Gordon also referred to this historical restoration of the Pentecostal experience. He stated that God has offered a higher position in this matter of the experience of the Spirit than the church has been able to occupy. He believed that the full experience of the Spirit was, and is, offered to each person at conversion, and that it is only from want of faith that a subsequent experience of the Holy Spirit becomes needful (Gordon 1964,86). Normally, the Pentecostal experience is received when one is convinced that it is a valid dimension of the full experience of the Spirit. Therefore, in terms of a renewal in the history of the church the Pentecostal experience *is* an experience "historically subsequent" to conversion for Christendom in general.

The above Protestant explanation of "subsequence" is nearly identical to that of Roman Catholic theologians on the subject. They stress the charismatic experience of the Spirit in terms of renewal, both historical and personal. Speaking for an international group of Roman Catholic theologians, Kilian McDonnell states that the differences between the early Christian community and the community of Christians in the contemporary church is to be found in a "difference of awareness, expectation and openness" (1980,28). Roman Catholics strongly emphasize that the Charismatic Renewal does not mean the church or Christians receive something they do not already possess, but rather "the renewal points to an expanded awareness, and this awareness and expectancy affect experience and the total life of the church" (1980,36). While it is recognized that the Spirit is sovereign and free, it is pointed out that He ordinarily deals with individuals "at the point of where they are, and that subjective dispositions in some sense affect experience" (McDonnell 1980,30). Where communities do not expect the Holy Spirit's outward-charismatic ministry, that ministry is not usually operative.

In terms of awareness and expectancy, faith is especially crucial for those holding to "actualization theologies." The "subsequence theologies" of classical Pentecostalism also stress faith and the already-present, indwelling Holy Spirit in the Christian life. This is contrary to the supposition of many non-Pentecostals. But "subsequence" is interpreted not only as a "historical necessity" for the contemporary church in general, but also as *personal necessity* for every Christian. Pentecostals believe that the experience of the full spectrum of the Holy Spirit's ministry is the *normative* Christian experience for both the early and contemporary church.

A Normative Experience

Classical Pentecostals would say the Pentecostal distinctive is a conscious-crisis experience with the Holy Spirit called the baptism in the Holy Spirit. It will be clear in the description of that experience by classical Pentecostals that "subsequence" is conceived in a different sense than the mere historical renewal of the Pentecostal experience to the contemporary church in general. They believe that this subsequent experience is normative for contemporary Christian experience. The theological underpinnings of this view were discussed in chapter two. The Assemblies of God statement on the Pentecostal experience is discussed here in order to bring into focus a classical description.[2]

A comment on the nature and purpose of creedal or confessional statements, like the Assemblies of God statement, before addressing the issue of "subsequence" in Pentecostalism is useful at this point. The Assemblies of God statement, "The Baptism in the Holy Ghost," like all creedal statements, focuses on particular problems, issues, or needs in the context of contemporary Christian thought and life. As such, they can never be viewed apart from the context of their authors or their existential historical moment. Nor should they be viewed as statements of "pure" theological truth or content. They are "contextualizations" of Christian truth, serving the church in its contemporary effort to understand the faith, to articulate it in accord with that understanding, and to obey it in practice. Such statements *do* focus on biblical content, but they also have a particular focus on the context of contemporary belief and practice in the particular historical moment. They are "selective" in nature and purpose as opposed to being "comprehensive" in nature and purpose.

Creedal statements, then, are the result of the church's response to Scripture in the light of particular issues and problems. Or, in other words, they are the result of fresh theologizing on the basis of Scripture about issues arising out of a particular historical context. Regardless of the particular ecclesiastical confession involved, such statements are never absolute statements, or complete statements; nor are they perennial in nature. This is true, not only because of their contextual focus, but it is also true due to the imperfect nature (though not necessarily incorrect) of all human articulations of divine truth (1 Cor 12:8). From time to time, therefore, they must be updated and sharpened through fresh theologizing on the basis of Scripture and the changing contextual problems facing the church. Chapter 5 discusses this "reinterpretation of dogma" phenomenon in detail.

With the previous introductory statement concerning the nature and purpose of confessional statements in general, the Assemblies of God statement can be analyzed in terms of its nature and purpose. The Pentecostal distinctives the statement articulates are those scriptural points about the Pentecostal experience which tend to preserve its uniqueness in a period of controversy. The *normative* nature of the experience ("all believers . . . normal experience of all in the early Christian Church . . . power for life and service") and the *distinct* nature of the experience (subsequence and evidence) are emphasized. The statement's purpose in preserving the distinctive nature of the Pentecostal experience is evident, as well as its reactionary-apologetic nature, in that a separate article exists for the evidence of the Pentecostal experience.

The distinct way the Pentecostal experience is described in the Assemblies of God statement is due to the historical controversy surrounding the experience and its distinctive—tongues.[3] Controversy was not so much over the fruit of the Spirit, which is also evidence of a genuine baptism of the Spirit, but on the "initial outward evidence" of the experience. Menzies states that the point of clarity on the evidence of the baptism in the Holy Spirit was not "merely sectarian narrowness"; rather, the motive was the preservation of a doctrine believed to be "basic to a full-orbed New Testament Church" (1971,125). The statement, then, should be understood in the context of its purpose—to preserve the distinctivenes of the Pentecostal experience—which in terms of the New Testament witness involved the outward charismatic ministry of the Spirit as well as His inward life-giving work.

Bruner's analysis of an earlier Assemblies of God statement focuses on the points above (subsequence and evidence) and a third point—"conditions"—in receiving the experience (Bruner 1970, 61,87-88,111).[4] However, the third point—"conditions"—appears to be arbitrarily extracted from the statement.[5] Bruner reads into the Keswickian-oriented statement the alleged "conditions" in order to carry out his polemic against the explicit Arminianism in the Wesleyan holiness tradition in Pentecostalism (1970,61). Furthermore, "conditions" are not indicated in the earlier Assemblies of God statement. Rather, the normativity of the Pentecostal experience, in terms of its availability and value for all Christians, is expressed. Bruner makes the statement carry more theological freight than its authors intended it to carry.

The relatively concise statement on the baptism of the Holy Spirit and its evidence is not intended to be a full statement on pneumatology. The doctrinal statement centers on the task of preserving the Pentecostal experience as a distinct conscious-crisis experience, in which the full spectrum of the Holy Spirit's ministry is kept in focus. This "preservation purpose" is evident in the Assemblies of God statement. One could say, then, that the matter of "subsequence" focuses not so much on the *time-sequence* as on the *full experience of the Holy Spirit* (of course, a logical subsequence is not in question here, that the Spirit's regenerating work logically precedes his charismatic work). The statement emphasizes the Pentecostal experience as "distinct" from conversion; it is on the neglected dimension of the Spirit's work in salvation history.

In referring to Dunn's study on the baptism in the Holy Spirit, Gordon Fee speaks somewhat indirectly to this idea of the full experience of the Spirit. He states:

> In a carefully argued exegetical study of all the relevant passages in Acts, Dunn (*Baptism in the Holy Spirit*) concluded that for Luke the real evidence (and chief element) of Christian experience was the presence of the Spirit. What seems to be important for Luke in this narrative is that the validation (and completion) of Christian experience in the initial spread beyond Jerusalem is tied to the Jerusalem church and signified by a dynamic quality similar to theirs. If Dunn is correct, and it surely is defensible exegesis, then the concept of subsequence is irrelevant. What is of consequence is the experiential, dynamic quality of the gift of the Spirit (1976,130).

The problem with subsequence appears to be asking questions of a text which is speaking of something else. The element of "time sequence" with regard to subsequence is not the important issue, or Luke's intention. Rather, the validation and completion of Christian experience is.

Fee then observes that if "subsequence" as "distinct from and subsequent to" cannot be established as being "taught" in the New Testament as the pattern for Christian experience, "there is a pattern is Acts which *may* be derived not only from historical precedent but also from the intent of Luke and Paul" (Fee 1976,130). Following Dunn's lead, Fee describes that pattern as focusing on the experience of the Spirit as a chief element in the process of Christian conversion, as well as its validating element. He states that in the Acts the presence or coming of the Spirit had a dynamic, charismatic nature (1976,131). He adds to this observation that Pentecostals see speaking in tongues as a repeated pattern in the New Testament (1976,131).

About the Pentecostal's attempt to preserve the dynamic dimension of the Spirit's ministry, Fee states:

> If in his attempt to recapture this New Testament pattern, the Pentecostal saw the dynamic element as "distinct from and subsequent to," he should not thereby be faulted. The fault perhaps lay with the church which no longer normally expected or experienced life in the Spirit in a dynamic way (1976,131).

The New Testament witness emphasizes a pattern of dynamic, Spirit-oriented Christian initiation which, in the eyes of the Pentecostal, is being restored in the contemporary Pentecostal Movement. The presence of examples of a subsequent charismatic experience in the Acts, whether exegetically sound or not, correspond with contemporary experience. Christians *are* experiencing a subsequent, dynamic experience with the Spirit which *is* identical to that of the first century church!

The parallel between the contemporary charismatic experience of the Spirit and that of the first century church may be more than coincidental, however. Luke's reason for recording those examples of a subsequent charismatic experience of the Spirit, where Christians did not experience the full dimension of the Spirit immediately upon conversion, could be that he intended to emphasize that the full reception or experience of the Spirit was *normative*. The same reason why contemporary Christians do not experience the full dimension of the Spirit—a matter of faith-awareness, faith-expectancy, or faith-openness—could be the key to the interpretation of the often quoted "subsequence experiences" in the Acts (Acts 8:12-17; 9:1-19; 19:1-7). Luke intends by these incidents to emphasize the necessity of experiencing the full dimension of the Spirit's ministry—the dynamic charismatic dimension included—even if it is hindered for some reason. Imperfect dispositions, such as those mentioned above, would prevent the normal experience of the Spirit (Montague 1976,293-294).

The outward dynamic dimension of the experience of the Spirit, in terms of the Spirit's witness, appears to have played an important role in validating Christian experience, especially as the gospel moved across cultural and prejudicial frontiers (Acts 3,9,10,19). Green sees Luke's purpose with the problematic account of the Samaritans (Acts 8) as an effort to stress the links between the church at Jerusalem and the expanding circles of Christian outreach. The distance in kilometers was not as dangerous to the potential loss of unity in the early church as the "cultural distance" the gospel traversed. Green suggests that God did not give the supernatural manifestations of the Spirit—tongues and prophecy—to the Samaritans at once upon their conversion, so that Jerusalem representatives could come down and express solidarity with them. He explains:

> It was not so much an authorisation from Jerusalem or an extension of the Jerusalem church, as a divine veto on schism in the infant church, a schism which could have slipped almost unnoticed into the Christian fellowship, as converts from the two sides of the "Samaritan curtain" found Christ without finding each other (1975,138-139).

Green, therefore, states that the account is recorded for the purpose that it is not typical for Christian initiation (1975,137). The outward evidence of the Spirit's coming was that which validated Christian experience in such cases and was the means for preventing schism that might arise on the basis of the gospel's diverse cultural expressions as it took root in the cultures of Gentile peoples.

One may well ask why the Pentecost event itself (and the disciple's experience of the fullness of the Spirit) is not used here for the discussion of "subsequence." The Pentecost event marked the ushering in of the era of the Spirit in which the full experience of the Spirit is made possible for all Christians following that event. The disciples' example, while clearly illustrating the full experience of the Spirit, does not provide a normative "subsequence" pattern for Christian initiation now. Their unique position in bridging two eras of salvation history prevents this. Their example *does*, however, support a distinctive, conscious-crisis Pentecostal experience for the church today. The example of the disciples is valid according to hermeneutical principle for the *type* of experience but not the *time* of the experience. Dunn is correct when he states concerning their example:

> The epochal significance of Pentecost raises the whole course of salvation-history to a new plane. As the beginning of the new age of the Spirit, the new covenant, the Church, it is what happened at Pentecost and not before which is normative for those who would enter that age, covenant and Church. The (pre-Christian) experience of the 120 prior to Pentecost can *never* provide a pattern for the experience of new Christians now (1970,53).

Dunn does not deny that what happened in the lives of the disciples prior to Pentecost is not applicable today, following an extreme dispensationalism. He merely points out that the disciples occupied a unique position in the transition of dispensations and that the era ushered in by Pentecost is the normative context for viewing Christian initiation in the age of the Spirit.[6]

Dunn's view of the Pentecost event in the course of salvation history emphasizes the matter of subsequence in terms of a distinct, dynamic experience of the Spirit which is repeatable. But the event is not viewed as a pattern of Christian experience where "subsequence" is viewed as a *normative time-sequence* for contemporary Christian initiation. In their unique salvation history position, bridging the old and the new eras, the disciples' Pentecostal experience is clearly subsequent to their conversion. However, the "Gentile Pentecost" (Acts 10) does not involve disciples in a period of salvation history transition (of the same sort) like the 120. Therefore, their baptism in the Holy Spirit (Cornelius' household) is not a "necessary" subsequent experience, only in a "logical" sense is it subsequent to conversion. It appears that Dunn argues for the Cornelius-type, simultaneous but dynamic, experience of the Spirit as that which is normative for Christian initiation today.

Though the Pentecostal experience of Caesarea was simultaneous with conversion, and in spite of it taking place in the unlikely Gentile context of God-fearers, its validity is unquestioned when related to the Jewish Christians in Jerusalem. This is a significant point to recognize. The witness of the Spirit in the evidential manner of His coming at Caesarea was identical to that of His coming at Jerusalem. The Jewish Pentecost, therefore, represents that "normative pattern" in terms of the distinct, charismatic type of experience with the Spirit; it has validation-value for Christian initiation. The Gentile Pentecost, on the other hand, could represent the normative pattern in terms of time-sequence for Christian initiation today, post-Pentecost. Affective dispositions, the same factor which prevented the full experience of the Spirit in Acts, could be a major reason why the Gentile Pentecost is not the normative pattern for common Christian experience today. People just do not *expect* a Cornelius-type baptism of the Holy Spirit at the point of conversion today.

Dunn's view of the baptism of Jesus at Jordan is also in a salvation history context, and is especially supportive of the Pentecostal's view of a distinct experience of the Spirit apart from conversion. But it is supportive in the Keswickian sense, as an enduement of power for service. However, Dunn argues that "subsequence" with respect to Jesus' experience of the Spirit at Jordan, while hermeneutically possible in terms of the personal experience of Jesus, is a secondary matter (1970,24). The primary matter is the event as a pivotal point in salvation history. Dunn states:

> In other words, we are dealing not so much with stages in the life of Jesus, which belong to the same dispensation of salvation-history and so can be appealed to as the pattern for all who belong to the same dispensation; we are dealing rather with stages in salvation-history itself. The experience of Jesus at Jordan is far more than something merely personal—it is a unique moment in history: the beginning of a new epoch in salvation-history—the beginning, albeit in a restricted sense, of the End-time, the messianic age, the new covenant (1970,24).

In terms of the twofold hermeneutical task, it could be said that what the text "meant" was that the event pointed to the initiation of a new age and the initiation of Jesus into that new age. But in terms of "means," in the interpretation and application, the event may be described as a second experience of the Spirit for Christian initiation (Dunn 1970,24-25).[7]

Dunn's salvation history view of Jesus' baptism is especially supportive of the Keswickian view of the baptism of the Holy Spirit. His discussion of Jesus' previous experience with the Spirit, contrasting it with the empowering for ministry, strongly suggests the nature and purpose of the experience. Commenting on how the first baptism of the Spirit (Jesus') could be taken as typical for all later Spirit-baptisms, Dunn states:

> Pentecostals are right to recognize that Jesus' anointing with the Spirit was what equipped him for his messianic ministry of healing and teaching (Acts 10:38). This empowering for service should not however be taken as the primary purpose of the anointing—it is only a corollary to it. The baptism in the Spirit, in other words, is not primarily to equip the (already) Christian for service; rather its function is to initiate the individual into the new age and covenant, to

"Christ" (= anoint) him, and in so doing to equip him for life and service in that new age and covenant (1970,32).

Granted the Christian is not equipped in the sense that he initially receives the Spirit in the baptism of the Holy Spirit; he receives the Spirit at conversion. The baptism of the Spirit still can be conceived as an *initiation* (belated of course) to the new age. The Christian is ushered into the *charismatic dimension* of the Spirit's ministry. Initiation into that dimension is also an anointing and empowering for service. The Pentecostal, therefore, sees in Dunn's statement above a certain redundancy, both actual and conceptual. For the person baptized in the Spirit, the experience is *both* an initiation to the potentials of the age of the Spirit *and* an anointing or empowering for service in that age.[8]

The Pentecostal's claim that the Pentecostal experience is normative finds strong support in the New Testament. It emphasizes the "full" experience of the Spirit, both His inward life-giving ministry and His outward charismatic ministry. The "given" of an historical renewal of a neglected dimension of the Spirit's ministry has forced the issue of "subsequence" to the fore. The Assemblies of God statement on the baptism of the Holy Spirit shows the results of the doctrine being contextualized in a period of controversy. The issue of subsequence is tied to the purpose of preserving the full experience of the Spirit. The dimension which is neglected is in focus in the statement—the outward, charismatic dimension. The distinct, conscious-crisis experience which is believed to usher one into the new dimension of the Spirit's ministry—the baptism of the Holy Spirit—is that which is in focus.

The historical renewal of the Pentecostal experience and the effort to preserve its distinctive nature have caused Pentecostals to emphasize the evidence of "subsequence" in Acts. Bias in western culture and world view, which tends toward an emphasis of discrete categories and time sequences, perhaps, has much to do with the attention paid to the subsequence issue as well. Westerners tend to "see" more categories and divisions in the holistically-oriented biblical material than is warranted. "Subsequence" in the New Testament witness, however, is connected with Luke's purpose in emphasizing the complete experience of the Holy Spirit's ministry. The time element does not appear to be in the category of normativity but rather in that of abnormality, due to various "subjective dispositions" on the part of believers (or, perhaps, a sovereign decision on the part of God? Acts 8), which prevented the full experience of the Spirit. The complete experience of the Spirit in the New Testament is normative, and it is concrete in nature. It is a conscious experience and it is accompanied with charismatic phenomena.

What Is Their Unique Message? "God with Us"

In dealing with the subject of "evidence" for the Pentecostal experience, or just supernatural evidence in contemporary Christian experience in general, the following questions are important. First, Should there be evidence for this further experience with the Holy Spirit? Second, and more fundamentally, Should there be further evidence for the Christian experience *at all* beyond the written Word of God? Finally, Should the initial evidence for the Pentecostal experience be tongues? The first two questions are fundamental in evaluating evangelical criticisms of the Pentecostal Movement. The third question is only of secondary theological importance for many evangelicals. The first two questions address a prevalent theological orientation among conservative evangelicals—that of Protestant Scholasticism. This orientation is the antithesis to the theological orientation of Pentecostal theology.

The matter of the initial outward evidence of the baptism of the Holy Spirit has been reserved for discussion under this section dealing with the unique message of Pentecostalism. But it is not here because Pentecostalism's unique message is speaking in tongues. It is appropriate to treat it at this point because speaking in tongues is that phenomenon which so commonly represents the dynamic experience of the Spirit in Pentecostalism. That the Spirit's coming in the Pentecostal experience is an *evidential* coming, points to both a *chief criticism* of the Movement and its *chief contribution*.

"Evidence": Bankrupt Faith or New Testament Faith?

The chief criticism mentioned above concerns the Pentecostal claim that the baptism of the Holy Spirit is accompanied by the initial evidence of speaking in other tongues. Often the criticism is part and parcel of a dispensational view that limits outward Pentecostal-charismatic type phenomena and the miraculous to the apostolic period only. The notion of "evidence" to critics holding such a dispensational view often is an indication of a bankrupt faith on the part of the Pentecostal. They say that one should be content with the authority of the written Word alone. This statement, at first glance, sounds quite Reformation-based. But such a view reveals the influence of post-Reformation Protestant Scholasticism. It points to the absence of statements regarding the "witness of the Spirit" and the outward charismatic working of the Spirit in conservative evangelical theology.

The criticism of the "evidential" coming of the Spirit reveals a weakness in evangelical theology and also brings to the fore the unique Pentecostal contribution (unique in terms of contemporary evangelical theology). The Pentecostal would simply reply to the evangelical charge that he has weak faith because of his doctrine of evidence, "Isn't Christianity the demonstration of God's power?" Or, he would ask, "Has not the kingdom of God broken through into this present age?" Or perhaps more specifically he might ask, "Isn't the Holy Spirit's witness, both inward and outward, to be expected today?" The Pentecostal contribution, therefore, concerns the dynamic experience of the Spirit, and His active witness in validating Christian experience today.

In the Introduction this emphasis on the dynamic dimension of the Christian faith was referred to as the "eighth principle," which Pentecostalism adds to the seven evangelical principles. Pentecostalism believes in the continuing activity of God today, by means of the inward and outward ministry of the Holy Spirit. It is concerned with the ontic principle of theology, the immediacy of the presence of God, the "thereness" of God in Christian experience and mission. The Pentecostal sees the validity of his Pentecostal experience today, its contemporaneity, to be founded on biblical theology and the witness of the Spirit. He is not reluctant to admit the latter, as it is together with the former a renewal of a Reformation principle—the indivisible nature of Word and Spirit. The notion of the Spirit validating Christian experience in contemporary times is a New Testament concept.

The Pentecostal's emphasis on the evidential coming of the Spirit presents a bothersome theme for conservative evangelical theology. Pentecostalism's pneumatology brings a pervasive dynamic orientation to its theology as a whole. The evangelical criticism concerning "evidence" points to the uniqueness of the Pentecostal message itself. It points to the dynamic nature of the Christian experience, as opposed to the cerebral, "faith-alone" nature of Protestant Scholasticism. The distinctive Pentecostal message, therefore, brings a corrective to the pervasive influence of post-Reformation Scholasticism in evangelical theology. Pentecostalism's message of "God with us," the renewal of the dynamic experiential dimension of the Christian faith, is a corrective to the western distortion. Under the influence of the Enlightenment an expression of the faith arose which reduced it to a noetic, rational system of belief, effecting a separation of Word and Spirit. At the root of the evangelical criticism of Pentecostalism, therefore, is a theological orientation which rejects the notion of "evidence" as either superfluous or anti-faith. The problem is with evidence *per se*, not merely the evidence of tongues.

Of course, speaking of the "eighth principle"—the dynamic dimension of the Christian faith—is just another way of saying that Pentecostalism brings fresh attention to the activity of the Holy

Spirit in Christian experience and mission today. If its formally articulated theology does not do so, the phenomenon of the Pentecostal Movement itself brings to light the neglect of pneumatology in western theology. The doctrines of biblical revelation and biblical authority are in focus when discussing the "evidence" of the Pentecostal experience. But a scholastic view of these doctrines is ill-equipped to evaluated Pentecostal phenomena. We have already illustrated its inadequacy in confronting certain issues in contemporary mission theology (e.g., the African Independent Church Movement).

The impact of Protestant Scholasticism in evangelical theology is clear when Bernard Ramm explains that in his preparation of the book, *The Pattern of Religious Authority*, he found that the doctrine of the internal witness of the Holy Spirit had almost disappeared from evangelical literature and theology (1959,7). The dynamic nature of both biblical revelation and biblical authority are important with regard to the Pentecostal doctrine of evidence. Pentecostals focus on the activity and witness of the Spirit at "this end" of biblical revelation, not only in connection with the authors of Scripture in the apostolic period.

The contrast of the theological orientations above may be illustrated by comparing the historic Reformed view of biblical revelation with the Reformed scholastic view. A chart showing this contrast is found in the Appendix. The diverse approaches to Scripture illustrate the contrasting theological orientations discussed here. The historic Reformed view emphasized the *function* of Scripture in its saving purpose. Scripture was dynamic in nature, it was enlivened by the Spirit. The Reformed scholastic view was preoccupied with the *form* of Scripture, the written text, and was static in nature. It represented a rationalistic approach to Scripture which resulted in the concept of the dynamic Word of God being reduced to its written form only (Pomerville 1980,95). These contrasts are important to recognize so that the Pentecostal orientation to biblical revelation and authority may be brought into focus. A principle contrast in the above mentioned chart is the activity of the Holy Spirit in the historic Reformed view and His absence in the Reformed scholastic view, with the exception of His work with the authors of Scripture. In its dynamic view of biblical revelation and authority, then, Pentecostalism follows in the tradition of historic Reformation theology.

In Bruner's *Theology of the Holy Spirit: The Pentecostal Experience and the New Testament Witness*, he argues against the doctrine of the initial evidence of the baptism of the Holy Spirit and the supposed necessity of evidence (the Pentecostal's requirement of evidence). The argument centers on the Wesleyan holiness stream of Pentecostalism, which in Bruner's view violates *sola fides* most. The inclusion of "evidence" in the Assemblies of God doctrinal statement on the baptism, in his view, detracts from the Reformation formula of saving faith, or *sola fides* (1970,115). The idea of evidence *per se* receives specific attention in the argument and is always in a pejorative context. The experiential dimension is also invalid with respect to a verification of Christian experience (1970,82). Only propositional statements from the text of Scripture are valid in this regard. Anything outside of "simple faith" in Christ is, in Bruner's view, an occasion for criticism. However, the scholastic, rationalistic view of *sola fides* in Bruner's argument is not that of the Reformation.

In Bruner's view "evidence-less" faith is what *sola fides* and *simplex fides* (apart from the evidence of Scripture, that is) signify. All of this discussion, however, is not about the conversion experience. It is in connection with the Pentecostal's subsequent experience of the baptism of the Holy Spirit and its evidence. The whole discussion against "necessity" of evidence made in connection with saving faith is imposed on the theological issue of evidence in regard to the Pentecostal experience. Not only is faith held to be "evidence-less" in terms of personal conversion, but the activity of God the Holy Spirit in contemporary times is also to be "evidence-less." This view reveals not only a very static view of faith but also a scholastic, noetic view of revelation and biblical authority. An underlying theological orientation shapes the theological argument—Protestant Scholasticism.

George Peters's evaluation of the twentieth century revival in Indonesia, *Indonesian Revival: Focus on Timor*, represents an argument against the miraculous and New Testament charismatic phenomena in contemporary times. It reflects Peters's strong dispensational position. However, the same underlying theological orientation that was evident in Bruner's criticism of Pentecostalism's "evidence" doctrine is found in Peters's evaluation of the Timor revival. To expect New Testament phenomena, or to show an interest in the supernatural, is interpreted as anti-faith. According to Peters, it is an indication of weak faith![9] The scholastic dichotomy of Word and Spirit, and Scholasticism's limitation of the Spirit's role in contemporary supernatural manifestations are evident when Peters states:

> If miracles are made *necessary* for our age to verify the power of the Gospel of Jesus Christ, we show on the one hand the bankruptcy of our faith in the Word of God written, and on the other hand we reflect negatively upon the sufficiency of God's past revelation and manifestations (1973,60).[10]

While the miraculous is never spoken of in normative terms, but only to meet the needs of animistic peoples in Peters's argument, it appears that dispensationalism alone is not the reason for the reluctance to admit to the probability of supernatural, New Testament phenomena. In spite of the clear references to such phenomena in the New Testament, and his own admission as to their biblical nature, Peters chooses to explain away the supernatural phenomena of the Timor revival. He attributes them for the most part to the "mentality" of non-western peoples, or to nativism (1973,63-71). This somewhat astounding matter of attributing supernatural phenomena in a non-western expression of Christianity to nativism, rather than to a New Testament expression of the faith, was also noted in the African context. The pervasive and subtle influence of Protestant Scholasticism appears to be part of the reason (along with a latent prejudice against Pentecostalism and a latent ethnocentrism).

A theological orientation which sees revelation as static in nature appears to control Peters's evaluation of the miraculous phenomena of the Timor revival. Anything beyond the rational-propositional proof of the written Word of God, in terms of Christian experience, is seen to militate against an alleged Reformation "faith-alone" stance. Such a position, however, is not representative of the Reformation but of post-Reformation Scholasticism. *Sola scriptura* and *sola fides*, in the context of the Reformation, do not even address the matter of the supernatural evidence of the Holy Spirit in His outward ministry among men and women.

The Bible-Only Mentality

Is Scripture the only evidence for validating Christian experience? Does *sola scriptura* mean that the only criterion for validating Christian experience is the biblical text? What of the period prior to the inscripturation of the New Testament? Was not the oral tradition that was taught and the preaching of the kerygma authoritative? Was it not the Word of God? What of the whole prophetic tradition of the Old Testament? What of the Reformation doctrine of the *testimonium*, the witness of the Spirit (Ramm 1959)? Would none of these constitute the "Word of God," due to the fact that revelation was not written? Is the concept of biblical authority to be tied only to the text of Scripture? All of the above questions are leveled at a view of revelation which is static and tends to limit divine revelation to its objective dimension—Scripture.

In an article entitled, "Is 'Scripture Alone' the Essence of Christianity?" Bernard Ramm outlines a scholastic view of biblical revelation which is prominent in conservative evangelicalism. He calls it: "the Bible-only mentality":

> The Bible-only mentality confuses the *sola scriptura* of the Reformation with criteria of theological scholarship. The Bible-only mentality makes the record of revelation more primordial than the original revelation; it makes the history Scripture reports of second order to the scriptural report. The Bible-only mentality in principle reduces theology to the simplicities of proof-texting theological convictions. . . . Finally, a Bible-only mentality virtually equates spiritual reality with the text of Scripture itself, whereas the Scripture is a pointer to or witness to that reality (1977,116).

Ramm speaks of a reality, a dynamic acting of God beyond the written Word of God. He is not demeaning Scripture. Rather he is putting it into the perspective of God's dynamic activity among mankind. A reductionistic view of revelation, "the Bible-only mentality," is evident in both Bruner and Peters when they discuss the matter of supernatural evidence in contemporary times. Equating the text of Scripture with spiritual reality eliminates the Reformation *testimonium* and effects a separation of Word and Spirit. Ramm states concerning the *testimonium* (the ontic witness of the Spirit) "The *testimonium* may occur wherever God's truth exists. It is not bound to truth in written form" (1959,66).

Sola scriptura is a phrase coming out of theological disputations with Roman Catholic theologians on the subject of the ultimate reference of authority. The debate contrasted the authority of the church with the authority of Scripture. It did *not* contrast the authority of Scripture with the authority of the Holy Spirit! *Sola scriptura* was never intended to mean Scripture alone in the sense of alone or apart from the Spirit. The Bible-only mentality eliminates the witness of the Spirit in the doctrine of revelation, replacing it with rational proofs and argumentation about Scripture's authority. The witness of the Spirit and faith are subordinated to human reason in that mentality; the ontic principle is replaced by the noetic.

Reformation theology had no such dichotomy of Word and Spirit.[11] Calvin strongly affirmed the priority of the testimony of the Spirit;[12] his view of the Word and the Spirit in inseparable relationship is clear in his doctrine of Scripture's self-authenticating nature.[13] Furthermore, Calvin believed that the preaching of the Word of God *was* the Word of God in dynamic living form. Preaching was another form of God's accommodation, a way that God condescended to communicate by means of human instruments. Clearly, he viewed the Holy Spirit active at the preaching-end of Scripture just as He was present at the writing-end of Scripture. God was active at both ends of biblical revelation; Word and Spirit were inseparable (Pomerville 1980,47).

It is that activity of God the Holy Spirit at this contemporary end of revelation which points to the distinctive of the Pentecostal Movement. This emphasis on the activity of God in turn points to the Movement's capacity for giving contemporary mission direction. The two criticisms of the Movement's claim to an "evidential" coming of the Spirit (Bruner's and Peters's) revealed the influence of Protestant Scholasticism on their view of Christian experience and mission. It is a view which severely distorts the nature of the Christian faith itself and impairs its impact among non-western peoples. The essence of Christianity is not merely intellectual commitment to a written revelation. It concerns a dynamic encounter with God the Holy Spirit in connection with that written revelation. Revelation concerns not merely knowledge and information; it refers to the *activity* of God the Holy Spirit (Kraft 1979,179-180).

The Pentecostal's emphasis on evidence, therefore, is not due to bankrupt faith. It is due to his emphasis on the dynamic experience of the Spirit. The evidential coming of the Spirit, the gospel with signs following (Mark 16:20), is not only a valid means for authenticating Christian experience, but it is also an effective means for evangelism and mission among animistic peoples. The issue of "necessity' of supernatural signs is not within the purview of men but of God. He alone knows what is "necessary" in bringing men and women to a saving knowledge and experience of Jesus Christ. A faith which looks to both the inward and outward evidence of the Holy Spirit in Christian experience today is in accord with the New Testament witness. It is New Testament faith. There is no Reformation principle against the notion of "evidence" for the baptism of the Holy Spirit. The question remains, however, whether the witness of the Spirit in that experience involves speaking with tongues.

The Evidence Points to "The Evidence"

In an article entitled, "The Evidence Points to the Evidence," D.V. Hurst surveys the experiential and biblical evidence for tongues as the initial, outward evidence of the baptism of the Holy Spirit. He asks several prior questions before addressing the question of the initial evidence of the baptism of the Spirit. One of them is, "is it [speaking in tongues] evidence of the baptism of the Spirit *at all*?" (1968,22). Then he points to the millions of contemporary "Bible-believing" Christians who confess they have had an experience after the New Testament pattern. Then he points to the clear references concerning the experience of the Spirit in the Acts and Epistles. Therefore, he speaks of two categories of evidence: *biblical* and *experiential*.

In this chapter a survey of the biblical evidence has shown the baptism of the Holy Spirit to be a "distinct" experience, a conscious-crisis one, dynamic and evidential in nature. That it was evidential in the New Testament is shown by the fact that it was a means for validating Christian experience (Dunn 1970,66). This is the case, especially, in prejudicial and cross-cultural contexts, as the gospel spread beyond its Jewish confines. As Green states, the experience of the Spirit in New Testament times was of a "concrete nature" (1975,146). According to the New Testament witness there is no problem with an evidential coming of the Spirit, nor are there any grounds in Reformation theology that would preclude an evidential coming of the Spirit. In answer to Hurst's first question above, Is tongues evidence of the baptism of the Holy Spirit *at all*? Both the New Testament witness and contemporary experience produce an unquestioned affirmative answer. Hurst's last question, Is speaking in tongues *the* initial outward evidence? brings to the fore the issue of tongues as the unique evidence of the Pentecostal experience.

The biblical evidence for the Pentecostal baptism of the Spirit has been discussed thoroughly by Pentecostals and their critics. The New Testament support for the Pentecostal position derives from the historical precedent of the occasions of the Spirit's coming in the Acts. The New Testament witness's contribution to this question concerns the hermeneutical use of historical precedent (Fee 1976,131-132). According to the New Testament witness, the historical precedent may be summarized as followed: 1) the presence of the Spirit was the main characteristic of Christian conversion and practice; 2) in Acts and in the Pauline churches the charismatic dimension normally accompanied the reception of the Spirit; 3) speaking in tongues was a repeated expression of that charismatic dimension; and 4) on the basis of the New Testament pattern Christians today may expect that dimension as an integral part of their conversion (Fee 1976,131-132). Fee concludes about the use of historical precedent:

> If the Pentecostal may not say one *must* speak in tongues, he may surely say, why *not* speak in tongues? It does have repeated biblical precedent, it did have evidential value at Cornelius' household . . . and—in spite of much that has been written to the contrary—it does have value both for the edification of the individual believer (1 Cor 14:2-5) and, with interpretation, for the edification of the church (1 Cor 14:5,26-28) (1976,131-132).

Furthermore, the initial evidence of tongues took place at crucial points in Luke's history. It occurred at the Jerusalem Pentecost, the central event for the rest of Luke's history of the church (Allen 1960,17; Montague 1976,271-272). And it occurred at the "Caesarean Pentecost," which marked the transition of the gospel from the Jewish cultural context ("Jerusalem and in all Judea and Samaria") to the Gentile world ("and to the ends of the earth") (Acts 1:8). The crucial nature of the Caesarean outpouring of the

Spirit is seen in Peter's recounting the incident when he is questioned by Jewish believers about the validity of the Gentile Christian experience (Acts 10:45-47; 11:15-17; 15:8-9). The evidential manner of the Spirit's coming is the crucial argument for the Jewish believers.[14] The evidential, outward witness of tongues is connected with the idea of authority, the authority of the Spirit. Its use in validating Christian experience points to the importance of the prophetic tradition in the experience of the early Jewish Christians.

MacDonald notes that the former crucial outpouring at the Feast of Pentecost is significant because "This was the first perceptible expression *from within* the disciples [speaking in tongues] that they had been filled with the Spirit" (1964,4). The "initial" evidence from the disciples themselves at Pentecost, therefore, was speaking in tongues as the Spirit enabled them (Acts 2:4). However, Pentecost's significance and the evidence of speaking in tongues among the proselytes of the Diaspora go beyond the personal experience of the disciples with the Holy Spirit.

The Pentecost event has primary theological significance for salvation history itself. It is the third great work of God in salvation history. It follows Creation and Incarnation, and marks the beginning of a new time phase in salvation history, the "last days." In the "last days" the Holy Spirit is powerful and active in the church until the Parousia (Cullmann 1964,73). A chief characteristic of this age of the Spirit is the universal witness of the gospel. The tongues are significant in that they symbolize that universal witness at Pentecost (Acts 2:4-11), and the ever-expanding movement of salvation history which encompasses the whole Gentile world. The appearance of tongues at both Jerusalem and Caesarea, *transitional outpourings of the Spirit*, point to the phenomenon as a significant and unique New Testament evidence.

In addition to the biblical evidence of tongues, which involves biblical precedent-pattern and prominence in the context of salvation history, the experiential evidence for tongues is significant. The belief that the Pentecostal experience, the baptism of the Holy Spirit, is accompanied by the initial, outward evidence of speaking with other tongues is held by the majority of classical Pentecostal denominations (Sandidge 1976,138). They do not hold that tongues is the only evidence, but that it is the only *initial* evidence. Some classical Pentecostal groups, neo-Pentecostal groups, and the Catholic Charismatic Renewal in general deny that tongues is *the* sign for the Spirit's baptism. Catholic writers, however, point to glossolalia as the *first* spiritual gift to be operative upon the "release of the Spirit."[15]

While tongues is not uniformly held to be the initial evidence of the baptism of the Holy Spirit in the Pentecostal Movement in general, glossolalia is a common practice. Other gifts of the Spirit are also believed to be the initial evidence of the baptism of the Spirit. One could say about the Pentecostal Movement in general that it is characterized by a belief that the Spirit's coming is accompanied by a perceptible outward evidence.

Dynamic, Continuing Revelation?

The question surfaces in connection with the "experiential" evidence of tongues in the lives of millions of contemporary Christians, why should this New Testament witness of the Spirit be disparaged in theological argument today? Why does not the witness of the Spirit have the credibility today that it had at Cornelius' house, or with the first century church in general? The reason why such questions must be posed is due to the estrangement of western Christianity and the Spirit. The experiential dimension of the faith had evidential value for the early church because of its nearness to the prophetic tradition, the renewal of that tradition in Jesus, and its renewal in their own experience. Their view of divine revelation was far from being static; it was dynamic, and at the advent of Jesus it was seen to be renewed and continuous.

According to Yehezkel Kauffmann the fall of Jerusalem was the great watershed of the history of Israelite religion. The life of the people of Israel ended and the history of Judaism began. The exile brought a central focus on the written Word of God; the age of compilation and canonization began. Israel's questioning as to whether God's presence was with them, in view of the fall of Jerusalem and the exile, caused the spirit of prophecy to die. Emphasis was on the objectified Word (written Word) rather than on the dynamic Word of prophetism (1972,447-451). This was the stance of many in the first century Jewish community.

Judaism's concentration on the written Word, and their identity as a people being tied to the fact of their custodianship of the Scriptures, may have been the focus of Jesus' allusion in John 5:39-40, "You diligently study the Scriptures because you think that by them you possess eternal life. These are the Scriptures that testify about me, yet you refuse to come to me to have life." Jesus' statement is filled with irony; as the Living Word stands before the custodians of the written Word, they do not recognize Him! Their static, "high view" of Scripture was devoid of the living dynamic of the prophetic spirit (2 Cor 3). Bromiley states this "high view" of Scripture in Judaism carried with it a threefold danger:

> In the first place it tended to abstract the divine nature and authority of the Bible from the human authors and situations, i.e., from the whole movement of God's saving work in and through the history of

Israel and the persons concerned. Second, it clearly abstracted the
Bible from the objects of its witness, thus being left with a mere
textbook of doctrine, ethics and ceremonial. Third, in rejecting Jesus
Christ it refused the witness of the Holy Spirit, so that in its reading
the Old Testament was deprived of its living power (1958,206).

For the early Christian (Jewish) church, however, the authority of
the Old Testament Scriptures was seen in the context of faith and
the witness of the Holy Spirit. It had experienced a renewal of the prophetic tradition in Jesus and in its own experience (Acts 2:17-21). For
it, the Scriptures were linked with the Holy Spirit's work in witnessing
to Jesus Christ (Rogers 1977,17).

A parallel to Israel's earlier view of dynamic revelation
(prophetism) and first century Judaism's somewhat static view of
revelation are those views of Pentecostalism and post-Reformation
Scholasticism respectively. In the post-Reformation period, under
the barrage of questions leveled at the Christian's world view, the
dynamic view of revelation shifted to Scholasticism's apologetic,
static, and text-centered view. A "high view" of Scripture in
evangelical circles today often refers to a view of biblical revelation
which parallels the Judaistic view. It emphasized the written
"form" of Scripture at the expense of its dynamic, functional
nature. The living prophetic voice of the Spirit is silent under the
"captivity of the Enlightenment." The three dangers Bromiley
mentioned above tend to be repeated in conservative
evangelicalism, with the exception that the second danger (the
abstracting of the Bible from the object of its witness) manifests
itself as the abstracting of biblical revelation. Its dynamic,
functional nature is denied (John 5:20-32,39). Rather than
Scripture's authority resting in the witness of the Spirit, His
speaking through the written Word as He transforms the lives of
believers, its authority is perceived as resting in the "form" of
Scripture, in arguments concerning the perfection of the text.

This emphasis on an objectified and static view of revelation has
to do with a demise of the role of the Holy Spirit and His activity in
contemporary Christendom. Pentecostalism believes that
revelation is dynamic, because the Holy Spirit continues to be
active at "this end" of biblical revelation. Revelation is a divine
activity, not simply the finished product of that activity (Kraft
1979,184). The discussion of this theological point is continued in
detail in chapter six. Pentecostalism testifies to, and exemplifies,
the fact that the continuing activity of the Spirit is not limited to
His inward work with the written Word. His activity also involves
His outward charismatic work in the lives of believers (Acts 1:1-5;
John 14:12-14).

The witness of tongues among millions of Pentecostal Christians
is valid evidence for the Pentecostal belief that the initial evidence

of the baptism of the Holy Spirit is speaking in tongues. To say this is not to say that every manifestation of tongues today is Christian, or is of the Holy Spirit. This was not true in the first century and it is not true today. Those biblical guidelines given in the Epistles, as well as the gift of the Spirit—the ability to distinguish between spirits—are to be used by the people of God.[16] However, the witness of the Spirit today is biblical evidence and is a valid means for verification of Christian experience within the biblical guidelines.

A point of difficulty in conservative evangelicalism's dealing with tongues as "evidence" is the subjectivism involved. An authority of the Spirit appears strange in a theological tradition so highly impacted by Scholasticism. The Pentecostal Movement represents a "corrective" influence for contemporary mission at this point. Also the possibility of Pentecostalism providing a theological contibution emerges here. As an established Christian tradition which is experiencing renewal of a neglected dimension of the Spirit's ministry, their contribution is obvious. It is a renewal that emphasizes the experiential dimension of the Christian faith. In terms of mission, this emphasis on the experiential dimension is relevant for mission strategy among the non-Christian animistic-oriented peoples of the Third World. It is that dynamic, powerful dimension of the Spirit which is crucial in evangelizing the animist. Rational arguments about biblical doctrine do not meet this challenge, regardless of how "sound" they may be.

PART TWO:
Pentecostalism: A Missions Contribution

5

The Pentecostal
and Mission Strategy

The contribution that Pentecostalism makes to contemporary mission theology concerns the discipline of theology itself. Considering its emphasis on the experiential dimension of the Christian faith, it may seem to be somewhat paradoxical that Pentecostalism has a "theological" contribution to make. Hollenweger notes that its contribution is not in the area of "dogmatic" theology, but rather in the area of "religious practice" (1972,500). While Hollenweger does not agree with classical Pentecostal's theology concerning religious practice (the tongues issue), he does view the experiential dimension of the faith as a theological dimension. Pentecostalism emphasizes the fact that theology is a practical discipline concerned with Christian experience and the activities of men and women engaged in mission. Thinking of mission strategy as mission "theologizing" points to the purpose of Scripture in providing direction for Christian obedience in life and ministry.

However, the idea of "theology" is often confined to theoretical reflection and theological systems which have been worked out in previous periods of the church. Confining theology to an historical *product* has produced a dichotomy between theory and practice in theology. Theology in scholastic tradition tends to leave the impression that mission strategy does not qualify as "theology." This notion has severely impacted mission strategy and its practice.

In contemporary mission literature the theologizing done in the arena of mission is often viewed as pure pragmatism. This charge of pragmatism intends to focus on the alleged lack of theological/biblical orientation to mission theologizing, not the philosophy of pragmatism. The critics are not so unkind as to level the charge of William James-philosophical-pragmatism (no absolutes, crass relativism). The misconceived criticism is due to missiologists and theologians failing to recognize the dynamic, continuous nature of theology and the validity of using insights of the social sciences in mission theologizing. The roots of this misconception are discussed in this chapter, focusing on the occasion when Pentecostals and the "church growth" school of missiology are accused of pragmatism and a lack of theological orientation. The theological framework from which this criticism emerges is often Protestant Scholasticism. A static view of theology and revelation are basic to the above misconception. The chapter discusses the nature of Pentecostal theology as a dynamic theologizing. It shows how that theological orientation provides insights and direction for contemporary mission theology. The Pentecostal's view of theology is that it is a dynamic, continuing biblical process. His view of revelation is that it is dynamic in nature.

Mission Strategy: Pragmatism or Theologizing?

A frequent criticism of church growth oriented schools of missiology is that their mission strategy lacks theological sophistication and support. Their focus on evangelistic results, in terms of men and women converted and made responsible members of multiplying churches, has been characterized as "American pragmatism." Their scientific focus on the context of mission and the advocacy of the use of the social sciences in mission strategy has also led to this charge (Wasdel 1980,1 and Padilla 1977,14). Some of the emphases which have been the occasion for criticism of the church growth school of missiology are: 1) the optimum growth of the church and the multiplication of churches; 2) a priority on evangelism as accomplished communication—men and women reconciled to God; 3) the focus on receptive people; 4) the necessity of research on the church and its mission; 5) the homogeneous unit principle; and 6) people movements. This configuration of emphases has been referred to as church growth strategy, or a "theology of church growth" (Hesselgrave 1978a,173).

Frequently the theological and biblical adequacy of this view of mission strategy is questioned because of its non-sectarian nature (i.e., that it is not related to a particular confessional system of theology). Also the use of research techniques appears to be problematic. In short, its in-mission or praxis origin is the point of criticism (Conn 1977,12 and Padilla 1977,14). It is important to note that the biblical nature of church growth mission strategy is not in question.[1] Rather, it is the in-mission use of Scripture, the theological methodology which is in question (Conn 1976,45-46).

While not emphasizing the scientific approach to church growth, Pentecostals also could be characterized as having a church growth oriented mission strategy.[2] As well as some emphases similar to those given for the church growth school, characteristic emphases of Pentecostal mission strategy are: 1) the planting of indigenous churches; 2) the evangelization of the humble, responsive masses; 3) the mobilization of the laity in witness; 4) spiritual gifts; 5) the spiritual dynamic of supernatural power in the power-encounter of mission; and 6) the development of spiritual leadership. Pentecostal mission strategy has also been characterized as pragmatic and lacking theological sophistication, but for some different reasons than those mentioned above. Pentecostals would fall under the criticism of having a non-sectarian theology, as well as having a mission strategy of a pragmatic nature. But the charge of pragmatism in their case relates more to their pneumatology. Some of the more prominent reasons that non-Pentecostals give for the pragmatic nature of Pentecostal theology are their experience orientation, their emphasis on the leading of the Holy Spirit in mission strategy, and the manner in which Scripture is used (Hesselgrave 1978a,45,65).

The charge of pragmatism primarily concerns the Pentecostal's belief concerning the active guidance of the Holy Spirit in mission. A response to the gospel is often considered evidence of the leading of the Holy Spirit. Classical Pentecostal missiologist Melvin Hodges believes mission strategy must be flexible in order for the church to take advantage of each opportunity for evangelism.[3] However, this flexibility, due to the leading of the sovereign Spirit, the chief Strategist, also means that certains biblical principles are inviolable (Hodges 1977a,146).[4]

Both of these church growth oriented schools of mission strategy are clearly committed to a biblically-oriented strategy of mission but somehow not in the sense that their critics would want them to be. Both are charged with the improper use of Scripture. Both are charged with a pragmatic approach to strategy, with a flexibility that appears to be outside of the boundaries of a sectarian system of theology. Critics find their theology originating in the encounter with the missionary task itself. Their theological horizon, however, is not the context of mission, like some conciliar theologies of mission. For these schools the world does not set the theological agenda. Rather, the authoritative starting point is clearly Scripture.

Certainly both church growth missiologists and Pentecostal missiologists are trained in their respective theological traditions. But in the opinion of their critics their mission theology does not reflect those theological systems. When they engage in mission, do those missiologists holding to church growth principles really discard their theological traditions because of the American value of pragmatism? Should Pentecostals be written off as theologically deficient enthusiasts because they speak of the leading of the Holy Spirit in mission strategy? Or does the problem rest with their critics, who perhaps are unable to see beyond their own sectarian theological tradition and concept of theology?

In contrast to the view of theology as a static theological deposit, a dated theological tradition, all of the above "symptoms" of a supposed theologically deficient mission strategy indicates a different view of theology. They indicate a view in which theology is a dynamic, biblical process of reasoned reflection. They indicate the use of a "biblical theology" methodology in a different phase of theological work from that of dogmatic or systematic theology. This theology represents a dynamic interaction between Scripture and the missiologist who is immersed in a mission context. It represents a search for biblical solutions to contextual problems in the execution of mission. The criticism of this dynamic, biblical theologizing stems from the failure to tell the difference between theology the cultural-historical *product* and theology the continuing biblical *process*.

The content of both a sectarian systematic theology and a biblical theology of mission functions as presuppositions which guide the missionary engaging in this fresh theologizing. Although this theologizing takes place in the context of the missionary endeavor, focusing on specific problems of mission, these problems are not the hermeneutical horizon. They are not the controlling, authoritative issue that determines the direction of theologizing. Nor do the creeds of the church, or a traditional theological deposit determine the orientation of the theologizing. The hermeneutical horizon, that authoritative starting point and guide, is Scripture.

Thinking of mission strategy as *theologizing* helps in bringing biblical solutions to many of the problems involved with the concept of "strategy." For evangelicals it brings the concept of mission strategy clearly within the confines of biblical authority. Thinking of mission strategy as "biblical" activity in the context of mission brings the concept into focus as a biblical theologizing. This theologizing involves a twofold task (a descriptive-historical task and an interpretive-theological task). That twofold task in turn involves a twofold fidelity (a fidelity to biblical revelation and a fidelity to the cultural context of mission). The identification of mission strategy as a valid phase of theological activity also closes the gap between mission theory and mission practice. It outlines the relationship between systematic theology and dynamic, biblical theologizing in the total theological enterprise.

The charge of pragmatism, or lack of theological orientation, in mission work is sometimes valid. However, this is not because of a dynamic, biblical theologizing on the part of the missionary. The charge of pragmatism draws attention to the methodological pitfalls involved in this dynamic theologizing. Sometimes the view of mission strategy is taken from the secular definition of "strategy."[5] At times the indiscriminate use of insights from the various social sciences are the occasion for the charge of pragmatism. The danger is not that insights from the secular sciences are used. Rather, the danger is in removing mission work from its theological-biblical base by failing to recognize mission strategy as preeminently *theological activity*. As theological activity it requires that mission decisions and strategy must be intentionally related to Scripture at all times.

Because of the various usages of the term "strategy," and some of its misleading connotations, it is necessary to let the term be defined by the concept of "theology" for various important reasons. Viewed as theology, or theologizing, the term "strategy" is immediately characterized as "biblical thinking" about mission. It is thinking that is related to Scripture in a special way (the previously mentioned twofold biblical task). The biblical "givenness" is indicated in the term "theology," in spite of the differences of opinion as to hermeneutics in that enterprise. When we approach the theological enterprise from an evangelical persuasion, the place and role of Scripture is somewhat precise, at least in terms of its authority. We know that to discuss "theology" we must be confronted with the content of Scripture and that it plays an authoritative role. Any thinking about God's mission in the world must be biblical; that is the "bottom line" of the doctrine of biblical authority (Berkouwer 1975,105). Viewing mission strategy as "theology," then, focuses on the particular way that the Bible is related to theology. The term "theology" implies a hermeneutic, or biblical methodology (in evangelical theology), which can be used to evaluate the various terms used in missiological literature which *appear* to be synonymous with the term "strategy" when it is coupled with the term "mission."

Viewing mission strategy as biblical theologizing provides a constant reminder that such thinking is to be under Scripture's authority, even though it involves the use of extra-biblical knowledge and insights. Often mission strategy loses its biblical orientation, or it is heavily impacted by the missiologist's world view or science when it is not recognized and articulated as a theological process.

The term "strategy" as a secular term has connotations which, if emphasized, are misleading when the word is used in a theological or missiological context. Strategy may be defined in such a way as to infer that it only has to do with thinking prior to an action or event and exclude any thinking *during* the execution of an action (Dayton and Frazer 1980,7,19). Strategy is thereby differentiated from "tactics" in its secular usage in that it involves planning and broad principles utilized prior to an action. Tactics, on the other hand, deals with carrying out general plans and principles. On the basis of this definition of strategy any biblical thinking done while engaged in a missionary task would not be mission "strategy," nor would it be "theology." From a theological viewpoint, however, this is an erroneous conclusion. The conclusion is derived from the secular usage of the term "strategy," not from a theological evaluation of the activity of the missionary. Would not tactical, biblical thinking done by a missionary engaged in mission be "theology?" Actually, according to the secular usage, strategy-as-planning and principles would represent mission theology-theory, and tactics would represent a dynamic phase of theology, mission theology-practice.

The definition and usage of the term "strategy" should not be allowed to determine the guidelines and nature of this crucial missiological issue. The dichotomy between strategy and tactics above contributes to a divorce of Scripture's influence on tactical thinking during the execution of the missionary task which is actually a biblical theologizing.[6] This apparent dichotomy has been the occasion for the charge of pragmatism with regard to church growth mission strategy. Whether thinking about mission is *prior* to missionary activity itself, *during* the activity, or *following* it, it is still biblical thinking and therefore is "theology" (Thielicke 1974,196-199). The time when the thinking is done in relation to the missionary task does not change its nature.

The dynamic, pragmatic nature of the activities involved in mission strategy is often not recognized as "theology," because of a preconceived idea of theology as a static deposit. Also, missiologists often employ secular concepts or paradigms to describe missionary activity which tend to distance that activity from its theological-biblical base. The charge of pragmatism, therefore, concerns a failure to recognize the true nature of theology. Mission strategy involves a dynamic, biblical theologizing in the context of mission.

Theology as Theory and Practice

In introducing the topic, "The Theology of Mission," David Bosch observes that the theology of mission can never be isolated from the practice of mission. He sees "theology of mission" as involved with the basic presuppositions and underlying principles which determine the practice of mission. Both theologies of mission and "practical mission work" are viewed in a relationship of creative tension (Bosch 1975,2-3).[7] Bosch brings into focus the danger of crass pragmatism in the practice of mission (the absence of theological orientation). But he also introduces the possibility of a danger in the other direction—in the direction of theology. He states:

> There is a risk (and it is more than imaginary) that the practice and the theology of mission can become so estranged from one another that theological reflection can come to reject any practical application almost as a matter of principle (1975,3).

This would mean that any fresh theologizing done in the context of mission would be suspect, because of its dynamic and practical nature. The danger in the other direction is that theology be separated from the practice of the church until it becomes a closed-world of abstract reflection (Thielicke 1974,23). This danger denies the mutual influence that exists between "theology" and "practice." Also it often results in the irrelevancy of that theology in terms of the issues immediately concerning the church in mission. It just does not address them directly.

The danger of a dichotomy developing between mission theory and mission practice was illustrated dramatically by Hendrik Kraemer when he refused to write another theoretical essay on "Syncretism as a Theological Problem for Missions" for Gerald H. Anderson's *The Theology of the Christian Mission* (1961). Kraemer stated that his reason for not writing the essay was his conviction that "writing theoretical essays time and time again on syncretism as a theological problem for missions has no use whatever" (1961,179). Kraemer saw that the essays did not change mission practice because they remained "theological museum pieces" (Kraemer 1961,179). They were innocuous because the tendency was to treat "theological problems" as theoretical affairs (Kraemer 1961,179-180).[8] Apparently for Kraemer, the separation between theory and practice was an established fact.[9]

Kraemer viewed a theological concept as not merely a matter of intellectual speculation but, rather, as "the most practical thing in the world" (Kraemer 1961,180). He viewed syncretism as a basic theological problem for *both* missiological thinking and for missionary strategy. However, because the subject was bracketed as a "theological problem" in the proposed essay title, he was of the opinion that no "practical" effect would result. The view that theology was a theoretical affair was entrenched. So it appears today when such practical theologizing done in the course of mission is suspect. Because it does not fit within a particular confessional or sectarian system of theology, it is not considered "theology!"

Because of the universal nature of the phenomenon of syncretism and the increasing contact of the Christian faith with non-Christian religions, Kraemer advocated bands of emic (indigenous) and etic (culturally-outside experts) theologians to deal with the problem. These bands of theologians were to do "second phase," fresh theologizing on the basis of the unique problems encountered in each religiocultural area of the world (Kraemer 1961,180-181). This second phase theologizing-as-practice is emphasized when Kraemer stated:

> Theology in itself (and that is what the isolated treatment of syncretism as a theological problem for missions often amounts to) is *not theology in full but an amputated specimen of theology.* Full theology includes expression in action and new forms of life, for the Christian truth, notwithstanding all its exclusiveness, is also all-inclusive (1961,181-182; italics mine).

Fresh theologizing involves both the "dated" nature of theology-theory, in terms of its historical-cultural contextual focus, and the demands of the contemporary context with its new issues. The contemporary context for theological reflection calls for a contemporary expression of Christian truth. Actually, it is the first phase of theologizing for the emic theologians, a dynamic biblical process. For the western theologian it appears as a "second phase" theologizing because it is done in relation to his culturally-conditioned theological product in western systematic theology.

Bosch also observes the tenative and imperfect nature of all theology (1975,4). This is the occasion for its dependence on practice. Practice brings theology to face its functional role in the life and mission of the church. In so doing, practice gives theology the occasion for growth in terms of increased insights. Bosch and Kraemer rightly observe that "it is on the frontiers where faith meets unbelief that theological reflection becomes most active" (Bosch 1975,6). Theology grows from crossing such frontiers. Therefore, mission theology should be characterized by its dynamic and contextual nature and not criticized for this quality.

In elaborating on the possible danger that theology may be regarded as the opponent to practice, or as its opposite, Bosch says that not all theology is "theology" (1975,6). He explains that some theology is not in the formal shape of "conciliar statements" and "ponderous publications." But nevertheless, it has to do with those basic presuppositions and underlying principles which determine the activities of the church in its mission (Bosch 1975,6). It is clear that Bosch regards the *practice of mission* as "true, living theology," even though this theology does not take a systematized form. However, he states that such theology also must be articulated and not just exist "implicitly" somewhere in the background, like some contemporary mission strategy (Bosch 1975,7). The pitfall here, as mentioned previously, is the loss of theological orientation and the danger of crass pragmatism. Bosch's discussion about theory and practice, therefore, illustrates the relationship between the two phases of theological reflection —systematic theology and a dynamic, biblical theologizing.

The nature of "doing theology this way" is often denied because of its aparent non-confessional nature and lack of theological appearance as a formalized theology. However, it should be recognized as a valid and necessary phase of theological reflection. Theology as theory and practice is not to be perceived as mutually exclusive but rather, mutually influential and dependent. Both theory and practice are valid phases of theological activity. Systematic theology provides theory, theological presuppositions, and principles which serve to guide missionary practice. These phases close the gap between theory and practice. Dynamic, biblical theologizing provides fresh insights and *prescriptions* as it reflects on biblical revelation in terms of new contexts and new questions that are confronting the church in its mission. Practice thereby enriches the whole theological enterprise.

Bosch's discussion about the relation of theory and practice highlights two theological perspectives which occasion the criticism that church growth mission strategy is theologically deficient. In effect, both perspectives divorce theology from mission practice. One of the perspectives involves church growth missiologists. The other perspective involves the critics themselves. Both perspectives evidence a theological deficiency.

The first "pragmatic" perspective concerns those church growth missiologists who fail to explicitly consider and articulate their mission strategy theologically. Some who espouse church growth principles often fail to articulate their theological presuppositions and methodology. A dangerous dichotomy exists in the thinking of those who take their understanding of mission strategy from the secular term "strategy." Strategy is related only to planning and the application of principles in pre-missionary activity, not to the practice of mission. This tends to divorce strategy in its wider application (the practice of mission) from Scripture. Often a secular theory, model, or paradigm is used which controls mission activity without examining its presuppositions in the light of Scripture. Theological work beyond that of "proof-texting" is necessary in the implementation of secular models in mission strategy. Otherwise a result is a questionable theological credibility. Also the potential of an unrestrained influence of the science or the missiologist's world view on methodology is present. In other words, the pitfall of crass pragmatism is present, even though it is unintentional.

A pragmatic dichotomy of mission theory and practice also

occurs with those missiologists who claim to have a theologically-oriented mission strategy. In this second perspective the sectarian issue is in focus. It is the perspective of critics who hold a theological dichotomy because they fail to recognize strategy as a dynamic theological process, practiced in solidarity with theology-the-culturally-conditioned product. Because *their* particular confessional system of theology is considered absolute and perennial, and because it is "dated," focused on another era and its problems, the system is inflexible. It does not lend itself to addressing different contemporary problems, so theologizing outside of that system is considered invalid. However, because of its western orientation and rationalistic nature, it finds itself not only irrelevant but inappropriate to its non-western, supernatural-istic context. The theological deficiency here involves the dichotomy of theory and practice. Theology is left in the dimension of theory; it is left on the bookshelf. This, in turn, results in distancing theology from the contemporary life and mission of the church. Such a separation tends to contribute to the theological poverty of both systematic theology and mission strategy.

Recognizing Phases of Theologizing

C. Peter Wagner's definition of strategy is of a general nature and is not so restrictive in its application as in the dichotomy above. It is therefore more useful in a theological context:

> Strategy is a mutually-agreed means to achieve the ends which have been determined by a particular group. Good strategy will be concerned with broad principles as well as specific tactics, but it will not lose sight of the determined goal (1971,16).

Wagner does not deny the difference between strategy and tactics, they are viewed holistically. There is no rigid dichotomy. This definition can be used to illustrate the different phases of theological activity. "Biblical thinking" which takes place prior to mission—theology as a culturally conditioned product (systematic theology and biblical theology)—represent one general phase of theologizing. "Biblical thinking" which takes place during mission—theology as a dynamic process (fresh biblical theologiz-ing)—represents another phase of theologizing.

In secular usage, "strategy," in distinction from tactics, represents goal-oriented theoretical thinking of a broad scope. It deals with principles, planning, and conceptual action. It is usually done prior to an action. This usage could illustrate a prior phase of theologizing, involving both systematic theology and biblical theology. These provide the theological presuppositions which condition both mission planning and action.

On the other hand, "tactics" also represent a goal orientation but, immediate goals as they relate to the ultimate goal or strategy.

Tactics represent thinking of narrower scope, which is situational and more practical in nature. It deals with execution, improvising, and coping in concrete action. It is usually thinking done during engagement of an action and is conditioned by the specific problems of engagement. Tactics are dependent on strategy for the necessary general orientation that insures their effectiveness in moving toward the ultimate goal. This secular definition of tactics illustrates, somewhat, the nature of the fresh theologizing mentioned previously. It takes place in the context of mission. It represents a necessary continuous phase of theologizing. It involves the dynamic process of theology.

The necessity of recognizing two general phases of theological reflection, at least, does not derive from the term "strategy," however. The two phases grow out of the nature of theology as a continuing response of the church to both Scripture and its environment. Both systematic theology and biblical theology (the biblical science, especially when understood as the domain of the biblical historian only) are time and culturally conditioned theological products. Biblical theology, in the sense of the theology *in* the Bible and the Bible's structure of theology, is in a special canonical sense normative. But it is still time and culturally conditioned. Therefore, a dynamic, continuing biblical theologizing must be done. Hermeneutics involves both an historical *and* an interpretive task. Both tasks are necessary in order to apply biblical content to contemporary questions and problems requiring a Christian response. A fresh phase of biblical theologizing is a necessity in every age and every culture.

James Smart points to the early 1960s as the time when a truncated view of biblical theology (the biblical science limited to the historical task only) began once again to include the interpretive-theological task. Smart cites the pressure of the sociocultural needs of the American community and the Vietnam war as the occasion for its emergence (1979,130). Theologians recognized that biblical theology in terms of what Scripture "meant" (the descriptive-historical task) alone was inadequate. The "means" dimension of Scripture (the interpretive-theological task) for contemporary American society was imperative.

Dogmatic theology, however, is clearly time and culture conditioned. It does not hold the same normative position as does biblical theology. It represents the partial, culturally conditioned, limited statements of the church which are focused on the theological issues of other times. In view of this fact, Berkouwer speaks of the necessity to "reinterpret dogma" (1977,216). This reinterpretation Berkouwer states, "usually assumes a fundamental distinction: the distinction between form and content, between the formulations of dogma and the truth that is expressed in those formulations" (1977,216,218). That distinction is the occasion for the reinterpretation of dogma. Different phases of theological reflection, therefore, are necessary because of the limited and time-bound nature of theological statements in general. A dynamic phase of theologizing is necessary. The need for such dynamic theologizing is much more critical in another cultural context, where the world view, value system, and needs, which theology must address are diverse.

Berkouwer notes in some detail the Roman Catholic response to "reinterpretation" of dogma. He states, "After all, truth formulated *infallibly* ought to be relevant for all time" (1977,218). But he notes that among Roman Catholics there has been a deep awareness of the historically conditioned nature of the church's dogmatic statements. The activity in reinterpreting dogma with even the Roman Catholic Church, then, is significant evidence for the necessity of a dynamic, continual theologizing. Distinguishing between the unchangeable affirmation (truth) and the changeable representation of truth (its form) represented a hermeneutical challenge for the Roman Catholic church. They had to recognize different phases of theological work. It was necessary that the affirmations of the church be reinterpreted in order to address contemporary issues (Berkouwer 1977,220).

For the Protestant church, reinterpretation of the confessions of the church from earlier centuries for current theological reflection brought tension. The confessions were obviously time-bound (Berkouwer 1977,224). The necessity for such a reinterpretation concerned even the central issues of the faith. In detail Berkouwer discusses how that the ancient christological formulations and the trinitarian formulations are subject to reinterpretation (1977,226, 227,258). In that discussion he advocates a non-Cartesian theology, a theology which has for its hermeneutical horizon Scripture, rather than a confessional-creedal horizon. Berkouwer advocates a fresh theologizing which has Scripture as its authoritative starting point and controlling orientation in such "reinterpretation" (1977,233-236,259-261). Berkouwer points to the nature of theology itself as the reason why "reinterpretation" or fresh theologizing must take place. He states:

> As a matter of fact, theology shows little sign of serene immobility. There is restless searching going on, a groping for ways to understand the gospel more clearly. We should not expect too much from theology; it will at best only give us incomplete knowledge and inadequate understanding. If we forget that theology is always going to be partial, travelling along the way without ever arriving finally, we will be upset by theology's continued movement, and others will be alarmed and disturbed by it, seeing it as a threat to established truth (1977,262-263).

Berkouwer affirms the necessity of a continuing theological task, noting that the necessity rests in the incomplete and imperfect nature of all theological reflection (1 Cor 13:12). Objections to such theologizing often rest in the misconception that dogmatic formulations are somehow absolute and perennial. Those objections result from a failure to recognize the validity of different phases of theological work. The criticism leveled at mission theologizing arises out of this misconception and failure. They are often rooted in a scholastic view of theology.

It is helpful at this point also to recognize that the discussion of the reinterpretation of dogma is related to the concept of "contextualization." A dogmatic theology needs reinterpretation precisely because it is a *contextualized theology*. The act of reinterpretation is a re-contextualization of the Christian faith in contemporary times, under the pressure of the new issues which the ancient statement does not address adequately.

Therefore, mission strategy involves two phases of theological activity. The first is a theoretical phase involving theological products, representing the presuppositions that support and give strategy theological orientation. Systematic theology gives theological orientation from one's cultural perspective, how a people ultimately understand theology in general and God's mission in particular. Biblical theology gives theological orientation from the perspective of what one perceives the biblical view of God's mission to be. Cultural perspective is also present here, but emphasis is on how the biblical writers understood the structure of theology and God's mission. The second phase is a practical phase involving theology of a more immediate, fresh and contemporary nature. It represents a dynamic process where biblical revelation is the hermeneutical horizon (as in the biblical theology above). Contextual questions of mission are the focus of theological activity.

Contemporary missiologists and theologians who object to and criticize mission theologizing often do so because of its lack of correspondence to a particular confessional system of theology. Criticism also arises because it often challenges traditional theological affirmations in those systems. While commending the church growth writers for having a sound biblical theology underlying their mission practice, Roger Greenway states:

> Most of church growth missiology's theological bases have been worked out *after* the methodological insights and missions principles were arrived at through field observation and experience. Very often they were defined more in opposition to the arguments raised by opponents of church growth than in relation to a recognized system of theology (1976,46).

This statement illustrates both the criticism that church growth mission strategy is "pragmatic' in nature, and in terms of the sectarian issue, that it does not appear to be related to a "recognized system of theology." Greenway is positive in his treatment of church growth missiology. But from his Reformed perspective he states that missiology's theology and organization is "seriously deficient" (Greenway 1976,46).

On the basis of Greenway's admission that sound biblical theology underlies the missiology he criticizes, it appears that the criticism of theological deficiency rests on *how* its theology was attained (the pragmatic nature of the theology). Also its relation to a system of theology is an issue. One wonders if critics doubt that church growth missiologists *have* theological presuppositions and traditions which condition their approach to the task of mission. Perhaps it is just the kind of non-sectarian theologizing that they engage in which is so objectionable (fresh biblical theologizing).

Obviously, trained missiologists *do* have theological traditions which function as a basis from which they do their theologizing in mission. Furthermore, it is readily admitted that the church growth school is engaged in sound biblical theology. But whatever one decides about these questions of prior theological bases for mission theology, the phenomenon of a theology of mission developing from theological grappling with the contemporary issues of mission and interacting with the arguments of systematic theologians is in fact how all theology develops—systematic theology included. The valid, firsthand biblical theologizing done in the context of mission and sharpened by interaction with systematic theologies should not be seen as a "serious deficiency." Rather, it should be viewed as the process of normal theological development which every theology undergoes, mission theology included.

How Is Mission Strategy "Pragmatic?"

The thesis of this chapter is that mission strategy is "theologizing." This thesis is reiterated in the statement, "mission strategy is 'biblical' pragmatism."[10] The phrase biblical pragmatism emphasizes the dynamic, biblical nature of theology. Mission strategy represents that theologizing in which Scripture is functional in providing the church with guidance for its mission in the modern world. In considering mission strategy as biblical pragmatism, therefore, the combination of the two terms aids in illustrating the role of Scripture and the contextual nature of this dynamic theologizing.

In terms of its contribution to evangelicalism, Pentecostalism directly addresses the question, How is mission strategy pragmatic? This question draws attention to the dynamic, continuing nature of theology and the necessity of applying Scripture to the contemporary life and ministry of the church. It points to the incarnational nature of theology, to its contextual nature and focus. The question focuses on the second of the twofold fidelity of theology—fidelity to cultural context. It has to do with the second hermeneutical task—the interpretive-theological task. Mission strategy is a continuous, biblical theologizing whereby contemporary problems of mission find biblical solutions. Scripture is functional in mission by means of the interpretive-theological task of hermeneutics.

The Interpretive-Theological Task and the Spirit

The Pentecostal's belief that the Holy Spirit continues to work at the modern end of divine revelation is a chief reason why he is able to respond so readily to the interpretive-theological task. He believes that revelation is dynamic and continuing in nature (revelation with a small *r,* the continuing ministry of the Spirit as opposed to revelation with a capital *R,* i.e., Scripture). This belief also allows him to respond positively to the matter of incarnating the Christian faith in other cultural contexts. The Holy Spirit, the Supreme Strategist, is present to guide in that work. The Pentecostal's orientation points to two dimensions of revelation which are crucial for mission strategy—its dynamic-continuous nature and its incarnational nature. Both of these dimensions of revelation are crucial for the hermeneutical task and theology's fidelity to the context of mission.

There are various reasons why the interpretive-theological task may be neglected, as well as the ministry of the Spirit. While Pentecostalism emphasizes the dynamic nature of Scripture and revelation, Protestant Scholasticism represents a fundamental distortion of them. Theology, Scripture, and revelation are all transformed into *static products.* It is at this point especially that mission theology's fidelity to the cultural context is seriously compromised. Because theology has been contextualized in western culture, in its scholastic form the functional purpose of western theology has been eclipsed. Theology-theory has been separated from theology-practice. In terms of mission theologizing this theological orientation represents a fundamental and serious distortion.

D.F. Strauss contended that the doctrine of the witness of the Spirit (the *testimonium*) was the "Achilles' heel of the Protestant system," due to the twofold possibility of the perversion of the doctrine—fanaticism and rationalism (Berkouwer 1975,64). In the first possibility the Spirit may be the source of a new revelation which may oppose Scripture. In the second possibility, rationalism, the danger arises from a failure to distinguish between what is from the Spirit and what is from one's own mind working within a particular world view. In both possibilities Scripture is pushed to a secondary position. The latter danger and perversion of the doctrine of the *testimonium* became a reality in the post-Reformation period under the influence of the intense rationalism of the Enlightenment and Common Sense philosophy. While not denying the danger of the former perversion, fanaticism, the perversion which is the present handicap of conservative evangelical mission theologizing is rationalism. Ramm states concerning the latter perversion, rationalism, that "a fanatical 'objectivizing' of Scripture can be as detrimental to its proper understanding as a frightful 'subjectivizing'" (1961,99).

Numerous theologians have identified the influence of Protestant Scholasticism in fundamentalism and conservative evangelicalism, especially in their apologetics. In a previous chapter Ramm was quoted as saying that he found the doctrine of the internal witness of the Spirit to have almost disappeared from evangelical literature and theology (1959,7). The scholastic penchant for rational argumentation supplanted the "witness of the Spirit"—the *testimonium*. Ramm states that the union of Word and Spirit is the theological ground for Calvin's theory of the *testimonium* (1959,17). The danger of rationalism is its tendency to conceive of revelation solely as a static product (revelation with a capital *R*) and not as a dynamic work of the Spirit with Scripture (revelation with a small *r*). The heart of the danger in Protestant Scholasticism is the severe limitation of the "subjective" work of the Holy Spirit with the Word at the contemporary end of revelation. Ramm states, "Here [its view of revelation] is the danger of fundamentalism, which turns revelation into court-reporting and does not see it as the divine Person in *conversation* with sinners" (1961,26). We could add, "and does not see it as the divine Person in conversation with *Christians*," not limiting the divine speaking to the salvation experience.

In a discussion about Scripture's authority Ramm lists three erroneous theories on "certainty": 1) Romanism—the infallible church is the source of certainty; 2) the enthusiasts—certainty rests in the immediate revelation by the Spirit; and 3) the apologist—Scripture's certainty is determined by rational evidences (1959,12). The separation of Word from Spirit is involved in them all. The apologists' approach to certainty represents the scholastic distortion of revelation discussed here.

In his book *Fundamentalism*, James Barr states that two streams of tradition feed conservative evangelicalism: 1) Protestant orthodoxies of the seventeenth and eighteenth centuries, their dogmatism and 2) Pietism, the deepening of the spiritual life

(Keswick convention). The two streams each provide emphasis in different areas in evangelicalism. The first represents the theology; the second, the practical expression of Christianity (Barr 1978,188-189). Barr identifies the intellectual leadership of fundamentalism with the Princeton theologians Warfield and the Hodges. These, Barr states, drew their philosophical position from Scottish Common Sense philosophy of Britain and Darby mainstream dispensationalism (1978,iv). Barr thinks that "Fundamentalism distorts and betrays the basic true religious concerns of evangelical Christianity, and it does this especially through its *intellectual apologetic*" (1978,v; italics mine). He points to the theology of the Hodges and Warfield, scholastic theologians of the post-Reformation period, as those who "moulded the set of ideas we now know as fundamentalism" (Barr 1978,262).[11]

Barr sees the "scholastic" stream of tradition in evangelicalism impacting excessively on its theological methodology. While he notes that the laity probably follow the pietistic model and influence, theologians and apologists follow the scholastic model. Often paradoxes arise in conservative evangelicalism, especially in fundamentalism, because of the influence of the two streams of tradition. The warm personal, emotional view of conversion and the devotional nature of the Christian experience are mixed together with a cold intellectual-apologetic approach to doctrine. The excessive impact of reason in theological methodology represents such a paradox. Barr sees the paradox in the fundamentalist view of biblical authority:

> The attempt to support that faith [evangelical] upon an intellectual apologetic is itself from the beginning a sign of abandonment of the inner core of that faith. Evangelical faith is betrayed by the fundamentalist apparatus of argument. For faith it substitutes dependence on rational use of evidence; and in place of the religious functioning of the Bible it takes, as primary guarantee of the authority of scripture, the absence of error, especially in its historical details (1978,339).

Evangelical methodology, therefore, does not appear to be consistent with evangelical belief and practice. It supplants the fundamental issue in the evangelical's approach to Scripture, faith, in the context of the witness of the Spirit.

The danger in the unconscious mix of contrasting streams of tradition is seen in the scholastic priority of reason over faith. Barr states that evangelicals evidence the impact of the Enlightenment in "their craving for intellectual recognition and their flaunting of the rationality and erudition of conservative apologists" (1978, 129-130). He feels that the objectivist, intellectualist attitude is one of the most unattractive features of their literature (1978,130). Perhaps its unattractiveness is due to its inconsistency, in that such rationalistic methodology is not in keeping with faith and the *testimonium* in the evangelical approach to Scripture.

The paradox is in even greater proportions when Barr notes a tendency toward fundamentalist rationalism in Pentecostalism. He states that in view of the central place that "experience" plays with the group, and not orthodoxy, the manifestation of rationalism is even more paradoxical (Barr 1978,209). Pentecostalism's whole orientation to the ontic presence of the Holy Spirit, its "God with us" orientation, is threatened by the "scholastic stream" of tradition. It has much more to lose in terms of theology (pneumatology) than other evangelicals if the distorting effect of Scholasticism's rationalistic methodology is not identified. Any development of Pentecostal theology has to contend with the influence of the "scholastic theological paradigm." The crucial doctrine of revelation is an area which needs fresh attention from a non-Cartesian, biblical, and Pentecostal perspective.

The Interpretive-Theological Task and a Dynamic Concept of Revelation

The functional nature of Scripture and theology points to the dynamic and continuing nature of revelation (revelation with a small *r*). The reason why a dynamic and continuing view of revelation is affirmed here is to call attention to the scholastic distortion of the concept and its importance for the interpretive-theological task. To affirm that revelation is continuing is not a denial that the Canon is closed. Nor does it advocate a pneumatic exegesis, the desire for extra-biblical revelation. Nor is it an advocacy for an existential approach to Scripture. Rather, it marks a return to the Reformation view of revelation as dynamic and continuous in nature. In view of the axiom of "Word inseparable from Spirit," it marks a reaffirmation of Calvin's view of the *testimonium*. Berkouwer states that the *testimonium* "is not to be isolated to [*sic*] the Spirit's witness to Scripture, both Bavinck and Kuyper rejected this" (1975,45). The *testimonium* is connected with the whole Christian life, pervading the salvation that appears in Christ (John 15:27; 16:8, 13). This view of the *testimonium* affirms that revelation involves a continued divine speaking (revelation with a small *r*).[12] The above theologians, therefore, give a picture of the continuing ministry of the Holy Spirit in connection with the Word in the Christian life. Pentecostals, of course, fully subscribe to this view.

Following Luther and Calvin, Ramm holds to a dynamic view of the Word of God (Hebrew *dabar*), stating that Jesus' character is revelation, not just His words. He states that there is a dynamic, ontic dimension to the revelation in Christ (1961,112). Jesus is the "living Word." Charles Kraft states concerning Christ's claim in John 14:6 ("I am . . . the truth"):

Personal truth and revelation are not static. A true person will speak truly. But *our understanding of truth (especially in the biblical sense) should not be reduced to a concept of "true information"* . . . . As Jesus did the truth, related truly in living the truth, he truly and truthfully revealed *God*—not simply information about God. We need to learn to *distinguish between such dynamic revelation (and truth) and the information that is inevitably a part but never the whole of either* (1979,179).

The dynamic dimension of the Holy Spirit cannot be separated from the informational product. Revelation is the ontic, activity of God the Holy Spirit.[13]

Apologetic treatments of the doctrine of revelation have reinforced a static view of the concept in evangelical literature. This takes place through the use of rational arguments which emphasize the objective nature of revelation. Ramm's book, *Special Revelation and the Word of God* (1961), represents numerous arguments in which the static view of revelation is supported. But Ramm does include some balanced statements on the nature of revelation in this book (1961,158,160). However, the preponderance of the argumentation is either directed against the view of revelation in Liberalism, in neo-Orthodoxy, or in Roman Catholicism (1961,135-136,139,142,152,164,173ff). What often results in an apologetic treatment of the doctrine is that it is a one-sided treatment.

While describing the wide scope of the concept of special revelation, in an apologetic-oriented statement, Ramm notes the dynamic dimension of the concept. But the emphasis on the continuing nature of revelation concerns the informational product:

The particular form of the "hereness' [of revelation] and abiding character of revelation *is its conceptual aspect*. Certainly the word "revelation" is rich in meaning. God's word to the prophet is revelation; God's act is revelation; the illumination of the Spirit is revelation; the return of Christ is revelation. The concept of revelation in Scripture is too rich to be easily schematized; *it is also rich enough to be applied to the conceptual side of revelation* (1961,151).

The concept involves divine speaking, divine action or event, and of course, divine product—the written divine Word. But in the apologetic treatment of the doctrine, Ramm consistently represents revelation in its informational mode, arguing for its superiority. A lack of explanation at points which deal with the dynamic nature of revelation also reveals the apologetic treatment (Ramm 1961, 140-141). The description of the dynamic dimension is obscure in the treatment, with vague references to the Holy Spirit. In the apologetic treatment, therefore, the dynamic dimension is not denied; it is trivialized.

Often in the curious mix of traditions in evangelicalism, especially in the apologetic mode, the influence of western world view and scholastic methodology on theologizing impacts adversely on the crucial doctrine of revelation. It is generally represented as a static product, as information. Kraft cites the bias of western world view as the reason for limiting the concept of revelation to the written mode.[14] Kraft also notes that together with the western focus on "knowledge as information" (the noetic view of "knowing" obscuring the ontic "knowing") are the "underlying fear of subjectivity" and the desire to know objectively (1979,183). He points to static orthodox views of revelation as the outcome of western world view (1979,185-186).

Revelation is both information and encounter with the Spirit of God (Ramm 1961,158). Kraft clarified the issue when he stated that revelation is a divine, continuing activity and not simply the finished product of that activity (1979,178-185). Any limiting of the concept of revelation to the products of that activity violates the Reformation axiom of "Word inseparable from Spirit," as well as the doctrine of the *testimonium*. In a balanced statement Ramm states, "Revelation is event *and* interpretation, encounter *and* truth, person *and* knowledge" (1961,160). Revelation is activity and this activity leaves a product, special revelation cast into written form. But special revelation is also a "powerful coming of God as well as a concrete coming of God" (Ramm 1961,21). While space prohibits a further clarification of the issue at this point, using Ramm's previous tact, we may say here that the *concept of revelation is also rich enough to be applied to the dynamic side of revelation and encompass the outward charismatic ministry of the Spirit too* (revelation with a small *r*).

Limiting the concept of revelation seriously effects mission strategy. It presents a picture of revelation in which the activity of the Holy Spirit in His missionary role is obscured. The outward charismatic ministries of the Spirit among God's people are also eclipsed. The factor of the gospel witness being confirmed by "signs following" is also eliminated. Such a serious restricting of the ministry of the Holy Spirit cannot but retard the ongoing mission in the world. This is especially so among the majority of the unevangelized, those influenced by Animism.

The concepts of Scripture and theology are distorted when the dynamic dimension of the Spirit is missing in revelation. The Reformation emphasis on the ontic principle of theology and Scripture's functional nature emphasizes the truth that they have to do with the activity of God in the contemporary moment. The idea that revelation, Scripture, and theology have a dynamic dimension validates contemporary contextualization efforts. Divine activity can be expected in those efforts. This is important for those cultures where efforts to contextualize the gospel involves power-encounters with the spirit world. The view of Scripture as enlivened by the Spirit when proclaimed, self-authenticating and sufficient to accomplish its redemptive purpose, would encourage and incite evangelistic efforts among animistic-oriented societies. Fear of syncretism would be replaced with the realization that the Word of God is living and powerful, a Word that has power to transform men and cultures when it is proclaimed with the enablement of the Holy Spirit.

The "real" authority of the Scripture in such societies will never be rationalistic arguments concerning the historical accuracy of a "book," even if it is a holy book (important as the historical nature of the Bible is, methodologically speaking). The supernatural witness of the Holy Spirit in the heart, the demonstration of the Word of God in transforming behavior, and the Word confirmed with "signs following" could only be adequate authority in those circumstances. Furthermore, in any circumstance only God is an adequate witness for God. The Christian faith concerns the present activity and rule of God, not merely an intellectual faith. This is the corrective message of Pentecostalism for an Enlightenment-impacted Protestant faith.

6

The Pentecostal and
Contemporary Mission Issues

This chapter discusses the activity of God in mission, a key issue in missiological debate, how God is active in mission today. Is He immediately and primarily involved in revolutionary movements which challenge social and political injustice? Or, is He active mediately, through the church as it engages in Great Commission missions? Thus, modern mission is experiencing a crisis regarding an understanding of the providence of God. How is God active in our world? Is He active in a redemptive mission? The various theological responses to these questions bring major issues of contemporary mission theology into focus. Pentecostal theology has much to contribute in resolving this crisis regarding the Providence of God.

For the Pentecostal, the church's mission is characterized by the continuing charismatic activity of the Holy Spirit. Rather than a somewhat deistic view of God's activities in the world that sees His activities primarily in sociopolitical movements, the Pentecostal perceives God to be immediately and explicitly involved in the world. While he would not deny the sovereign activity of God in the movements of history and His influence in sociopolitical movements among mankind, the Pentecostal clearly sees God's redemptive activities articulated in the New Testament and identifiable in the world. God's acts are mediated through the church by the enablement of the Holy Spirit. These acts primarily concern what has been called "Great Commission mission," the proclamation of the good news of Jesus Christ, the discipling of the nations, and the establishing of churches.

The church is not only enabled for its mission by the Spirit, but it is the medium through which the triune God has chosen to manifest His power in redemptive mission. To say this is not to equate the

129

kingdom of God completely with the church nor to abandon a trinitarian view of mission. Rather, it emphasizes the incarnational means of God's revelation and the importance of the church as the vehicle for bringing that reign of God to the hearts of men and women and their societies. To say the church empowered by the Holy Spirit is active in carrying out God's mission is to point to the true nature of trinitarian mission.

The Scripture is the Pentecostal's primary and authoritative criterion for identifying the activity of God in the world. But that criterion also involves the quickening ministry of the Holy Spirit. The Word of God is a dynamic, living Word. For the Pentecostal, the "heavens are not as brass"; the prophetic voice is not silent as he engages in mission. God's activity in the world is not just theoretical, "muted activity," the work of an "anonymous Christ" in the events of history. The Spirit speaks in the preaching of the written Word and through prophecy, tongues, and interpretation of tongues. The latter, revelation with a small *r*, are subordinate to the written Word. Furthermore, the Holy Spirit illumines the proclaimed Word and continues to minister by guiding theological responses to the issues and problems of contemporary mission.

Mission Issues with Pneumatological Gaps

Contemporary mission issues clearly reveal a major problem —pneumatological gaps in mission theology. These gaps arise because mission theory is inconsistent with mission practice. Mission practice inevitably reflects deficiencies in mission theology (mission theory). The correction comes when the issues force missiologists to examine Scripture afresh. As they do this, the neglected doctrine of the Holy Spirit is repeatedly resurrected in one way or another. It is *that* dimension of trinitarian mission which is increasingly in focus today.

The following description of contemporary mission issues focuses on those where pneumatology is neglected. The treatment of these issues is not merely due to the selection of a Pentecostal missiologist. These issues are *representative* issues of contemporary mission theology. This points to an orientation gap in western theology where the doctrine of the Holy Spirit is neglected. Chapter 3 described that theological distortion in western theology and the resulting neglect of the Spirit in the history of mission theology and practice. Generally speaking, the non-experiential view of the Christian faith, the static view of theology and revelation, and the erosion of the sense of the supernatural are all linked to the under-development of pneumatology in western .Christendom. A predominantly rationalistic, although orthodox, view of the Christian faith has developed. In that view, for all practical purposes, after the conversion experience God ceases to be active in the affairs of men. This position views God's activity in the world in any other way as problematic.

The subjective dimension of the Christian faith is often addressed in pejorative terms in evangelical literature (particularly in dispensationalist-oriented literature), as though it is anti-faith in nature. But the subjective must not be denigrated because that distorts the fundamental character of the Christian faith. Any neglect of the experiential dimension of the faith touches everything else. It impacts negatively on our devotional life and on our theology. In the last analysis, the neglect of the subjective dimension of Christianity involves our view of the activity of God in Christian experience and our view of God's activity in the world. This kind of theological reductionism impacts negatively on mission theory and practice.

Evangelicalism's failure to recognize its theological heritage and the impact of Protestant Scholasticism upon itself, especially its pneumatological hiatus, results in the loss of a major "evaluative perspective" for viewing Pentecostal movements and their mission phenomena. For example, in *The Christian World Mission: Today and Tomorrow*, J. Herbert Kane treats the Pentecostal-Charismatic Movement as a problem when he discusses it under the section entitled, "Continuing Problems." He does not believe that the Movement is part of the solution to an experiential void in contemporary evangelicalism, a renewal movement filling an enormous theological gap left by scholastic orthodoxy. Kane states that the popularity of the Charismatic Movement is partly due to the impact of existentialism! He states, "Existentialism in philosophy and theology, with its emphasis on personal experience, has created a climate in which this kind of experience-oriented movement can thrive and grow" (1981,267). Kane misses the fact that both existential theology and the Charismatic Movement are responses to an overly rationalistic, static-oriented orthodoxy.

To attribute the popularity of the Movement, even in part, to the impact of existential philosophy and theology rather than to a genuine renewal of the Spirit in a valid dimension of the Christian faith, reveals how entrenched static orthodoxy and its rationalistic-apologetic is in the western world. Kane's treatment of the Charismatic Movement for the most part is objective, and he does mention the great neglect of the Holy Spirit in evangelicalism (1981,270-272). But he shows no awareness concerning the theological roots of that neglect. Existential theology is a symptom of the neglect; it is not the Movement's cause nor its crucible. Nor is there any mutual influence connecting the two phenomena, other than the fact that both existential theology and Pentecostalism emphasize Christian experience. To point out that similarity is no more relevant than to point out that existentialists breathe the same air as the Pentecostals! Rather than the view that Pentecostalism is a continuing problem in missions, the crucial issue is the nature of God's activity in western Christendom and the demise of the experiential dimension of Christianity.

The Problematic Activity of God in Mission

The western silence on the Spirit in the face of the current issues in mission has provided a crisis regarding the doctrine of the providence of God. The fact that both the providence of God and the kingdom of God are problematic in contemporary mission theology is symptomatic. They provide a major theological context in which contemporary mission issues are discussed here.

The Kingdom and God's Activity

The theme of the kingdom of God has emerged as a source from which theological responses are being made to mission problems. Some of the problems addressed by this theme are: the nature of the church's mission, social justice, poverty, religious renewal, and the contextualization of the Christian faith in the varied cultures of the Third World. But the Kingdom theme is given various interpretations in mission theology. The question arises, How is God's reign manifested in mission today?

The kingdom of God theme directly addresses the issue of the manifold activity of God in the world today. It has a theological affinity with the doctrine of the providence of God, which concerns God's all-inclusive presence and rule in the world. The mission problems mentioned above all concern how God is active in contemporary mission. The Pentecostal's view of the kingdom of God represents a unique paradigm in modern Christendom for the approach to, and solution of, these problems. If it is true that the Kingdom theme is a significant biblical dimension for the solution of these problems, then it is reasonable to assume that the neglect of that theme would result in mission problems with significant pneumatological gaps. In other words, if the Kingdom is "hidden" in any way to contemporary evangelicalism, it must not only retard mission, but it also must inevitably result in mission problems where a deficiency in pneumatology is endemic.

In an article entitled, "Preaching the Kingdom of God," I. Howard Marshall finds the contemporary "silence" on the kingdom of God rather surprising, because it is universally agreed by New Testament scholars that the theme is central to the Gospels and the teaching of Jesus Christ. Marshall attributes this silence to the lack of expectancy of contemporary Christians and their loss of belief in divine intervention in history. He also cites the difficulty in defining the concept because of its "already" and "not yet" references in the New Testament (1977,212).

In C. Peter Wagner's *Church Growth and the Whole Gospel*, he mentions that the "kingdom idea" was resurrected in evangelicalism shortly after World War II. He discusses the irony involved in the fact that the kingdom of God was central in Jesus' preaching and teaching but seldom mentioned in evangelical circles. Wagner attributes this to distortions arising from the "social gospel," dispensationalism, and cultic-apocalypticism—any of which provided a false justification for its neglect in evangelicalism (1981,2-3). Another possible reason for its neglect in contemporary evangelicalism is the theme's pneumatological implications. Wagner identifies two categories of "signs" of the kingdom of God:

> *Category A: Social signs or signs applied to a general class of people.*
> These include (1) preaching good news to the poor, (2) proclaiming release to the captives, (3) liberating the oppressed, and (4) instituting the Year of Jubliee ("acceptable year of the Lord").
> *Category B: Personal signs or signs applied to specific individuals.*
> These include (1) restoring sight to blind people, (2) casting out demons and evil spirits, (3) healing sick people, (4) making lame people walk, (5) cleansing lepers, (6) restoring hearing to deaf people, and (7) raising the dead (1981,16).

Category *B* signs are easily identified with a Pentecostal expression of the Christian Faith. They involve the outward charismatic ministry of the Holy Spirit. Evangelicalism may have avoided the Kingdom theme, and to an extent their social obligations, because type *A* signs are linked with the social gospel. But they could have also neglected that central theme of Jesus' ministry because of the type *B* signs which characterize and support Pentecostal theology. Without a doubt, the kingdom of God theme emphasizes two greatly neglected areas in conservative evangelicalism—the social and pneumatological implications of the gospel. Pentecostals neglect the former area with other evangelicals. Of course, the latter refers specifically to the outward charismatic nature of pneumatology. It is that "hidden dimension" of the kingdom of God in evangelicalism which brings the Pentecostal contribution to contemporary mission into focus.

The frequent mention of the kingdom of God theme and its biblical and theological articulation throughout this study indicates its importance for the development of pneumatology and mission theology. The biblical theme of the kingdom of God represents the theological underpinnings of Pentecostal theology. The kingdom of God represents the dynamic reign of God in the world. The Kingdom in its biblical sense designates God's supernatural breaking into history in the person of Jesus Christ. The Kingdom is synonymous with the activity of God; it is a more pregnant expression for God himself. In the new age of the Spirit, Scripture shows God's power and activity among people to involve the third person of the Godhead, the Holy Spirit. The coming of the new age is characterized by a new full dimension of the Spirit of God. That work of the Spirit among believers involves both an inward life-source dimension and an outward charismatic dimension (Grassi 1978,7-8; Montague 1976,32,366). The outward charismatic dimension of the Holy Spirit's ministry is identified in Scripture with the concept of the Kingdom. It is God's redemptive, mediated activity in and through the church.

A Crisis in the Doctrine of the Providence of God

G.C. Berkouwer devotes a chapter to this crisis in the doctrine of the providence of God in his *Studies in Dogmatics: The Providence of God* (1952). He cites three motifs which have occasioned its demise in the western world: the scientific, the projection, and the catastrophic (1952,17). The first motif, the scientific, has appeared repeatedly in this study. It is primarily cultural and has eroded the sense of the supernatural in the western world. The second motif, projection, is the most radical. It has been used by Marx, Feuerbach, Nietzsche, and Freud to dispose of the truth-character of religion and has provided a rationale for its tenacity in history. The motif is expressed in the following ways, "religion is the projection of man surrounded by the powers of nature," or "theology is anthropology," or "religion is the opiate of the masses," and so on (Berkouwer 1952,19-20). Berkouwer's third motif, the catastrophic, is especially relevant for a discussion of the crisis in connection with contemporary mission theology. It simply has to do with the catastrophic terrors and sufferings of humanity, and the deplorable conditions under which a majority of the human race exists in the modern world. The doctrine of providence must address how God is active in such a world. In turn, mission theology must articulate how God is active in carrying out his mission today, and also what the church's response should be in such a world.

The catastrophe motif and the resulting crisis of providence became prominent in mission circles as the leaders of the "younger" Third World churches became more involved in the worldwide missionary movement. They began to tell of their struggles with poverty and social injustice. Especially in ecumenical circles this struggle of part of the worldwide church became the focus of mission theology. The history of the International Missionary Council (IMC) after World War II reveals a growing consciousness on the part of the worldwide missionary movement toward the deplorable conditions of the emerging nations. The agenda of the IMC began to show an increased concern for the social, economic, and racial injustices taking place in the world. This attention to the socioeconomic and political dimensions of the church's mission challenged mission theology to be relevant to a new emerging world. A valid aspect of the church's mission in the world was coming into focus; mission theology needed to address that dimension of the church's mission in the new world.

The crisis concerning the activity of God in the world became acute, however, when the conditions of the Third World began to dominate the agenda of mission thinking. In other words, the crisis in the context of mission—the poverty, the violence, and the oppression—began to impact excessively on mission theologizing. These issues themselves became the hermeneutical horizon for mission theologizing. The world, it was said, sets the agenda for mission. Great Commission mission was swallowed up in the concern for humanization. In a sense, the "catastrophic" nature of the context of mission and its pressing needs eclipsed confidence in the activity of God through Scripture, the true hermeneutical horizon for mission theology. In the last analysis, the methodological shift of horizons from Scripture to the "world" constituted a compromise in biblical authority. God's "speaking from the world" became the norm rather than God's speaking from Scripture. This phenomenon brings to mind the previously cited historic "ebbs of the Spirit" in salvation history. A diminishing sense of the active presence of God resulted in an increased attention to more "objective" revelation (in that case the written Word). God's active redemptive presence appeared to subside, so a deistic-providential emphasis replaced the former.

The crisis of providence in contemporary mission, however, involves more than an eclipse of the activity of God as mediated by Scripture. God not only is said to speak from the world, but His immediate activity is said to be found in revolutionary movements in the world. The eclipse of the mediated activity of God through the church, through the ministry of the Holy Spirit, becomes complete. We must now discover where God is active in the world and join Him in order to participate in God's mission (Bassham 1979,68). For many, it was no longer clear where God was working in His redemptive mission. The catastrophic needs of the context of mission, in some circles, led to an abandonment of the mediated activity of God in mission (Great Commission Mission) for a search for His immediate activity in those contextual events.

The crisis in the doctrine of the providence of God, therefore, provides the basis for some crucial missiological issues. What *is* mission? Is it a search for God's presence in the sociopolitical movements of mankind and an alignment with those movements? What then is the role of the church? What is the role of Scripture? What of "Great Commission" mission, the church sent into the world to proclaim God's salvation from sin? What about evangelism? In *The World Council of Churches and the Demise of Evangelism*, Harvey Hoekstra speaks of a reconceptualization of mission in conciliar theology after the integration of the IMC with the World Council of Churches (WCC). "New mission" was then characterized by the above crisis about the manner of God's activity in the world. It gave humanization as the primary emphasis of mission. Hoekstra shows how this "new mission" resulted in the demise of evangelism and Great Commission mission in the history of the WCC (1979,12,21,26-27,69).

The methodological error arising out of the crisis in providence was the forfeiture of Scripture as the authoritative starting point for mission theology.[1] The redefinition of mission is directly related to the conciliar "contextual" hermeneutic. In the quest for relevancy, mission theologizing was excessively impacted by its context, resulting in a compromise of biblical authority. This compromise effected the very agenda for mission itself. The redefinition of mission is directly related to the crisis in the nature of the activity of God in mission. Bassham states:

> This new understanding of mission radically changed the traditional view of God and his relationship to the world. No longer was mission accomplished primarily through the church: the new emphasis stressed that God's primary relationship is to the world and it is the world, and not the church, that is the focus of God's plan. The value of this insight, as stated and developed, tended to overlook completely the meaning and importance of God's covenant with his people and the call to "the obedience of faith for the sake of his name among all the nations" (Rom. 1:5) (1979,69).

New mission's pattern of God-world-church now replaced classical mission's pattern of God-church-world (Bassham 1979,69). Under the pressure of the "catastrophic" context of mission and a faulty hermeneutic, what began as an effort to discover the true, holistic nature of the church's mission led to a fatal redefinition of mission. That redefinition excluded Great Commission mission as the meaning of mission for the contemporary world.[2]

The idea of missions (plural), as the church sent into the world to make Jesus Christ known as Lord and Savior, persuading men and women to become His disciples and responsible members of His church, was replaced by the idea "the church is mission." In the contemporary world that mission, therefore, means humanization. Everything the church is called to do is mission. The capitulation to the pressures of the context of mission is evident in that the very goal of mission itself is considered negotiable. A tactical matter concerning the emphasis of mission is allowed to alter basic mission theory. The compromise in biblical authority allowed such a strategic error.

The "new mission" ("mission" in the singular), therefore, refers to everything the church is sent into the world to do. It is the comprehensive term for the church's task in the world. However, Lesslie Newbigin stated concerning the two terms "mission" and "missions":

> Any progress in thought and action depends on being able to discern and state *both* the relation between things *and* the distinction between things. Or to put it another way, it depends upon being capable of looking at one thing at a time without thereby falling into the illusion of thinking that it is the only thing that exists (1960,23).

Newbigin gave a prophetic warning during the period when the integration of the IMC and WCC was being discussed. He stated:

> Now it is my plea that if ecumenicity is not to mean Christianity without its cutting edge, one of our needs today is to identify and distinguish the specific foreign missionary task within the total Mission of the Church understood in ecumenical terms (1960,23).

A failure to differentiate between "mission" and "missions" in conciliar theologies of mission *has* taken the cutting edge off of the Christian faith. In broadening mission to everything the church should do without discrimination, it has resulted in a practical reduction of the concept of mission. That which especially should not be neglected, the narrower view of mission—Great Commission mission, is neglected. This has been documented in the subsequent history of the WCC's Committee on World Mission and Evangelism (CWME) (Hoekstra 1979 and Johnston 1978).

Missio Dei and "New Mission"

Therefore, one of the most fundamental and crucial issues of contemporary mission emerges from the context of the problematic activity of God in the world—the nature of the church's mission. The theological springboard for the redefinition of mission is the *missio Dei* (mission of God) concept. The idea itself does not provide a basis for the redefinition of mission as "new mission." But its use by conciliar missiologists represents a deviation from its original meaning in contemporary discussion, as well as a deviation from its traditional use (Roman Catholic missiology). In fact, in its emergence in Protestant mission circles, at the meeting of the IMC at Willingen in 1952, it pointed to a solution to the crisis about the activity of God in the world. *Missio Dei* arose in connection with a discussion of the trinitarian view of mission (Rosin 1972,6-7). That view specifically involves the principle of "delegated" mission and the roles of the Son and the Spirit in commissioning the church in mission. But the concept's modification and interpretation by some conciliar missiologists reflect the crisis that was present with regard to the problematic activity of God in mission.

H.H. Rosin did a critical literary study of the *missio Dei* concept in order to determine its original meaning and function in Protestant missiological discussion ("Missio Dei": an examination of the origin, contents and function of the term in Protestant missiological discussion, 1972). His study supports the contention that the phrase *missio Dei* originally referred to the trinitarian view of mission. Rosin shows that the concept was subsequently used by conciliar missiologists to support their "new mission," in which humanization was their goal. They contended that the immediate activity of God in the movements of liberation was the manner of God's activity in the contemporary world of mission.

Georg F. Vicedom's *Mission of God* brought the phrase, *missio Dei*, into popular use in Protestant missionary circles. Vicedom placed the origin of the phrase at the Willingen Conference of the IMC in 1952 (1965,5).[3] For Vicedom the phrase, *missio Dei,* clearly had a trinitarian content and belonged with trinitarian theology and terminology (Rosin 1972,9). The Willingen Conference centered on the trinitarian basis of the missionary enterprise, emphasizing the source of mission as the triune God and the primacy of the activity of the Godhead in mission (Rosin 1972,9-10).

Missio Dei in the trinitarian sense refers to God as the protagonist of mission (He sends), but also that He is the One who is sent. The Son is sent (the Incarnation), and the Holy Spirit is sent (Pentecost) (Rosin 1972,14-15). The idea of "delegation" is prominent, therefore, along with incarnation in the trinitarian view. The Son is sent (Gal. 4:4-6); the Holy Spirit is sent (John 14:16); and the disciples are sent (John 17:18). Nowhere in the trinitarian understanding of mission is the church eliminated because mission originates in God, or because it is to be understood primarily as the activity of God.[4] The church has a mission too, because it is commissioned and sent into the world by Christ and empowered by the Holy Spirit for the task (Rosin 1972,17,21).

Vicedom complained that the phrase *missio Dei* underwent a modification and interpretation in the hands of some conciliar missiologists. Their treatment of the concept resulted in a deviation from its original meaning. From the trinitaran usage, denoting what God was doing mediately through the church in the proclamation of the gospel, the phrase was used to accent what was happening in historical development (Recker 1977,186).[5] Such a vague use also has resulted in bypassing the instrumentality of the church in mission. In the attempt to describe the contemporary immediate activity of God among mankind, His mediated activity through the church was neglected. Rosin shows the danger of taking the concept out of its salvation history context, with regard to the definition of mission:

> By extending the concept *"missio Dei"* limitlessly (defined as "the history" or the "dynamic revolutionary events" or the "sum total of all the good that is being done") the term loses its original meaning entirely and comes finally to signify everything except what it literally means: *God's (special) "mission."* For this after all indicates an action, which does not point indiscrimately [sic] to all kinds of happenings in the world, but only to one incomprehensible event, namely that God, the creator of all things submerged himself in his own world as a stranger...who in this world pursues a very special, hidden road in order to liberate it (1972,34).

The limitless use of the term affects adversely *the crucial midpoint event* of salvation history—the incarnation, crucifixion, and resurrection of Christ—the heart of the missionary message. The primacy of evangelism in the concept of mission is thereby eclipsed, and the role of the church in mission is trivialized. "Mission is God's or Christ's but not ours," proponents of such a use of *missio Dei* say. It is proposed that mission is to be found in the anonymous immediate activity of God in the history of mankind's struggles for human dignity and justice, not in the contemporary proclamation of the gospel.

The crux of understanding the *missio Dei* issue is the ability to differentiate between God's immediate activity and His mediated activity in the world. When this is done, the misuse of the concept in the support for "new mission" is evident. The twofold view of the activity of God is simply not a matter of "either/or." Newbigin's counsel with regard to "mission" and "missions" also applies to God's manifold activity in the world. One must discern and state *both* the relation between things *and* the distinction between them. One must be capable of looking at one thing at a time without falling into the illusion of thinking that it is the only thing that exists.[6]

The question, Can a distinction be drawn between God's providential activity and God's redeeming activity? must be answered in the affirmative *methodologically*. The critical question is not whether all of the activity of God in the world is one or not, as Recker states (1977,186). Of course, that historical activity of God is one *in essence* with His redemptive activity. But the problem concerning God's activity in mission is its *recognition by men and women*; it is an epistemological issue, not one concerning the ontological nature of the activity. The question concerns how the activity of God may be discerned and differentiated in mission theology. The issue does not concern theological speculation primarily but, an eminently practical matter—how God is involved among men and women in his redemptive activity.

A further reason why there must be a differentiation made

between God's providential activity in history and His redemptive activity is the *revelational nature* of the latter. Because God's redemptive activity is revelational activity, it necessarily requires the response of faith. It could therefore be hidden activity. The biblical description of God's activity necessarily separates God's providential activity in history from His mediated redemptive activity—not in essence but necessarily for human observers. A parallel discussion, one involving methodology primarily, concerns the nature of general history and salvation history. Some theologians use the German terms *Historie* and *Geschichte* to differentiate between the providential activity of God in history and His redemptive activity respectively. Methodologically speaking, in terms of historical critical methodology, salvation history is not completely unveiled by such methods. The reason is because salvation history is not only "historical" in nature, but it also is revelational in nature. The inadequacy of the historical critical method is due to its inability to plumb the depths of the supernatural dimensions of the *acts of God* in history.

Another reason for differentiating between God's providential activity and His redemptive activity is that in the latter God has chosen to act mediately through the agency of men and women. This choice sets apart God's redemptive activity. The mediated nature of God's redemptive activity is in keeping with the nature of divine revelation itself—it is incarnational. God co-opts men and women to represent Him; He condescends to speak through them (Recker 1977,192). This biblical picture of God's use of human agency in His redemptive purpose conflicts with the *ordo saludis* of "new mission": God-world-church. In its trinitarian sense, Samuel Volbeda affirms the agency of men and women in divine mission when he says:

> Even a slight acquaintance with Scripture will indicate that the idea of sending and being sent is one of the fundamental categories of Scripture. Revelation itself is mediated by God's sending such as He chooses to use in its communication and effectuation....
>
>   God - Revelation - Missionaries - People
>
> Without missions, revelation would never come home. God always picks out some men and sends them....(Recker 1977,194-195).

Therefore, by God's choice mission is characterized as mediated divine activity. By means of the enabling power of the Holy Spirit the church engages in mission*s*. This affirms the formula: God-church-world.

The somewhat extended treatment of the concept, *missio Dei*, here is warranted because it is the "Trojan horse," as Rosin puts it, by which the "walls" of the traditional trinitarian theology of mission were breached. But the distortion of the concept and its use as a vehicle for "new mission" are not the only reasons for discussing it. The concept illustrates the crisis in western mission theology about the activity of God in the world. That crisis establishes a *major context* for understanding contemporary mission issues; it represents a basic common denominator for contemporary mission problems. They have a crucial pneumatological dimension.

One could ask how such a major theological shift could take place in an area as fundamental as the church's mission. Of course, the reasons are numerous. Was it the catastrophic nature of the needs of the church in the Third World? Certainly the methodological or hermeneutical error contributed to the shift from Great Commission mission to the nebulous, limitless use of *missio Dei*. At least these matters can be understood from the viewpoint of Third World theologians. The contextualization phenomenon itself is an explanation for the shift from their perspective. For them, theologizing in mission represented an effort to make theology relevant to a new context of needs. In so doing they emphasized the need for a more holistic view of mission. Certainly the neglect of the socioeconomic dimension of mission in the West was a contributing factor, even though the resulting mission theology neglected, and in some conciliar theologies omitted, the evangelistic mandate. The excessive impact of the context of mission on the content of mission theology took place in the absence of biblical authority, however. This arbiter and check to the pull of the context in theologizing was not present due to the use of a faulty hermeneutic. Scripture was not the authoritative starting point for theologizing.

But one could ask, If there were a strong conviction as to God's redemptive activity through the preaching of the gospel, and an equally firm conviction concerning the mediated, transforming activity of God in the church, would such a shift have taken place? If there were a firm belief in, and experience of, the charismatic activity of God the Holy Spirit in worship and mission would there be such an intensive search for His presence elsewhere? Would there be the limitless idea of *missio Dei*, a view of the undifferentiated activity of God in the world? Under the circumstances of a dynamic experience with the redemptive activity of God, could a shift from trinitarian, Great Commission mission to "new mission" take place? Does not the shift itself point to a spiritual malaise? Could it not represent a theologizing in mission which is due to the participants' contemporary experience of the Spirit being in an "ebb stage?"

The crisis in providence and the emergence of *missio Dei* as an alternative to the mediated redemptive activity of God through the church indicates an underlying pneumatological hiatus in conciliar theology. Perhaps since the activity of God was so problematic, was of such an esoteric nature, the notion of discovering His activity elsewhere was not so strange under the circumstances.

Since the signs of the Kingdom in terms of the redemptive activity of God the Holy Spirit (category *B* signs) were so obscure, theologizing gravitated toward an emphasis on the more "objective" signs of God's activity in history. This would be the case, especially, in view of the catastrophic needs of the context of mission in the Third World. On the part of western theologians, the shift could be explained also as a desire to show solidarity with the "younger" churches of the Third World.

In the brief discussion of the problematic activity of God and the *missio Dei* concept, a number of significant mission issues have emerged. Chief among them is the nature of mission itself; its holistic nature, encompassing both the evangelistic and cultural mandates, is problematic. The limitless use of *missio Dei* calls the church's role in mission into question. It also brings into focus the problem of discerning whether Scripture sets forth a priority of mission activity among all the good works the church could do in the world. The conciliar theologies of mission emphasize the neglected mission issue of ecumenism. Theological method in mission strategy is also an issue arising from the pressing needs of the mission context of the Third World. The issue of contextualization, with its pitfalls, is evident. The praxis nature of mission strategy (mission theologizing) brings the theological issue of biblical authority into the arena of contemporary mission issues.

Finally, in view of the crisis in the manner of God's activity in mission and the confessed trinitarian basis of mission, the Holy Spirit's role in mission appears as an issue. Those theologies of mission focusing on the undifferentiated use of *missio Dei*, and which also utilize the Kingdom theme but yet fail to articulate the role of the Holy Spirit, point to the pneumatological hiatus in contemporary mission theology. However, both the biblical and Pentecostal perspectives of the Kingdom bring pneumatology into the arena of mission problems.

The phenomenon of independency movements in the Third World, furthermore, is an issue that has been in focus repeatedly in the wider context of this study. At times they were in focus in connection with the contextualization issue, with indigeneity. At other times they arose directly in connection with the deficiency in western pneumatology (e.g., their causation). Such movements must be viewed as a challenge to our pneumatology. They also would come under the "major context of mission problems"—the problematic activity of God in the world. The movements present a challenge to western notions of orthodoxy, and call for a practical, cross-cultural view of orthodoxy (Watney 1982,2). The African Independent Church Movement brings the question of the unity and diversity of the Body of Christ into focus in its international dimensions. This issue of ecumenism also has an important pneumatological dimension.

In summary, the identification of a major theological context of contemporary mission issues has gone a long way toward their solution. The catastrophic circumstances of the context of mission in the Third World brought the whole church to realize that a holistic view of mission was needed for twentieth century mission. However, the hermeneutical error that arose in response to those needs, and the ill-conceived view of *missio Dei* that was used to support "new mission," resulted in a compromise of the heart of "God's special mission"—Great Commission mission. The Pentecostal Movement is a chief source from which to emphasize God's special mission, as mediated by the activity of God the Holy Spirit through the agency of the church. As a "people of the Spirit," Pentecostals represent a source for dispelling the confusion concerning the activity of God in the world of mission. By means of the Kingdom motif, which has been prominent throughout this study, this biblical motif is used in the next chapter to provide a Pentecostal perspective for the issues raised in this chapter.

7

The Pentecostal and
the Kingdom of God

This chapter summarizes the Pentecostal contribution to contemporary mission theology by giving Pentecostal perspectives of contemporary mission issues. The kingdom of God motif provides a biblical perspective which is needed to approach the problems of contemporary mission. The motif is inseparably related to pneumatology, so a Pentecostal perspective also emerges. Therefore, it is instrumental in bringing new insights to a major context of contemporary mission issues—the problematic activity of God in mission. The kingdom motif also helps to clarify the Holy Spirit's role for a trinitarian view of mission. The issues of the holistic nature of the missionary enterprise, its priority, and the role of the church in mission are addressed by the Kingdom motif in a significant way. The Kingdom motif brings into view a major issue of contemporary mission—the poor. This social issue can be examined, therefore, from the perspective of a major biblical theme. Pentecostal prescriptions for mission theology emerge, therefore, from the Kingdom motif.

The Kingdom without the Spirit?

In chapter 6 the discussion of *missio Dei* illustrated a failure in distinguishing between God's immediate providential activity in the world and His mediated redemptive activity. This resulted in a mission emphasis in which the cultural mandate or "humanization" dominated. Any approach to mission which neglects the mediated redemptive activity of God, "the Great Commission mission," contrasts starkly to the Pentecostal perspective of mission. The Pentecostal perspective is founded on the biblical concept of the kingdom of God. The Kingdom motif emphasizes

145

the dynamic, evidential experience of the Spirit—the mediated activity of God through the church. Pentecostalism provides insights into this experiential dimension of the Christian faith; in this sense it functions as the "third corner" of Christendom.

With respect to the mission of the church, the Kingdom idea's scope is clearly comprehensive in Scripture. It concerns both the evangelistic mandate (the narrow view of mission—evangelism or Great Commission mission) and the cultural mandate (the wider view of mission—social dimension). The latter mandate is the primary emphasis of most conciliar theologies of mission. The former points to the area of Pentecostal emphasis and contribution. The cultural mandate functions also as a challenge to Pentecostalism's inadequate biblical response to the wider mission of the church.

The Kingdom perspective puts contemporary mission problems in a biblical framework from which fresh theologizing can provide solutions. But the Kingdom theme is often used in theologizing about mission without articulating the role of the Holy Spirit. This theme is used to support the wider view of mission by emphasizing the immediate providential activity of God in social and political movements. The need to specify that activity in terms of the Holy Spirit does not appear to be crucial in those cases. The concept of *missio Dei* used improperly, in its undifferentiated sense, puts the emphasis on the activity of God the Father. However, a biblical theology, as well as the Kingdom motif, requires a description of the role of the third person of the Trinity for a true trinitarian view of mission. The description of His role brings the holistic nature of mission into focus, and it points to the biblical priority of mission.

When the Kingdom theme is treated apart from the role of the Holy Spirit, mission theology is severely impaired, even distorted. The published documents of the World Council of Churches' Committee on World Mission and Evangelism (CWME) conference at Melbourne in 1980 reveals the typical silence on the ministry and role of the Holy Spirit in conciliar theologies of mission. A conference on evangelism and mission gathered to discuss the mission perspectives of a theme like "Thy Kingdom Come," you would expect, would have much to say about the Holy Spirit's role in mission. But the scarcity of pneumatology in the conference documents is curious.

In the plenary presentations only Ernst Käsemann broached the subject, due to his treatment of the New Testament concept of the Kingdom in its eschatological context. While Käsemann expresses the signs of the Kingdom in terms of the outward ministry of the Holy Spirit *in the New Testament* (category *B* signs), most of his *contemporary* applications of the concept concern the social and political dimensions of the Kingdom (category *A* signs) (1980, 64-66). Apparently for Käsemann, the signs of the Kingdom today only involve the preaching of the gospel, ecumenical openness, and social justice (1980,70). The latter two signs of the Kingdom were typical of the focus of the whole conference.

The section reports make scattered references to the Holy Spirit but, only about His inward work in regeneration, revelation, and strengthening the believer (1980,194-196). When mission in the wider sense (social justice) is linked with the Kingdom theme, emphasizing the undifferentiated activity of God, the result is a relatively sparse mention of the work of the Holy Spirit. The Kingdom concept is no guarantee that the missionary role of the Spirit and a holistic view of mission will be considered. Since the concept of the Kingdom is comprehensive, one may choose to only emphasize one aspect of God's activity, either His immediate providential activity or His mediated pneumatic activity. The limitless use of *missio Dei* under the alleged purpose of attaining a holistic view of mission appears to function as a "smoke screen" for an obvious bias in pursuing humanization as the goal of mission. But the crucial question is, Does Scripture indicate a priority for mission? If biblical authority means anything this question must be answered.

Even evangelical approaches to the Kingdom theme can neglect the role of the Holy Spirit for a number of reasons. George Eldon Ladd's otherwise excellent survey of the kingdom of God theme in *The Presence of the Future* (1974) is an illustration. He is unusually silent on the role of the Holy Spirit. His thesis chiefly concerns the truth that the kingdom of God is the dynamic, redemptive activity of God himself in history. But his chief omission is "how" God acts and works in history apart from Jesus Christ himself. Ladd's silence on the Holy Spirit is counterproductive to his purpose of showing that the Kingdom breaks through into contemporary history in the person and mission of Jesus Christ (Ladd 1974,xi). Ladd does not describe the Kingdom concept as God's activity in the world by means of the Holy Spirit's dynamic ministry, both in and independent of the church.[1] In what appears to be an almost studied manner he avoids the mention of the third person of the Trinity. In certain obvious pneumatological contexts references to the Holy Spirit are missing. Although such terms as "power," "signs," "exorcisms," and "healings" are mentioned, they are not related to pneumatology (Ladd 1974,183). The topic, "The Kingdom: Supernatural," is discussed without a solitary reference to the Holy Spirit (Ladd 1974,188-194).

Perhaps the fact that the christological context of the Kingdom is consistently in focus in Ladd's treatment is the reason for the omission. But given the fact that Ladd primarily confines his treatment of the Kingdom to the Old Testament, the ministry of Christ, and the mission of the Twelve and Seventy pre-Pentecost, the silence on the Spirit is still conspicuous. In the solitary reference to Pentecost, where the Kingdom's powers were said to be no longer limited to Jesus and His close disciples, pneumatology is even avoided! The coming of the Kingdom to all believers is spoken of as "Jesus returning in the Spirit" (John 14:16-18) and believers being "delivered from the dominion of darkness and transferred into the Kingdom of Christ" (Col 1:13). The only mention of the third person of the Godhead is a reference to Romans 14:17 (Ladd 1974,272-273). The lone paragraph and an "aside" reference involving one sentence (Ladd 1974,271), represents an incredible paucity of references to the Spirit in a biblical study of the kingdom of God.[2]

The neglect of the Spirit in discussions of the Kingdom theme in exegetical studies of Jesus' preaching in the Gospels may be due to several reasons. A failure to recognize *a change of terminology in the use of the Kingdom concept in the Bible*, and a *failure to recognize a major transition in salvation history itself* are common reasons why the Spirit is neglected.

The Biblical Reinterpretation of the Kingdom

In an article entitled, "The Concept of the Kingdom of God in the Preaching of the Apostles," Donald E. Macomber observes that in the Book of Acts the preaching of the Kingdom and the preaching of the gospel were one and the same. He explains, "In the progress of doctrine in the New Testament, the term 'kingdom of God' is, in Acts dropping out for the term 'gospel'" (1958,356). In various New Testament references to the term "kingdom"[3] Macomber shows that the concept is linked with the *preaching of the gospel and the name of Jesus Christ* (1958,356-358). With regard to the content of the disciples' preaching the result is the same: the Kingdom and the gospel are one (Macomber 1958,359). I. Howard Marshall agrees concerning this reinterpretation of the Kingdom concept by saying, "What these changes in terminology indicated was . . . a realization that the saving action of God was to be unpacked in terms of the work of Christ, in his ministry, death and resurrection" (1977,213). He states further, "The person in whom the Kingdom was revealed replaced the Kingdom in Christian preaching" (1977,213). However, Jesus "unpacked" the Kingdom concept in terms of the *Holy Spirit* too.

George T. Montague states that Jesus prepared the disciples for the above reinterpretation of the Kingdom by His own reinterpretation. This happened just after His resurrection and just prior to Pentecost (Acts 1:1-8). The passage Montague refers to (Acts 1:8) states that Jesus spoke to the disciples about the kingdom of God over the period of forty days (Acts 1:3). The disciples were expecting the coming of the Kingdom on Jesus' own word. Furthermore, they were instructed to wait for the promised Kingdom in Jerusalem. After all, did not Jesus say, "I am going to send you what my Father has promised; but stay in the city until you have been clothed with power from on high" (Luke 24:49)? They thought this promise of the Kingdom meant that they would be enthroned to judge the twelve tribes in "the Kingdom" (Montague 1976,269). But Jesus disregarded these expectations and spoke to the disciples concerning the power of the Holy Spirit in the context of their mission.

Furthermore, when we look in Luke's Gospel for a promise of the Holy Spirit like that mentioned in Acts, no text that warrants the salvation history importance of "the promise" is forthcoming. Instead, we must look for texts which have to do with the "Kingdom" (Montague 1976,269). Acts 1:8 also parallels the Great Commission passages in the Gospels which involve the *preaching of the gospel and the power in Jesus' name* (Matt 28:18-20; Mark 16:15,17; Luke 24:47; John 20:21,31). The Kingdom theme is a mission theme; it concerns Great Commission Mission! It involves the activity of the Holy Spirit in the world of mission.

What this change of terminology means is that after Pentecost the redemptive activity of God is mediated primarily through the preaching of the gospel and the manifest power of the Holy Spirit in Jesus' name. The church empowered by the Spirit demonstrates the Kingdom's presence by the preaching of the gospel, which is confirmed by signs and wonders (Mark 16:15-17,20). It is in this saving activity of God the Holy Spirit, through the agency of the church, that the priority of mission is found. The priority of proclaiming the gospel, Great Commission mission, dominates the church's mission in the Book of Acts. Scripture does put emphasis on the evangelistic mandate, God's "special" mission.

Recognizing a Salvation History Transition

While it may not have been so evident to the disciples then, it should be clear for the modern student that Acts 1:8 contains a pneumatological statement. Because of the Pentecost event and Jesus' lead in reinterpreting the Kingdom as the Holy Spirit's power in the church, we must understand the Kingdom in terms of the Spirit. Jesus' interpretation of the Kingdom clearly linked the ministry of the Holy Spirit with the church's mission.[4] The prominence of the Holy Spirit's presence and role in Acts 1:8 points to the passage's transitional nature for salvation history. The Age of the Spirit was dawning for the church. In Jesus' answer to the disciples' Kingdom question, the matter of the coming Kingdom in consummation (Acts 1:11, its "not yet" dimension) is subordinated to the presence of the Kingdom and the imperative of mission in the "time between the times" (Acts 1:8, its "already" dimension). The "unpacking" of the Kingdom concept in terms of pneumatology, in the transition of salvation history, points to centrifugal mission in the power of the Holy Spirit.

The Pentecost event (Acts 2) is a pivotal point in salvation history. Boer states:

> At Pentecost a distinct period in the divine economy of redemption was introduced, the characteristic feature of which is the presence of the Holy Spirit. We may therefore say that after Creation and Incarnation the outpouring of the Spirit is the third great work of God (1961,66).

Recognizing that a transition in salvation history is taking place in the Acts 1:1-8 passage allows us to understand the Kingdom concept in terms of pneumatology. Pentecost means the church is not only confronted with the *fact* of the Holy Spirit's presence, but with the *power* of His presence, and the *effects* of His presence. The power and effects of His presence in Acts is primarily concerned with the witness of the church. Boer states concerning this "coming of the Kingdom with power":

> The being filled with the Spirit at Pentecost manifested itself in *irrepressible speaking* about the great works of God that came forth from the human spirit wholly seized by the divine Spirit. Pentecost momentarily placed in sharp and dramatic relief that the Church that had come into being in her New Testament form is a speaking, proclaiming Church and that she addresses all men and all nations with her message (1961,102).

In effect, therefore, Pentecost confirms that the Kingdom equals the proclamation of the gospel. The New Testament church's reinterpretation of the Kingdom emphasizes the *evangelistic mandate's priority* in its mission. Jesus' reinterpretation also points in this direction. The Kingdom in pneumatological terms has to do with the witness of the church in the Spirit's power and the universalization of mission under His direction.

Pentecost represented the renewal of the Spirit of prophecy, a tremendous flow of the Spirit after its ebb in salvation history.[5] Boer notes that there are two types of speaking occurring at Pentecost. There was the speaking in other tongues under the enablement of the Spirit, which was accompanied with signs, and the preaching of the gospel by Peter under the same enablement.[6] Boer interprets Pentecost in a salvation history context, emphasizing the priority of the proclamation of the gospel in the church's mission in "time between the times." Not only is the priority of mission established by this interpretation, but also the instrumentality of the church. The focus on the ministry of the Spirit in the New Age, therefore, brings attention to the *mediated redemptive activity of God through Great Commission mission.*

Boer notes that both of the above "speakings" of the church establish the "central task" of the church. That task is to witness to the great works of God in the power of the Spirit in the "last days." He sees the proclamation of the gospel and the outpouring of the Spirit as signs of the end (Boer 1961,103). Therefore, both the preaching of the gospel and the outpouring of the Spirit are "signs of the Kingdom." They represent two major dimensions of the Holy Spirit's ministry in the Age of the Spirit: His life-giving ministry through the Word, and His charismatic ministry in connection with that Word. While Boer holds that the speaking in tongues is a "passing sign," Montague sees such category *B* signs as typical of the messianic age.[7]

While there are passages of Scripture that may be interpreted to show that Christ is at work in human history, showing solidarity with the oppressed and needy, Scripture plainly states how Christ is active in contemporary mission. The Great Commission passages contain crucial statements concerning the church's mission in the world. Matthew and Mark's accounts specifically mention the presence of Christ as the church engages in God's "special" redemptive mission. This is not an anonymous presence; it is in connection with the two signs of the messianic age—the preaching of the gospel and the charismatic activity that accompanies this proclamation (Matt 28:18-20; Mark 16:15-20; Luke 24:47; John 20:21,31). Christ confirms the former by the latter (Mark 16:20).

When the issue of the poor in contemporary mission theology is linked with the Kingdom theme, the transition in salvation history mentioned previously (in connection with the Acts 1:8 passage) is prominent. The biblical references to the poor are tied to this new age of the Spirit. They are in the exegetical framework of salvation history.

The solidarity of Pentecostalism with the poor is often noted. Pentecostalism's phenomenal growth is often attributed to its ties with the poor and the working classes. However, it is clear that such solidarity with the poor is not due to overt mission strategy.[8] Pentecostals do not have a concern for social issues. In fact, the case is quite the opposite. Neglect in this area is often noted about Pentecostalism (Wagner 1973,137-138). It is no longer true that Pentecostals in general are only from "the other side of the tracks." Pentecostals are also frequently numbered among the middle class overseas. Since the neo-Pentecostal Movement and Catholic Charismatic Renewal, this is all the more the case. Is it true that the Pentecostals have a greater percentage of the poor in their ranks than any other Christian group overseas? Do they have greater ties with the poor and, therefore, greater growth? The solidarity of Pentecostalism with the poor is somewhat paradoxical in modern mission discussion, especially in view of the intense interest concerning mission and the poor. We might ask, If Pentecostalism's ties with the poor are not due to their mission strategy, or because of a particular value of social concern for that group of society, then why do they have such solidarity with them?

When theological reasons are sought for phenomenal Pentecostal growth, an alleged "preference of God for the poor" is emphasized. God's favor for the poor is supposed to be demostrated by the rapid growth of the gospel among them around the world (Wagner 1981,31). A common text used by both evangelical and conciliar missiologists (to support God's alleged preference for the poor) is Jesus' quotation of the Prophet Isaiah:

> The Spirit of the Lord is on me, because he has anointed me to preach good news to the poor. He has sent me to proclaim freedom for the prisoners and recovery of sight for the blind, to release the oppressed, to proclaim the year of the Lord's favor (Luke 4:18-19).

The question of interpretation immediately emerges about the emphasis of the Luke 4:18-19 passage, as well as other New Testament passages which are supposed to support the position that God has a preference for the poor. But, is God's preferential favor demonstrated in these passages, or does the key to Pentecostal growth rest with the poor themselves, with their ready response to the gospel? Somehow the Pentecostals, the poor, and phenomenal growth are all linked together.

The view of mission and the gospel narrowing down to focus on this economically deprived group is often treated in connection with the Kingdom motif in conciliar theology (CWME 1980,171). Conciliar theologians interpret the Luke 4:18-19 passage to refer to the socioeconomic poor; it is said to be a reference to the cultural mandate (the goal of humanization in mission). We are cautioned that the passage should not be "spiritualized," that it is a reference to the literal poor and oppressed. But the meaning of the Luke 4 text is confused when the "literal interpretation" versus the "spiritual interpretation" question is asked. *Both* interpretations are suggested. But this does not settle the question of the passage's intended emphasis. It is at this point where Wagner's two types of Kingdom signs emerged in his discussion of Luke 4:18-19 (type *A* social signs and type *B* personal charismatic signs) (1981,16). The twofold sign of the Kingdom shows both interpretations are possible in Luke 4:18-19. A critical question, therefore, is What was the intended meaning of the passage when it was spoken and written in its historical context?

The literal poor *are* addressed in the passage; the Spirit was upon Jesus to proclaim the good news to them. But are the poor set apart here because of their socioeconomic status? Or, are they mentioned because they represent the increased focus of the gospel in the new age, the class of people *who were ready to respond to the gospel in that age?*

The emphasis of Jesus' statement in the Luke 4:18-19 passage refers to a new period which was dawning in salvation history. The parallel passages in the synoptic Gospels support this:

> After John was put in prison, Jesus went into Galilee, proclaiming the good news of God. "The time has come," he said. "The kingdom of God is near. Repent and believe the good news" (Mark 1:14-15)! "Repent, for the Kingdom of heaven is near" (Matt 3:17).

That the poor represent *an enlargement of the gospel focus in the new age* is indicated by the transition of the ministry of John the Baptist to that of Jesus ("After John was put in prison"). The references to "the time has come" and "the kingdom of God [heaven] is near" also point to this. Both Matthew and Luke make the salvation history transition clear (Matt 11:1-13; Luke 16:16). Luke states:

> The Law and the Prophets were proclaimed until John. Since that time, the good news of the kingdom of God is being preached, and everyone is forcing his way into it (Luke 16:16).

The significance of the poor is *their affective disposition* which allows them entrance into the Kingdom—*repentance and faith* —not their socioeconomic class.

In view of the salvation history context of the Luke 4:18-19 passage and the twofold sign of the Kingdom in the passage, it should be interpreted as a reference to the evangelistic mandate. The passage refers to God's "special" mission, the universal proclamation of the gospel which was offered in the new age on the basis of repentance and faith. The context of the Kingdom and the poor in the other crucial references in the New Testament also support this interpretation.

The *real* question is not whether the statement concerning the poor in the New Testament *may be* used by way of an interpretive-application (the second hermeneutical task) to emphasize the church's responsibility to the poor. This would be a valid use and extrapolation of the Luke 4:18-19 text. Nor is the question whether God is concerned with the poor, this is obvious. The first question must be to ask whether the cultural mandate was *the intended meaning* of the statements when they were made in their historical context (the descriptive-historical task). Are all of the statements concerning the poor in the New Testament direct references to the cultural mandate? Or must they be differentiated in terms of groups? Is their meaning that God had, and has, preference for this socioeconomic group? Or, do these crucial references to the poor (those in the context of the Kingdom theme) represent people who are particularly responsive to the gospel? In other words, what *is* the emphasis of the New Testament concerning the poor? But first a word about the position that God has preference for the poor.

The idea that God has a preference for the poor approaches a theological absurdity, especially in the context of the New Testament. God is biased? Can one say this without a reference to the response of faith?[9] In *Rich Christians in an Age of Hunger: A Biblical Study*, Ronald Sider states:

> The poor are the only group specifically singled out as recipients of Jesus' gospel. Certainly the gospel he proclaimed was for all, but he was particularly concerned that the poor realize that his good news was for them (1977,66).

Sider takes Luke 4:18-19 to refer to the socioeconomic poor as a group which receives special concern from God and the ministry of Jesus. But at the outset the question should be asked, did Jesus have a preferential concern for the poor, or were they not in fact those who readily recognized that the good news was for them?

Sider notes that the preaching of the gospel was also the mission of Jesus. But due to the focus of his book he emphasizes what he considers to be an *equally important* mission of releasing literal captives and liberating the socially oppressed (1977,66,231). He refers to Jesus' healing the sick and blind in His ministry, according to Luke 4:18-19, but he does not give any New Testament examples where the literal social captives and oppressed are set at liberty. Does the lack of such New Testament references point to the primary nature of Christ's Kingdom as portrayed in the Gospels (it is not of this world, a political Kingdom—John 18:36)? Does this lack have a bearing on the interpretation of Luke 4:18-19? Is the obvious meaning a spiritual meaning, with reference to the oppressed and the prisoners? The New Testament is replete with exorcisms and deliverances from demon possession, but political and social deliverances are few and are clearly not the thrust of the Kingdom motif.

Sider quotes numerous Old Testament references in support of God's special concern for the poor. But even these contain references to the affective disposition of the poor in their response to God, or to the negative affective disposition of the rich and wicked who oppress the poor (1977,67,72-74). However, Sider's treatment does not emphasize this crucial dimension. When the affective dimension is not emphasized in viewing the rich, they are often unjustly stereotyped. The "rich-bad guys/poor-good guys" dichotomy is not helpful in deciding the "poor issue" in the New Testament. While consistently maintaining God's preference for the poor (1977,66-68,70-71,82), Sider is forced to admit that God in reality does not have preference for the poor (1977,73,83-84). The apparent contradiction emerges from the forced nature of the exegesis, and the theological absurdity involved with such a contention. Sider does, however, make an excellent case for God's judgment on those who oppress the poor. The neglect, mistreatment, and oppression of the poor is clearly condemned by Scripture; ministry to the poor is clearly a Christian duty (Sider 1977,59-85).

The key to understanding the references to the poor in the New Testament is not God's preferential favor, but the response of faith on the part of the poor. In the crucial New Testament passages concerning the poor (those in the context of the Kingdom motif),[10] persons who are *receptive* to the gospel message are referred to. The key to the "Pentecostal paradigm," *Pentecostals—the poor —phenomenal growth*, is the receptivity of the poor. Furthermore, rather than a *narrowing* of the focus of mission to a socioeconomic group, the crucial New Testament references concerning the poor refer to a *widening* of the focus of mission in salvation history. They refer to the universalization of the gospel (Matt 11:11-13). These crucial statements about the poor focus not on a "preferential group," or on an economic category; the New Testament message as a whole opposes this idea. Rather, the gospel is universally proclaimed without respect for persons or classes. It is offered without discrimination on the condition of "repentance and faith," whether to rich or poor. The "poor issue" concerns the central theme of the New Testament—the faith response of men and women to the grace of God that is revealed in the gospel (Eph 2:8). The context of the majority of statements concerning the poor in the New Testament (the crucial Kingdom references) is the evangelistic mandate, not the cultural mandate.

The idea that God prefers the poor and the use of New Testament passages concerning the poor as proof-texts to support that position illustrate the "pitfall" of the contextualization of theology. The excessive impact of the catastrophic context of mission on the content of mission theology distorts the New Testament teaching on the poor.

In Luke's Gospel the consistent themes accompanying issues of the Kingdom and the poor are: 1) the universal proclamation of the gospel (Luke 4:18-19,43; 7:22; 13:29-31; 14:15-24; 16:16; cf. Acts 1:8), and 2) the charismatic signs of the Spirit's power (Luke 4:18-19,31-43; 8:1-2; 9:2,11; 10:18; 11:20; 13:32). These signs of the Kingdom accompany the crucial "poor" references and are in keeping with what we previously stated about the reinterpretation of the Kingdom. At times, the Kingdom theme is more explicit and frequent in the parallel passages of Matthew's Gospel. Also there are numerous references and incidents referring to the "type *B*" charismatic signs of the Kingdom interspersed between the verses listed above.

The "poor," therefore, are consistently linked with the universal proclamation of the gospel in the new age. As a group their significance is not that they represent a particular socioeconomic class but that they represent the "common man." The poor represent the enlarged audience to whom the gospel message is now directly addressed in the new period of salvation history. There are references to the socioeconomic poor in Luke (10:30-37; 11:41; 12:32; 14:13; 18:22). But these references do not dominate the Gospel or the teaching of Jesus as do the crucial references in connection with the Kingdom motif. The salvation history poor, as the recipients of the gospel message in the new age, are characterized not by their material poverty but by their receptivity to the gospel message (Luke 6:20,24-25; 8:9-15; 9:2-6; 10:8-11, 21-22; 14:15-21).[11]

The significance of the poor, therefore, in connection with the Kingdom is that they are ready to respond to the gospel because of their humility and probable positive affective disposition toward repentance and faith—the crucial prerequisites for entrance into the Kingdom. The crucial "salvation history poor" references must be differentiated from the "socioeconomic poor" references. They refer to different mandates. Those references accompanying the Kingdom motif make up the group which dominate the teaching of Jesus.

A third theme which would logically accompany the Kingdom and the poor, beside the preaching of the gospel and the charismatic confirming signs of the Spirit, would be the *required faith response* to that message. Receptivity of the gospel is the consistent theme accompanying the Kingdom motif and the poor in Luke's Gospel. The *faith issue* is clearly the immediate context of the crucial Luke 4:18-19 passage also; the unbelief of the Nazarenes is the context of this passage, as well as the widow of Zarephath story.[12] The faith of the centurion foreshadows the age of the universalization of the gospel which would follow the period of Jewish particularization (Luke 7:1-10).

The answer to the question we asked previously about the nature of the New Testament teaching concerning the poor is twofold. The references to the socioeconomic poor teach the Christian duty to help the poor. They are references to the cultural mandate. However, the references which dominate the New Testament are those that are connected with the Kingdom motif and refer to the evangelistic mandate. The "Kingdom and poor" theme is consistently accompanied by the twofold sign of the Kingdom: the proclamation of the gospel and the charismatic signs of the Spirit's

power. The poor are representative of those who respond to the
good news in repentance and faith. These "Kingdom and poor"
references represent the broadening of mission in salvation history
and illustrate the basis upon which the good news of the present
kingdom of God may be received—repentance and faith. God is no
respecter of persons (Acts 10:34-35).

The early church reinterpreted the kingdom of God and thus
emphasized the proclamation of the gospel, the narrow view of
mission. This role of the church cannot be trivialized. For the
Kingdom is known by the dynamic activity of Christ in the church
as it proclaims His name in the power of the Holy Spirit. This view
of the resurrected Christ working with the contemporary church
points to the necessity for a clarification of roles in a trinitarian
view of mission.

The Kingdom and Trinitarian Mission

Both the concept of the Kingdom and that of trinitarian mission
have significant "pneumatological gaps" in Protestant discussions
about mission. The description and importance of the role of the
Holy Spirit is usually wanting in the evangelical use of the concepts.
Previously, our study of Ladd's view of the Kingdom illustrated
how the name "Holy Spirit" is studiously avoided. In contrast to
his view the term "kingdom" is often substituted for "Holy Spirit"
when describing some aspect of the Spirit's ministry in mission
(Shenk 1979,24-26). Although the Kingdom may be identified as "a
concept of the acting God," a discussion of both the Kingdom and
the nature of mission itself can take place with only a sprinkled
reference to the Holy Spirit here and there (Shenk 1979,23).
Usually, references to the Spirit are connected with Jesus' ministry,
or they are confined to the first century. It does not appear that this
is intentional, but rather a silence on the Holy Spirit results when
the Kingdom concept is not "unpacked" in terms of the full
ministry of the Spirit. Also, the trinitarian view of mission needs to
be understood in the same way.

Often when Pentecostals speak about the Spirit in this way it is
said that their interest is doctrinaire. Or, they are charged with
overemphasizing the Spirit in sort of a "monism of the Holy
Spirit" way. Bernard Ramm notes that "the standard objection of
historic Christianity and Reformed theology to all forms of
enthusiasm, fanaticism and Pentecostalism" is that they "build a
temple where Scripture permits only a tent" (1959,30). Pentecostals, however, are not alone in their apparent overemphasis of a
particular person of the Godhead. Both Roman Catholicism and
various Protestant denominations also do this (Spiceland
1980,144). Also it is understandable that Pentecostalism, a renewal
movement, emphasizes and brings to the attention of Christendom

that neglected reality of the Holy Spirit in Christian experience. As previously stated, this represents their contribution as the "third corner" of Christendom. Evangelicals usually emphasize the ministry of the Spirit in uplifting Christ. But Ramm asks whether the doctrine of the Trinity does not dictate a "Trinity-consciousness," a consciousness of all three persons of the Godhead (1959,28). Ramm asks a question that shows that there may be further biblical reason for the Pentecostal's emphasis of the Holy Spirit. He suggests a reason beyond pneumatology's historic neglect and the Pentecostal's particular doctrinal emphasis—a christomonism in evangelicalism. Ramm asks if it is true that Scripture teaches that Christian consciousness must be "Christ-consciousness," and not "Spirit-consciousness" (1959,29).

The previous discussion about the Kingdom concept clearly mentioned both the activity of God the Son and God the Holy Spirit in the church as it engages in mission. The contemporary silence on God the Holy Spirit's role in that mission has contributed greatly to the underdevelopment of trinitarian theology. As a by-product of Christology, historically the Holy Spirit's specific trinitarian role has been left undeveloped (Bray 1980,58-59). This may be the reason also for the intense reaction we feel concerning Ramm's suggestion about the Christian's Spirit-consciousness. The historic christological controversies and the undeveloped nature of pneumatology have helped to promote what appears to be an excessive Christ-consciousness. There is no doubt concerning the cruciality of Christology in those controversies concerning the Trinity in theology in general. But we must avoid a pitting of Christology's importance over against that of pneumatology. Rather the various roles of the persons of the Godhead must be identified in terms of their work in the church and mission.

The trinitarian controversies clearly affirmed the equality of the persons of the Godhead. But the Church Fathers also maintained that the persons of the Godhead were distinct though inseparable. And the same held true for their work.[13] It is a theological necessity to distinguish the various persons of the Godhead, as well as their particular work in the church. To do so does not mean that we are slipping into the errors of modalism, subordinationism, or tritheism. Spiceland supports this view when he says that "The trinitarian formulations were an attempt to express and preserve the threefold experience of God in Christ through the Spirit" (1980,149). He states further that "The entire apparatus of technical language about the Trinity results from the attempt . . . of the Christian Fathers to make sense of Christian life" (1980,149-150). The particular area of Christian life we must understand here is the experience of the Holy Spirit in the context of the church's mission. The contemporary silence on the third person of the Godhead in mission reflects the need for the Holy Spirit to be emphasized in order to make sense of mission and to avoid a practical subordinationism of the third person of the Trinity.

Missio Dei, *The Silence, and the Issues*

The switch from the trinitarian use of *missio Dei* to its limitless use (God's providential activity in historic events) not only reveals a pneumatological hiatus in western theology, but it also is a means for perpetuating the silence on the third person of the Trinity. It does so in that the misuse of the term results in a non-trinitarian emphasis, specifically a mistaken view of the role of God the Father in mission. He is viewed as originating, owning and carrying out this mission in the contemporary world to the point of detracting from the roles of the other persons of the Godhead. God the Son's role is often confined to the first century, the crucial midpoint of salvation history (Nababan 1980,3-4). Or, Christ becomes an anonymous presence in revolutionary movements in contemporary times. God the Holy Spirit's role in mission is seldom articulated. In Roland Allen's words this is a "neglect of one whole hemisphere" of pneumatology (and trinitarian theology), a crucial one for mission—the missionary role of the Spirit.

Therefore, along with a non-trinitarian use of *missio Dei* is the characteristic paucity of pneumatology. J. Verkuyl's *Contemporary Missiology, An Introduction* reveals this use of *missio Dei* and neglect of the Holy Spirit in mission theology. The brevity of the references to the Holy Spirit in His missionary role at crucial points of Verkuyl's theology is conspicuous (1978,105,108,111,145-146). The attempt to discern where the powers of the Kingdom are at work today, especially in liberation movements, betrays a loss of appreciation for the Holy Spirit's missionary role and ministry in contemporary mission. This is shown by the tendency to speak of the activity of God entirely as providential in a socioeconomic context. The signs of the Kingdom are typically social (category *A* signs). In Verkuyl's mission theology there are no clear references to the biblical signs of the Spirit (category *B* signs). These are either used figuratively or they are interpreted in social terms. Often a "cognitive leap" is made from healing in the New Testament, due to the power and agency of the Holy Spirit, to medical missions (1978,202,212-213). Therefore, how mission is "the self-revelation of the triune God in the Son *and in the Holy Spirit*" is neglected (Andersen 1955,60). This is the case in theologies of mission where the distorted view of *missio Dei* is influential. It is clear in Verkuyl's mission theology that the use of the Kingdom motif does not guarantee a full description of pneumatology. To do so would topple the whole idea of *missio Dei* in its misconstrued form.

A by-product of the neglected Holy Spirit in most conciliar theologies of mission is a neglect of evangelism. As previously mentioned, "new mission's" hermeneutical horizon, the sociopolitical context, is the dominating principle of conciliar theology. It lends itself to interpreting mission as humanization and the creation of a new world order (Hoekstra 1979,12). Part of this anthropocentric mission theology is the rejection of everything that tends to be "propaganda," that is, proclamation-persuasion mission (McGavran 1977,48; Hoekendijk 1977,48-49). *Kerygma* is held to mean the proclamation that "Shalom" has come; this Shalom is lived (*koinōnia*) and demonstrated in humble service (*diakonia*). The three are considered comprehensive "evangelism" (McGavran 1977,50-51; Hoekendijk 1977,50). Along with the unhappy redefinition of mission there is also an ill-conceived redefinition of evangelism.

While Verkuyl does emphasize both the evangelistic mandate and the cultural mandate, advocating a holistic view of mission, the evangelistic "cutting edge" of mission is blunted by his view of *missio Dei* and the Kingdom. Taking the goal of mission (*missio Dei*) to be the kingdom of God (1978,197), mission becomes everything God intends for the world (1978,200-201). There are no priorities of mission for they change with the context of history and the changing needs of men (Verkuyl 1978,203). In other words, the world sets the agenda for mission; the previously mentioned hermeneutical error, therefore, is also illustrated.

The one-sided use of both *missio Dei* and the Kingdom motif has perpetuated the eclipse of the Holy Spirit's role in mission. This in turn has eclipsed the area of mission in which He is central—Great Commission mission. The neglect of the mediated activity of God the Holy Spirit in mission has also called into question the instrumentality of the church by blurring the distinction between the church and the world.[14] The misuse of *missio Dei* trivializes the church's nature and role in mission and thereby denigrates the Holy Spirit's work in the creation of that community and in His missionary role in connection with it.

The emphasis that the church *is* mission, and that primarily God the Father does mission (*missio Dei*) amounts to a capitulation to "Christian presence" and service replacing conversion mission.[15] Through secular work and involvement in social issues and politics the church is said to be in dialogue with the world. As people join together with God in His mission in these diverse ways, there is unity in the church. All of these modes of mission are conceived to be valid mission structures (Bassham 1979,71). *Missio Dei*, the silence on the Holy Spirit, and the neglect of evangelism are all related in the paradigm of "new mission." The failure to identify and articulate the role of the Holy Spirit in mission and the failure to "unpack the Kingdom concept" in terms of pneumatology are fundamental to the shape of this "new mission."

The Holy Spirit's Missionary Role

What is the Holy Spirit's missionary role? And how does that role affect the issues of contemporary mission theology? These questions emerge from the discussion concerning the misuse of the *missio Dei* concept in contemporary mission theology. A trinitarian view of mission must articulate the activity of the third person of the Godhead. The biblical nature of mission cannot be completely brought into focus, nor can it be adequately stated, apart from a description of the Holy Spirit's role. Mission cannot be derived or defined from the church's task in a world of great need. It must have its source in the Father, Son and Holy Spirit—the trinitarian view of mission as set forth in Scripture. The recovery and further development of a trinitarian view of mission, in biblical perspective, must come to grips with this contemporary pneumatological silence. How is mission the self-revelation of the triune God in the Son *and in the Holy Spirit*? What specifically is the role of the third person of the Trinity? Does this question detract from the previously mentioned activity of the *resurrected Christ* in mission? Does it merely reflect the Pentecostal bias coming through, a provincial or doctrinaire interest?

Bernard Ramm addressed these questions when he said that Pentecostalism was frequently charged with attempting to "build a temple where Scripture permits only a tent." But in view of the pneumatological hiatus in western theology and the resulting missiological dilemmas, we might question whether a "tent" is either sufficient for contemporary mission theology or for a truly biblical theology. All indications are that the "temple" is the more appropriate metaphor for the missionary ministry of the Spirit, according to the New Testament. The previous discussion concerning the reinterpretation of the Kingdom concept by both Jesus and the early church supports this contention. Therefore, Pentecostal theology is not so provincial or doctrinaire in centering its attention on the Acts of the Apostles and the prominence of the Holy Spirit's work in that history.

Roland Allen stated that "It is in the revelation of the Holy Spirit as a missionary Spirit that the Acts stands alone in the New Testament" (1960,21).[16] George Peters also speaks of the crucial role of the Acts in providing a picture of this dimension of the Spirit's ministry in the church. He states:

> The superintendency of the Holy Spirit in missions is evident from the Book of Acts. Here it is also evident that the Holy Spirit was not only

resident in but also President of the early church. When this happens there is a mighty all-out horizontal push in world evangelism (1972,304).

As executive of the Godhead in this age the Holy Spirit is also the Supreme Strategist of world mission (Peters 1972,305). Vicedom states that it is through the sending of the Spirit that missionaries receive their power and their authority; it is through the Spirit that missions are linked with the *missio Dei* (1965,70). Vicedom states that the Holy Spirit continues the mission which God began in His Son until Jesus himself returns and terminates that mission (1965,56). Ramm also states that the Holy Spirit is executive of the Godhead in the church age, and as such He makes concrete and real the will of the Father and the Son (1959,30). The Son is the mediator and content of revelation, but "what the Son mediates is realized within the creature by the executive of the Trinity, the Holy Spirit" (Ramm 1959,31). The designation of the executive of the Godhead points to the Spirit's missionary role in the economy of salvation history.[17]

The dimensions of the missionary role of the Spirit are especially clear when we consider the significance of Pentecost for salvation history. An examination of the role of Pentecost in the initiation and universalization of mission reveals the Holy Spirit's central role after the earthly ministry of Christ. Jesus himself spoke of this executive role that the Holy Spirit would have with the church. He spoke of the coming of *another Paraclete* (John 14:16). The Holy Spirit was to be Christ's advocate, He was to stand in for Christ. He would empower the church and direct it in its mission as Jesus did when He was with them. In John 15:26 the Holy Spirit is given the name Paraclete again. Twice in that verse the Spirit is spoken of as being sent from the Father.[18] The double mention that the Paraclete comes from the Father denotes the *mission* of the Spirit. The Holy Spirit has a mission as executive of the Godhead. He himself, as well as those whom He empowers and sends in mission (John 15:27), bears witness to Christ.

The Holy Spirit's role in His universal mission is illustrated in Acts by the Pentecostal event and in His breaking through Jewish particularism. The Spirit was the One who opened the door to the expansion of the church among the Gentiles.[19] The Spirit's primary role in His universal mission is demonstrated in the early chapters of Acts. This is especially so in the Spirit's dealing with the Apostle Peter in chapter 10. The Spirit instructed him to make no distinction between Jew and Gentile in the offering of the gospel (Acts 11:11-14). The decisive event that validated the Gentile mission, for both Peter and the early church, was the outpouring of the Spirit in Pentecostal fashion on the uncircumcised Gentiles (Acts 10:44-48; 11:15-17; 15:8-9). After this crucial work of the

Spirit in breaking through cultural barriers the mission of the church spread to the Gentile world. The Spirit in each instance was initiating His mission and causing it to expand in ever-widening circles.

Pentecost, therefore, had epochal meaning; it marked an end of the age of national particularism and the return of God's redemptive purpose to the nations. The ethnic diversity brought about by the confusion of languages was reversed at Pentecost. Through the miracle of languages God began to restore the unity of the race which was lost at Babel. Pentecost was both a symbol of that unifying work of God and the actual beginning of the unification of the race.[20] The *Spirit was the agent of this restoration of unity*. The role of the Spirit in His mission, breaking through the barriers which separate people, points to the importance of pneumatology for ecumenism. A full-blown trinitarian view of mission is an ecumenical touchstone (Rosin 1972,11).

In summary, a trinitarian view of mission in biblical and salvation history perspective gives the Holy Spirit a primary role in contemporary mission. As executive of the Godhead He is Lord of the Harvest. This perspective focuses on the centrality of the church as the agent of mission. But the church is not to be characterized primarily by its instrumentality. It is the new creation of the Holy Spirit, a called-out people who belong to God and who also carry out His mission in the world. The missionary role of the Spirit, in biblical perspective, is related inseparably with the sending and empowering of the church in Great Commission mission. This sending, God's special mission, is characterized by the preaching of the gospel in the power of the Spirit with signs following.

APPENDIX

HISTORIC REFORMED VIEW

Approach to Scripture: non-Cartesian, Scripture is the first principle. Emphasis: the priority of faith and the function of Scripture, with a focus on the work of the Holy Spirit, in connection with the written Word of God. The self-revelation of God, due to His transcendence and incomprehensibility.

Nature of Scripture: christocentric, dynamic, holistic view of the Word of God—the Incarnate Word, the written Word, and the proclaimed Word. Scripture is a historical account of the acts and words of God. Inspiration: both the divine and human dimensions of Scripture are held in biblical tension, due to the incarnational model of divine communication, and the principle of accommodation. Scripture is "from God."

REFORMED SCHOLASTIC VIEW

Approach to Scripture: Cartesian, the categories of the mind, Aristotelian philosophy. Human reason is the first principle. Emphasis: the priority of reason and the form of Scripture; focus on the text and its precision. The activity of man in his use of reason to understand God's revelation. Reason is held to be analogous with truth as it is in the mind of God.

Nature of Scripture: the Word of God is static in nature, being synonymous with the written Word; it consists of propositional statements. Scripture is the "quarry" for systematic theology. Inspiration: the divine dimension of Scripture is emphasized, the human dimension is ignored or virtually denied. Authors of Scripture are as "penmen," the historical-cultural context of Scripture is not in focus.

Purpose of Scripture: to bring persons to salvation, and give guidance for the Christian life.

Authority of Scripture: authority is in the context of faith, and inner testimony of the Holy Spirit; there is no separation between Word and Spirit. The authority of God's written Word is God himself. Scripture is self-authenticating. God authenticates Scripture. Authority is functional in nature, the ability of Scripture to accomplish its redemptive purpose. "Certainty" is a matter of faith.

Role of the Holy Spirit: His role is extended from the authors of Scripture to the hearers and interpreters of the Word. The present inward work of the Spirit in the believer is emphasized.

Clarity of Scripture: those things necessary to be known, believed and observed for salvation are plain and clear in Scripture.

Purpose of Scripture: to provide inerrant information on all branches of learning, and a unified system of knowledge; the objective completeness of Scripture is stressed.

Authority of Scripture: authority is in the context of reason, the accuracy of the written text of Scripture; internal and external evidence, logical, rational arguments for its divinity prove its authority. Authority is abstract in nature. Man authenticates Scripture; rationalistic inerrancy is the guarantee for the divinity of Scripture.

Role of the Holy Spirit: His role is confined to the original authors of Scripture, according to Princeton theologians; his work at that end of revelation is emphasized.

Clarity of Scripture: the clarity of Scripture rests on logic rather than on its self-authentication; every subject upon which it speaks is clear and to be defended (Pomerville 1980, 96-97).

NOTES

Introduction: Missions from a Pentecostal Perspective

1. In Harry Boer's definitive study on the significance of Pentecost for missions, *Pentecost and Missions* (1961), he expresses surprise over the paucity of theological attention devoted to his subject (1961,12). David Bosch also states that pneumatology, in terms of the Spirit's out-directed ministry, began to be neglected as early as the second century. He states that the missionary dimension of pneumatology was rediscovered in the eighteenth century but that it played no significant role in Protestant theology (Bosch 1980,241-242).

2. Lindsell (1949), Kane (1976), along with Allen (1960) and Boer (1961), all support the thesis that the role of the Holy Spirit in modern missions and mission theology is greatly neglected.

3. Hollenweger (1972) emphasizes the common factor among Pentecostals as "all the groups who profess at least two religious crisis experiences (1. baptism or rebirth; 2. The baptism of the Spirit), the second being subsequent to and different from the first one, and the second usually, but not always, being associated with speaking in tongues" (1972,xix). Hollenweger leaves the option open for the evidence of the Pentecostal experience to be other charismatic signs besides glossolalia. Often the term "Pentecostal Movement" is confined to that group of sects within the Christian church which are comprised of classical Pentecostals, and it is therefore a reference to "the Pentecostal denominations."

4. Sandidge states concerning the term, "renewal," that "Charismatic Renewal" properly is a broad term, referring to the "worldwide resurgence of the experience of the Holy Spirit in all forms of Christianity including Roman Catholicism, the Orthodox Churches, mainline Protestantism and Evangelicalism" (1976,11).

5. The three main streams of Pentecostalism, both in the western

167

and non-western world, have various "tributaries" which can be identified. For instance, within the neo-Pentecostal and Catholic Charismatic streams one can differentiate: Roman Catholic Pentecostals, Orthodox Pentecostals, Anglican Pentecostals, non-Roman Apostolic-type Pentecostals (Irvingites), and Black neo-Pentecostals. All of the various tributaries of the Charismatic/neo-Pentecostal and classical Pentecostal streams are found in non-western cultures also. This is clear in the discussion of David Barrett's findings in chapter 1. See also Barrett 1982,782-783.

6. David Barrett adds two further classifications to Faupel's: Perfectionist-Pentecostals (Free Pentecostals, Deliverance-Pentecostals, Radical-Pentecostals, Revivalist-Pentecostals) who emphasize four crisis experiences—conversion, sanctification, baptism of the Spirit, and deliverance/ecstatic confession/prophecy/perfectionism or authority/discipling/shepherding; and Apostolic or Pentecostal Apostolics who stress the complex hierarchy of living apostles, prophets or other charismatic officials (Barrett 1982,127). Barrett's classification of classical Pentecostalism is given in full in chapter 1.

7. Piepkorn states, "If salvation and the work of Jesus Christ were the dominant themes of the Reformation movement that produced the Protestant denominations, then sanctification and the work of the Holy Spirit were the significant themes in the movements that resulted in the formation of Holiness and Pentecostal churches" (1979,xiii).

8. Menzies states concerning this claim, "It is the author's contention, after extensive interviews with Pentecostal leaders, evangelical churchmen, and representatives from the larger church world, that the Assemblies of God, largest of the American Pentecostal bodies, is indeed the most representative of the Pentecostal organizations, and can serve usefully as a microcosm of the Pentecostal Movement as a whole" (Menzies 1971,10). Faupel agrees with Menzies's claim, "He [Menzies] further points out in a footnote that others such as Bloch-Hoell, Nichol and Kelsey (all non-Assemblies of God men) have made the same claim for the Assemblies of God. By this, he means all of the issues and forces which have brought to bear on any part of the Pentecostal Movement have at some point affected the Assemblies of God as well. Despite initial reservations, this writer has come to accept this as basically true" (1972,21).

9. One such case which illustrates the point is the issue of the nature of revelation (see chapter 5). The Pentecostal believes that revelation is dynamic and continuous in nature. This is due to his or her experience with the gifts of the Holy Spirit today, and the activity of the Holy Spirit in connection with the written

Word—Scripture. However, care has been taken to differentiate between the continuous revelatory activity of the Spirit and that which resulted in Scripture. This is done by careful explanation concerning the latter's normative nature and by speaking of the former as revelation with a small *r*.

10. This thesis has been argued well in an historical study by Jack Rogers and Donald McKim in *The Authority and Interpretation of the Bible* (1979).

Chapter 1 An Emerging "Third Force"

1. In *The Pentecostals* (1972), Hollenweger states concerning the worldwide spread of Pentecostalism, "I believe that the statistics are mostly too low, not because they accord to individual denominations too few members—there are a few cases of exaggeration—but because there are large Pentecostal bodies which are unknown to the Pentecostals themselves, and about the size of which they have no information" (1972,63).

2. The characteristics that Sengwe mentions are: 1) Emphasis on the Holy Spirit in healing, prophecy, and revelation; 2) Legalism; 3) Schism; 4) A de-emphasis on education; 5) Mistrust in medicine and emphasis on healing administered by "prophets;" 6) A restoration of the "place" of the supernatural; 7) Rapid growth; 8) The authority of the religious experience; and 9) The involvement of the laity or discovery of community (Sengwe 1981,93-97).

3. Injecting a somewhat humorous, but instructive note in this regard, John V. Taylor refers to the Third World response to traditional western attempts at understanding indigeneity in that part of the world. He states, "On the whole the Christian leaders of Africa and Asia have been unimpressed, not only because they are reactionary or suspicious of our motives, but because they believe we are only playing at it. Their unspoken thought has been: 'Have these dear idiots any idea what they are asking for? If they met a truly indigenous worship, *they might be shocked, and if they allowed us to express our understandings of Christianity in our own way they probably wouldn't recognize it*" (1969,171).

4. However, in fairness to Sundkler it should be remembered that at the writing of his work the Charismatic Movement had not yet taken place in the denominational churches. That this evaluation of Sundkler's work is not too severe or inappropriate is indicated by Sundkler's own remarks in the 1961 edition of his work. Also its severity is necessary in view of the continuing counterproductive influence his work has today for an objective evaluation of the AICM.

5. Pentecostalism is in the same pejorative context when

Sundkler states, "Within modern Protestantism, especially in America, most of the secessions which have arisen from time to time have been caused by different interpretations of the Holy Spirit, and it is only to be expected that some of the same difficulties will arise in such African Churches as are the outcome of missionary efforts from Western Churches of Pentecostal, Apostolic Faith and Zionist type" (1961,242-243). In passing, it might also be noted that Sundkler's statement that "the same difficulties" might be expected in the African milieu ignores the radical difference between the western and African milieu in which the movements occurred. Their respective societal needs in terms of the gospel's application and the resultant cultural expression of Pentecostal Christianity would be quite different. The central orientation of African society and culture to the spirit world and the society's institutions for coping with that reality play a major role in the causation of the movements in the African milieu. Pentecostalism addressed a *severe* problem in the matrix of African society; it addressed the very core of African world view and African social structure. Of course, Sundkler's statement is directed toward the schismatic tendencies of the American Pentecostal Movement, but it ignores the issue of the causation of the respective movements from the standpoint of contextual need.

6. Oosthuizen states, "The African personality must be offered positive development in the Church, which means the Church must discard its foreignness" (1968,21). But at the same time he asserts, "The great task of the Church is to be the Church; not an ethnic institution, but the Church of Christ" (1968,21). The result of this tension between cultural-spiritual, or human-divine identity, is a rejection of the former. This occurs instead of accepting both identities in their biblical tension as the Incarnation illustrates.

7. With regard to utopian, messianic expectations, Peel states, "In Africa millennialism is one of the less characteristic features of independent churches" (1968,3).

8. In a statement which also illustrates the rational-static nature of scholastic theology, Oosthuizen states, "The God of the missions is too remote for a system in which men's 'gods' belonged to their lineage, and, although far removed, could be approached through their ancestors. The God in the Christianity with which they came in contact had much to do with their souls, and with certain individuals but not with them in all spheres of life and as a whole community" (Oosthuizen 1968,119).

9. Hollenweger links the origins of Bantu Independent Churches of South Africa specifically with the Apostolic Faith mission and the Christian Catholic Church in Zion, Illinois—Pentecostal bodies (1972,120-121).

10. In a direct reference to Pentecostalism Oosthuizen states, "The misunderstanding of the person and work of the Holy Spirit in Africa is not confined to the nativistic movements, many of the Pentecostal Churches revealing [*sic*] the same difficulty. These movements in Africa have been greatly influenced by Negro Baptist and Pentecostal sects from the United States" (1968,120).

11. One wonders about Oosthuizen's awareness concerning historic occurrences of charismatic renewal, when he states concerning glossolalia, "There is no evidence of glossalaly [*sic*] amongst the Montanists" (1968,140).

12. See Barrett 1982,39-104 where he uses a new methodology in categorizing Christianity in that he divides his statistics into three basic categories: 1) professing Christians (those who identify themselves as Christian, or confess Christ), 2) affiliated Christians (those claimed by the churches, total community), and 3) practicing Christians (those faithfully involved with the institutional life of the church) (1982,47). These categories each have their advantages and disadvantages with regard to identifying the scope of Pentecostalism.

13. Barrett describes the difficulty in determining the scope of the various Charismatic movements: "In many parts of the world, new Christian movements are beginning and growing rapidly, the largest example being the global neo-pentecostal and charismatic movements within the major older denominations. Such groups have little time or opportunity for self-analysis, and usually keep neither statistics nor exact membership lists. Further, many movements exist within the structures of older denominations, value their close relations with them, and oppose the collecting of statistics as tending to artificially crystallize their identity and to appear to divide charismatics from their non-charismatic fellow-Christians" (1982,55).

14. "Predominantly" in this estimate of Latin American charismatics means something well over fifty percent (Barrett 1982,69).

15. Barrett's White classical Pentecostal sub-types are:

PeA Apostolic, or Pentecostal Apostolic (stress on complex hierarchy of living apostles, prophets and other charismatic officials)

Pen Pentecostal (Protestant; Classical Pentecostal of unspecified type); charismatic, faith-healing (Classical Pentecostal sub-types include PeA, Pe1, Pe2, Pe3, Pe4)

Pe1 Oneness-Pentecostal or Unitarian-Pentecostal: 'Jesus only', sometimes unitarian, non/or anti-trinitarian

Pe2 Baptistic-Pentecostal or Keswick-Pentecostal: 2-crisis-experience (conversion, baptism of the Spirit)

Pe3 Holiness-Pentecostal: 3-crisis-experience (conversion, sanctification, baptism of the Spirit)
Pe4 Perfectionist-Pentecostal, Free Pentecostal, Deliverance-Pentecostal, Radical-, or Revivalist-Pentecostal: 4-crisis-experience (conversion sanctification, baptism of the Spirit, deliverance/ecstatic [sic] confession/prophecy/perfectionism, also authority/discipling/shepherding)" (1982,127).

Barrett's Non-White indigenous Pentecostal sub-types are:
"**peA** indigenous charismatic pentecostal apostolic (hierarchy of living apostles)
pen indigenous charismatic (pentecostal, spirit-dominated): Black/Third-World indigenous body of pentecostal type (charismatic, enthusiastic, faith-healing); in Africa, spiritual or zionist or spirit or aladura (praying) churches
pe1 indigenous charismatic oneness-pentecostal, unitarian-pentecostal
pe2 indigenous charismatic baptistic-pentecostal (2-crisis-experience)
pe3 indigenous charismatic holiness-pentecostal (3-crisis-experience)
pe4 indigenous charismatic perfectionist, free, radical- or revivalist-pentecostal or deliverance pentecostal (4-crisis-experience)" (1982,127).

16. See Barrett's discussion on "belief," in his *World Christian Encyclopedia*, (1982,53).

17. The conservative nature of the 100 million figure may be illustrated by comparing some statistics gathered in connection with the writing of this book apart from Barrett's source. The number of classical Pentecostals in the United States and Canada for 1979-80 was approximately 4,000,000. Barrett's survey indicates 3,225,701 (1982,215-216,720-725). The Assemblies of God alone make up one-third of Barrett's figure. Pentecostal statistics gathered for several other countries also differ. Brazil, a country where seventy percent of the Protestant community is Pentecostal (Miklaus 1982,117), shows a significant different statistic. Estimates of the number of Pentecostals in Brazil have been as high as ten million (Harrison 1981). Robert Niklaus reports eight and one-half million (1982,117). Barrett's survey, however, shows 3,915,210 (1982,191-193). The Assemblies of God alone report 3,350,000 baptized members (plus 2,750,000 "other believers") for 1980 (Division of Foreign Missions 1981,7). Barry Chant reports an estimated 60,000 classical Pentecostals in Australia (1981,1), while Barrett's survey is nearly half of that figure: 36,000 (1982,155-156). The reason for the discrepancy may be the rapid rate of growth—156 percent during the period of

1970-1980 (Chant 1981,1). Steve Durasoff estimates the Russian Pentecostal community to be from 500,000 to 600,000 (a very conservative figure) (1982,1), while Barrett's survey indicates a community figure of 120,000 (1982,696). One of the largest Pentecostal churches in the world is in Seoul, Korea; the Assemblies of God membership in Korea is 82,200 baptized members with 120,000 adherents (Division of Foreign Missions 1981,5). But Barrett's survey only gives 82,191 for the whole country (1982,444). His survey gives 296,624 for the classical Pentecostals in all of the Philippine Islands, but the Manila area alone has over 120,000 classical Pentecostals (Seleky 1982,1). Therefore, indications are that the 100 million figure for the worldwide Pentecostal Movement is too low.

Chapter 2 A Renewal Movement

1. In a statement that puts the two major dimensions of the movements in perspective, Brumback states: "Church historians are prone to interpret revivals solely on the basis of the earthly, rather than the heavenly. So often they emphasize the human element—the social, economic, political, or merely religious problems of the hour, while almost totally ignoring the divine element—the coming again spiritually, of the Lord to His people. The origin and growth of the present-day Pentecostal Revival has been attributed by many authors to mundane causes. It would be folly, of course, to deny the influence of these conditions upon this revival, . . . the conditions which all agree provide a background for the rise of the Pentecostal Movement. Nevertheless, any investigation, factual though it may be, which fails to yield the First Cause of this phenomenal revival has not "come to the knowledge of the truth" (1961,1-2).

2. Wallace's processional structure of religious movements (Steady State, Period of Increased Individual Stress, Period of Cultural Distortion, Period of Revitalization, and New Steady State) is a helpful framework for comprehending both the human and divine dimensions of a Christian movement. In discussing the variations within his basic structure of "revitalization movements," Wallace identifies the secular and religious dimensions of the movement. He notes that both secular action and religious action take place in differing degrees at different stages of the movement. Wallace emphasizes the importance of the religious or charismatic action in the earlier stages of revitalization, and the tendency for movements to become more secular in emphasis in the later organizational stage (1979,424,428).

3. Linton agrees that investigation of nativistic movements must go beyond the secular dimension of society, "An adequate

explanation of such movements must go beyond an analysis of the kind of deprivation involved to elucidate the social and cultural context out of which they grow" (1979:414). While Linton advocates a more holistic approach to the movements, he shows a presuppositional bias against the inclusion of the supernatural with regard to origins (Linton 1979,416-417).

4. Furthermore, the growth of the Movement is explained in terms of a discovery and exploitation of a "new means of communication" by White Christians which were "indigenous to North American Negroes." In other words, the phenomenal growth of the Movement, according to Hollenweger, was due to the White adoption of the new means of communications which Black culture provided—enthusiastic religion. This, of course, would require a major "paradigm shift" in western culture, a shift from a written-abstract orientation to the oral-dynamic orientation of the American Negro (Hollenweger 1972,xvii)!

5. Bloch-Hoell attributes the emotional heights of the Azusa revival to the number of women involved. He states that in the United States in 1936 there were 78.5 men to each 100 women. Therefore, he reports, "It is *reasonable* to suggest the marked preponderance of women is explained by the emotional or ecstatic character of the movement" (1964,60; italics mine). The chauvinistic stereotype is complete when he states that women feel attracted to such forms of religion (1964,60). While the ratio of men to women Bloch-Hoell cites is neither significant or relevant for his "reasonable suggestion," it is interesting to note that in 1980 among the twenty-nine million Pentecostal-charismatics in the United States, only forty-two percent of the tongues-speaking Pentecostal-charismatics were women (Kantzer 1980,28). A bias against the emotional, supernatural, and subjective dimensions of Christian experience verily "sticks out" in Bloch-Hoell's analysis of the classical Pentecostal Movement.

6. In another statement reflecting the "Jerusalem-Centrifugal" theory, Bartleman alludes to other revivals in the light of Azusa Street: "Los Angeles seems to be the place, and this the time, in the mind of God, for the restoration of the church to her former place, favor and power. The fulness of times seems to have come for the church's complete restoration. God has spoken to His servants in all parts of the world, and has sent many of them to Los Angeles, representing every nation under Heaven once more, as of old, come up for 'Pentecost,' to go out again into all the world with the glad message of salvation. The base of operations has been shifted, from old Jerusalem, for the latter 'Pentecost,' to Los Angeles. And there is a tremendous, God-given hunger for this experience everywhere. Wales was but intended as the cradle for the worldwide restoration of the power of God. India but the Nazareth where He

was 'brought up' '' (1980,90).

7. This dichotomous view of the worldwide Pentecostal Movement is clear from: 1) Hollenweger's typology of Pentecostal organizations (1972,71-72), 2) his discussion of the differences between the Charismatic Movement in Germany and the Pentecostal-free churches in Germany (1972,247-249), and 3) his preference for the Pentecostal Movement within the established churches with its corresponding criticism of the "come out" churches of American Pentecostalism (1972,15,24,253). Also evidence of the dichotomy is Hollenweger's methodology of beginning his history of the worldwide Pentecostal Movement with a chapter on the Charismatic Movement, "Pentecost Outside 'Pentecost:' Speaking with Tongues in the Traditional Churches of America" (1972,1). Therefore, when Hollenweger speaks of the "Pentecostal Movement" in the Preface to his work, *The Pentecostals*, he refers to the origins of the *American* classical Pentecostal Movement and does not support a "Jerusalem-Centrifugal" theory with regard to the worldwide Movement. From his critical, and at times somewhat sarcastic, view of the classical Pentecostal Movement in America, Hollenweger would especially avoid such a conclusion.

8. This term, *Heilsgeschichte*, is not to be understood as referring to a "metahistory," but to a Christian view of history in which process (not progress) and direction toward an *eschaton* is primary. It involves the concept of periodization, a recognition of epochs with significant acts of God taking place in those periods of history. It envisages a universal history, one in which God is at work with all of mankind. In that complexity and diversity, however, history has meaning and purpose (McIntire 1977,51-59).

9. As an "outsider" speaking of Pentecostalism in general, Henry P. Van Dusen emphasizes that it is a restoration of the ministry of the Holy Spirit, "They [the Pentecostals] share a common spiritual aim: to return, in deliberate imitation, to the content and practices of the early Christian church" (1958,113). He then notes, "many features of this 'new Christianity' bear striking resemblance to the life of the earliest Christian churches as revealed in the New Testament" (1958,112).

10. The Baptist World Alliance statement on the Charismatic Movement reflects this position: "1. The 'charismatic' movement [sic] is to be viewed in its historical perspective and in particular to be evaluated in the light of certain historical features of our time such as alienation, the reactions against scientism and rationalization, and the quest for mystical experience. . . . 2. Throughout the centuries the Church has owed much to periods of experiential religion which has been of value in correcting the

imbalances of a too rational, credal, or barren Christianity. The modern charismatic movement has met with a mixed reception among Baptists. Some have found in it a new experience of spiritual renewal. Others dismiss it as untrue to Baptist tradition" (McDonnell 1980,80).

11. After pointing out the missionary implications of the "upon all flesh" in Joel's prophecy, Hodges states, "probably we would be correct if we relate this outpouring of the Spirit to three different periods of time" (1974,3). The Day of Pentecost marked the beginning of the fulfillment of the prophecy (Acts 2:13-21). Hodges explains, "Peter declares 'this is that.' He relates the prophecy to the 'last days,' giving this meaning to the 'afterward' of Joel 2:28. The Day of Pentecost was 'the last days,' if we relate it to all of the centuries in which God worked with His people previous to that time" (1974,3). Although the prophecy is believed to have begun to be fulfilled at Pentecost in a salvation history context, the references to prophecies of signs and other details declared by Christ to occur at the time of his Second Coming and the millennial period point to a future period of fulfillment. Hodges states concerning that future period, "The prophecy without question has a direct reference to the Pentecostal revival that has taken place in the twentieth century" (1974,3).

12. Filson explains: "The new order is at hand, and the reference is not merely to a new civilization or a new period of the same sort of world history, but to God's new order, established by divine power as the climax of God's dealings with this world. . . . Similarly, in Acts 2:16 the gift of the Spirit is connected with the prediction of Joel 2:28-32 that in the last days the Spirit will be given. The fact that in the Greek text of Acts usually followed the reference to 'the last days' is not found in Joel shows that to the writer of Acts the phrase is no meaningless item, but is rather inserted precisely because the Apostolic Church regarded the gift of the Spirit as an eschatological event" (1950,75-76).

13. Bosch explains further that "The future, including the future *before* the end, is not empty but filled with the Kingdom. Admittedly the Kingdom is still hidden and can be perceived only by the eyes of faith; admittedly the form the Kingdom takes is still inchoate; yet this does not imply that the presence of the Kingdom is illusory. We live on the basis of the 'already' enroute to the 'not yet,' but in such a way that the challenge of the 'already' outweighs the vision of the 'not yet,'. . . Eschatology does not refer only to a future divine answer which we have to accept blindly or on authority; it also refers to anticipations in human experience now" (1980,236).

14. In view of the Kingdom being God's dynamic working in history, it should not be equated with the church. The Kingdom is

only acknowledged and realized in the church partially and imperfectly (Bosch 1980,222). Bosch states further, "She [the church] is a sign of the coming age and at the same time a guarantee of its coming. She lives on the border-line between the 'already' and the 'not yet.' She is a fragment of the Kingdom, God's colony in man's world, his outpost and bridgehead" (1980,225). Ladd is even more emphatic in avoiding an equation of the Kingdom with the church. He states that it involves one's basic definition of the Kingdom, "If the dynamic concept of the Kingdom is correct, it is never to be identified with the church. The Kingdom is primarily the dynamic reign or kingly rule of God, and derivatively, the sphere in which the rule is experienced. In biblical idiom, the Kingdom is not identified with its subjects. They are the people of God's rule who enter it, live under it, and are governed by it. The church is the community of the Kingdom but never the Kingdom itself. Jesus' disciples belong to the Kingdom as the Kingdom belongs to them; but they are not the Kingdom. The Kingdom is the rule of God; the church is the society of men" (1974,262).

15. Ladd quotes G. Gloege in this regard: "The Kingdom of God [*Gottesherrschaft*] is never something which can to some extent be separated from God, but is only a more pregnant expression for God himself" (1974,145).

Chapter 3 A Correction of a Western Distortion

1. Green states concerning 1 Corinthians 13:8, a passage often used as support for the position that the charismatic gifts disappeared with the apostolic age, "Still less can a passage like 1 Cor. 13:8 ("as for prophecies, they will pass away; as for tongues, they will cease...") be adduced to attest the supposed demise of these gifts. They will pass away only when 'the perfect comes,' i.e. [*sic*] at the Parousia—not at the end of the apostolic age or the formation of the New Testament Canon" (Green 1975,198)!

2. Latourette confirms that this theological misconception concerning the Great Commission existed in the Reformation period. He adds that Luther and Melanchthon both believed that the end of the world was so imminent that no time remained to spread the gospel throughout the world (1967,25). Stephen Neill suggests that the stance of the Reformers on the binding nature of the Great Commission may have been defensive in nature. Roman Catholic controversialists charged that "The Lutherans compare themselves to the apostles and the evangelists; yet though they have among them a very large number of Jews, and in Poland and Hungary have the Turks as their near neighbors, they have hardly converted even so much as a handful" (1964,221). Rather than admit they should have missions, they tended to say missions were not obligatory (Neill 1964,222).

3. Allen states concerning this inner motivation: "St. Luke fixes our attention, not upon an external voice, but upon an internal Spirit. This manner of command is peculiar to the Gospel. Others direct from without, Christ directs within; others order, Christ inspires; others speak external words, Christ gives the Spirit which desires and strives for that which he commands; others administer a dead letter, Christ imparts life. This is the manner of the command in St. Luke's writings. He speaks not of men who, being what they were, strove to obey the last orders of a beloved Master, but of men who, receiving a Spirit, were driven by that Spirit to act in accordance with the nature of that Spirit" (1960,5).

4. Warren is consistent in his personification of the Great Commission throughout the book (1976,26,29,45,67,136,172).

5. Horton notes regarding the disparate nature of the two world views, "So far as a confrontation of modern Christianity with traditional African religion is concerned, then, it looks as though the essential aspiration of the one is often the marginal aspiration of the other. . . ." (1979,250).

6. Oosterwal also observes that western dichotomizing tendencies have cut westerners off from a dimension of the Christian faith that is readily accepted by non-western societies: "In the West,. . .The biblical message becomes demythologized . . . but it has become fatal in the African and Asian setting, where the whole of life is (still) sacred and the world view is essentially a religious one. The Kingdom of God is a reality; its signs of healing, hearing the Spirit's voice, speaking in tongues, dreams and miracles of all sorts are tangible experiences of its presence" (1973,41).

7. Avery himself may betray a western bias against the supernatural when he says, "Evil spirits and curses of sorcerers are daily problems and fears; the wrath and blessings of the 'living dead' [ancestors] are present experiences. To preach that these forces do not exist is only displaying one's ignorance of the reality *from the African's viewpoint*" (1969,3; italics mine). That missionaries preached the spirit world did not exist, as well as Avery's mention that one must know reality "from the African's viewpoint," both reveal the anti-supernatural bias. It is not just a matter of understanding the African's viewpoint, if I have interpreted Avery's statement accurately, but the affirmation that the African's viewpoint about the existence of evil spirits is *biblically correct*. The provision of the Christian answer for that viewpoint is the crucial issue. However, Avery does mention the tremendous stress produced by western Christianity when he quotes Mitchell: "In short, Christianity was too western on the whole, too rationalistic and other-worldly to gain the confidence of its

adherents at their deepest levels of experience. This showed up most plainly in those times of personal crisis, such as barrenness and sickness when many baptized believers, thinking that Jesus Christ did not have any interest, or worse, the power, to improve their state of affairs, felt they had to visit the traditional healer" (1969,64). Mitchell goes on to contrast this western expression of Christianity with that of the African Independent Churches: "It is precisely to this spiritual malaise that the independent churches preached their naive, yet deeply biblical, theology of power. They proclaimed a God who acts, a Saviour who saves *in* the world" (Avery 1969,64).

8. The inadequacy of Barrett's "love theory," as well as theories focusing on social, political, and economic deprivation as the cause of the movements are evidenced in the continuation of the movements and in the circumstances in which they continue to emerge. H.W. Turner states that polygamy and economic deprivation are contributary rather than basic causes of the movements. He states that there are many instances where they cannot be applied. Ghana has the highest standards of living among African peoples, yet movements have proliferated during the very period of prosperity (Turner 1963,114). Also the wealthy are involved in the movements. The economic principle is applied to explain the prophet movements in political terms. There is some truth to this, especially in certain areas of Africa. But it does not account for the wide ranging phenomenon in Africa (Turner 1963,114). The inadequacy of the economic-political grounds for causation is seen in the continuing growth of the movements after the colonial period. Turner states that a deeper probe into causation shows that the movements represent a creative response to the breakdown of old forms of African society. The new movements represent groups which provide fellowship, security, and some sanctions and guidance for living, a life in which the African works out the expression of Christianity according to his own way of life (Turner 1963,115).

Chapter 4 An Experience with the Spirit

1. Dunn addresses the westerner's difficulty with (or aversion to) the experiential and subjective when he states: "It is a sad commentary on the poverty of our own immediate experience of the Spirit that when we come across language in which the NT writers refer directly to the gift of the Spirit and to their experience of it, either we automatically refer it to the sacraments and can only give it meaning when we do so . . . or else we discount the experience described as too subjective and mystical in favor of a faith which is essentially an affirmation of biblical propositions, or else we in

effect psychologize the Spirit out of existence" (1970,225-226).

2. (7) THE BAPTISM IN THE HOLY GHOST

All believers are entitled to and should ardently expect and earnestly seek the promise of the Father, the baptism in the Holy Ghost and fire, according to the command of our Lord Jesus Christ. This was the normal experience of all in the early Christian Church. With it comes the enduement of power for life and service, the bestowment of the gifts and their uses in the work of the ministry (Luke 24:49; Acts 1:4,8; 1 Cor 12:1-31). This experience is distinct from and subsequent to the experience of the new birth (Acts 8:12-17; 10:44-46; 11:14-16; 15:7-9). With the baptism in the Holy Ghost come such experience as an overflowing fullness of the Spirit (John 7:37-39; Acts 4:8), a deepened reverence for God (Acts 2:43; Heb 12:28), an intensified consecration to God and dedication to His work (Acts 2:42), and a more active love for Christ, for His word, and for the lost (Mark 16:20).

(8) THE EVIDENCE OF THE BAPTISM OF THE HOLY GHOST

The baptism of believers in the Holy Ghost is witnessed by the initial physical sign of speaking with other tongues as the Spirit of God gives them utterance (Acts 2:4). The speaking in tongues in this instance is the same in essence as the gift of tongues (1 Cor 12:4-10,28) but different in purpose and use (Menzies 1971,388).

3. Such controversy within the Movement was settled in the General Council of 1918 (Menzies 1971,129). Menzies states concerning this distinctive, "Many other evangelicals have accepted the concept of a filling with the Holy Spirit as an experience subsequent to conversion, but the Pentecostal touchstone has always been on the definition of the evidence" (1971,125).

4. Statement of Fundamental Truths, 1959, essentially the same doctrinal statement but missing the elaboration of "other" signs of the Spirit-filled life in the current up-dated statement.

5. See note 2. Why does Bruner arbitrarily separate "earnestly seek" from "entitled to" and "ardently expect" in the same sentence?

6. Dunn adds in qualifying his previous statement: "In one sense, therefore, Pentecost can never be repeated—for the new age is here and cannot be unshered in again. But in another sense Pentecost, or rather the *experience of Pentecost*, can and must be repeated in the experience of all who would become Christians. As the day of Pentecost was once the doorway into the new age, so entry into the new age can only be made through that doorway, that is, through receiving the same Spirit and the same baptism in the Spirit as did the 120" (1970,53-54; italics mine). Although Dunn means by this statement that each Christian today does experience

"Pentecost" at conversion, in that he or she is initiated into the same Spirit, the Pentecostal would find no fault with the above statement if it referred to the distinct, charismatic, dynamic repeatable Pentecostal experience of Acts 2:4.

7. In view of the sometimes crude and theologically inaccurate Pentecostal use and interpretation of Jesus' baptism, to support a "subsequent" experience (as though prior to that time Jesus did not experience the fulness of the Spirit!) Dunn's emphasis is helpful. He states, "The descent of the Spirit on Jesus effects not so much a change in Jesus, his person or his status, as the beginning of a new stage in salvation-history. The thought is not so much of Jesus becoming what he was not before, but of Jesus entering where he was not before—a new epoch in God's plan of redemption. . . . It is not so much that Jesus became what he was not before, but that history became what it was not before . . . " (1970,28-29).

8. Of course, the Pentecostal experience thus conceived does not involve a "quantitative" reception of "more" of the Spirit (this is only possible figuratively speaking, not theologically speaking). Rather it represents a qualitatively different relationship with the Spirit, and it should be viewed as the Spirit getting more of the Christian, not vice versa. The emphasis is on the Spirit's control of the believer, due to his new awareness, openness, and expectancy.

9. Peters states, "No aspect of the Timor revival has received more attention and wider publicity than the miracles that are supposed to have accompanied it. Such interest may be the result of massive publicity, but in general it seems to me that this unusual attention to the miraculous indicates that American Christians are so destitute of spiritual reality that they look for the spectacular to substantiate and bolster their own faith in the truth of the Gospel. The faith of the average Christian is evidently so bankrupt, and his life so empty, that he needs this kind of demonstration" (1973,57). Peters's position on present-day miracles is that they are a *possibility,* but not necessary, nor probable (1973,50-60,62). This position is maintained throughout the debunking of the Timor revival. The position is maintained in spite of his acknowledgement that there is no conclusive New Testament exegetical evidence that would preclude such supernatural manifestations. Nor, he states, would any New Testament truth be violated if all the miracles of the Book of Acts were to be repeated today (Peters 1973,58,60).

10. As in Bruner's argument, the issue boils down to the objection of any evidence for Christian experience beyond the written Word. The outward ministry of the Holy Spirit is admitted as a "possibility," but not a "necessity," nor even a "probability" today. This "domestication of the Spirit" is not absolute, however, as Peters mentions an exception to this dispensational rule. The exception would be when the gospel is introduced to a people for

the first time, pioneer situations in missions (Peters 1973,60). Another exception would be to counteract the "magical miracles" of an animistic people (Peters 1973,71). In view of the thousands of "unreached people groups" among the two and one half billion who are powerfully and pervasively influenced by Animism today, these "exceptions" appear to address the task of evangelism among the majority of the non-Christian world! According to Peters's own argument supernatural phenomena would not be the exception but the contemporary rule.

11. Jack Rogers states about Calvin, "Calvin strove for the Augustinian middle way of the church. He fought against two extremes. He rejected the rationalistic Scholasticism on the one side which demanded proofs prior to faith in Scripture. He rejected with equal firmness the spiritualistic sectarians on the other side who claimed leadings of the Spirit apart from the Scripture. For Calvin, 'Word and Spirit belong inseparable together'" (1977,27).

12. Calvin stated, "The highest proof of Scripture derives in general from the fact that God in person speaks in it . . . we ought to seek our conviction in a higher place than human reasons, judgements, or conjectures, that is in the secret testimony of the Spirit . . . the testimony of the Spirit is more excellent than all reason" (Inst. I, vii.,4).

13. Calvin stated about the self-authenticating nature of Scripture: "Let this point therefore stand: that those whom the Holy Spirit has inwardly taught truly rest upon Scripture, and that Scripture indeed is self-authenticated; hence, it is not right to subject it to proof and reasoning. And the certainty it deserves with us, it attains by the testimony of the Spirit. For even if it wins reverence for itself by its own majesty, it seriously affects us only when it is sealed upon our hearts through the Spirit. Therefore, illumined by his power, we believe neither by our own nor by anyone else's judgment that Scripture is from God; but above human judgment we affirm with utter certainty . . . that it has flowed to us from the very mouth of God by the ministry of men" (Inst. I, vii.,5).

14. Donald Gee states that Luke's explanation following the outpouring at Cornelius' house ("For they heard them speaking in tongues and praising God" Acts 10:46) "is so emphatic that it approaches a definite statement of the doctrine" concerning tongues (Gee 1949,3). Hurst also states about this evidence at Cornelius' house, "The root evidence supporting all action and conclusions was 'tongues.' The Holy Spirit was poured out, water could not be forbidden, and repentance was available to the Gentiles—all based on *the* evidence" (1968,27; italics mine).

15. Ranaghan states, "The gift of tongues is not the baptism of the Holy Spirit. Rather it is a consequence, normally the first

consequence, of receiving the baptism of the Holy Spirit" (1969,220).

16. See 1 John 2:18-23; 4:1-3; 2 Cor 12:9 and 1 Cor 14.

Chapter 5 The Pentecostal and Mission Strategy

1. In a summary of his book, *How Biblical is the Church Growth Movement*, J. Robertson McQuilkin asks: "Is Church Growth thinking biblical thinking? Yes, it is. This is not to say that all the people associated with Church Growth think biblically in all applications and interpretations of the principles. But the underlying presuppositions of the Church Growth Movement rest on a solid theological foundation grounded in the Word of God" (1973,62). The charge of pragmatism, then, is specifically related to the alleged improper theological base and improper biblical methodology.

2. In a statement which echos the church growth strategy of Donald McGavran, Melvin L. Hodges states, "Whatever other good things the church may do, its success in promoting the Kingdom of God must be measured by the number of people it can bring into vital relationship with Christ and the number of local units of the Body of Christ that it can produce" (1977a,144).

3. Hodges states, "The Pentecostal's deep conviction that the guidance of the Holy Spirit must be sought for each situation makes for flexibility and insures variety in method" (1977a,146).

4. At the beginning of his article, "A Pentecostal's View of Mission Strategy," Hodges states, "Pentecostals have roots imbedded in *The Book*. They strive constantly to follow the New Testament in every aspect of faith and practice. If follows that Pentecostal missiology should be based on biblical doctrine, experience and methodology" (1977a,142).

5. Many terms and phrases are used as synonyms for "strategy" or at least are used in a definitive way to describe the concept of mission strategy. Some representative terms in missiological literature are: "the missionary approach" (Bavinck 1960,79); "philosophy," "management theory," "planning," "pragmatism," "discovering God's strategy," and "incarnating the norms of the Bible" (Dayton and Frazer 1980,26,38,49,270,297-298, 365,443); biblical "paradigms for mission" (Shenk 1980,160); "practical missiology" (Anderson 1961,133); "the contextualization of the gospel" (Stott and Coote 1980,77-78); "mission theory" (Conn 1976,ii); "theology of mission," and "practice of mission" (Bosch 1975,1,3). The terms used to define the concept cover both activities prior to, and during the engagement in mission. The context in which the various terms are used infers a biblical hermeneutic. But often it is not articulated. Some of the terms connote a biblical hermeneutic; others are purely secular, signifying

nothing concerning the role of Scripture in the activity. The problem of pragmatism rests in the latter usage.

6. See Dayton and Frazer 1980,7,263,266-267,270-271,294-298, 344,365.

7. Bosch states further, "The practice of mission continually needs the critical orientation provided by the theology of mission. While theology of mission, in turn, is dependent upon practice without, however, exalting the utilitarian aspect, or 'effectiveness,' to the status of the highest norm (as expressed in the statement: 'It works, therefore it's good'!)" (1975,3).

8. Kraemer explains, "With this tendency I heartily disagree. To me a 'theological problem,' if really of fundamental significance, is an eminently *practical* affair demanding new *decisions* and followed by new *action*" (1961,180).

9. Kraemer states, "One more article on syncretism as a theological problem for missions will not cause the least change, because theology and spiritual strategy are usually kept neatly separate" (1961,182).

10. Why bother with the term "pragmatism?" When modified with "biblical," its careful use would be a corrective to the imbalance caused in theological thinking by scholastic-oriented theology. It emphasizes the chief difficulty with the scholastic orientation—its static, theoretical, and reductionistic nature. This static, theoretically-oriented theology militates against the second hermeneutical task, which deals with the application of biblical truth in practical situations. Such a view of theology tends to fail to see mission strategy as theological activity and, therefore, distances that activity from its authoritative source—Scripture. With theology "on the book shelf," often a pragmatism results in which a philosophical theory from the social sciences controls mission activity and thought. Scripture, therefore, plays a secondary role. In addition to the term's corrective purpose, it has positive connotations which illustrate the true nature of mission strategy. Mission strategy is not only guided by the Word, but it is also guided by the Spirit himself. In this sense, one may speak of a "pragmatism which is Spirit-directed and Spirit-filled" (Conn 1976,84).

11. This view of the influence of the above theologians is also supported by Jack Rogers and Donald McKim in their book, *The Authority and Interpretation of the Bible* (1979), an historical study of the doctrine of Scripture.

12. Ramm states, "As in all instances of revelation and inspiration there is the accompanying inward work of the Holy Spirit—an insight we owe to Calvin's exploration of the witness of the Holy Spirit as not only a feature of individual salvation but *as*

accompanying the giving of special revelation" (1961,44; italics mine).

13. Ramm especially focuses on the *preaching of the gospel* as the Word of God (1961,116,118,149). He states, "So in the preaching of the gospel out of the pages of the New Testament the modality of the incarnation as special revelation is continued; and when men believe this witness by responding to it with saving faith, then Christ comes also to the heart" (1961,116).

14. Kraft states, *"In keeping with this emphasis of western culture* [the western high value on information], *we have both accepted the informationalizing of revelation and often lost our ability to imagine that it could be anything else"* (1979,179).

Chapter 6 The Pentecostal and Contemporary Mission Issues

1. Some of those participants at the Third Assembly of the WCC at New Delhi in 1961 recognized the danger of a theological methodology which started from the context of mission. Bassham states that some of the participants saw a "basic methodological difficulty . . . in this way of approaching mission theology" (1979,68). Bassham states further that they thought the idea of participating in God's mission in the world "ran too much risk of breaking away from the necessary controls (theological, liturgical, canonical) that the Church has painfully developed in the course of its history...The method of searching for God's presence in contemporary situations runs the danger of assuming a 'second source of revelation' (in 'the world') uncontrolled by the theological criteria provided by the given revelation in Christ" (1979,68-69).

2. The WCC study report on the missionary structure of the congregation, "The Church for Others," reveals this reductionistic view of mission: "We have lifted up humanization as the goal of mission because we believe that more than other positions it communicates in our period of history the meaning of the messianic goal. In another time the goal of God's redemptive work might best have been described in terms of man turning towards God . . . the fundamental question was that of the true God, and the Church responded to that question by pointing to Him. It was assuming that the purpose of mission was Christianization, bringing man to God through Christ and His Church. Today the fundamental question is much more that of true man, and the dominant concern of the missionary congregation must therefore be to point to the humanity in Christ as the goal of mission . . . "(Hoekstra 1979,69). The statement above does not focus on an attempt toward understanding mission in its holistic sense, evangelism and humanization; it represents an effort of reducing mission to only humanization today.

3. Rosin states that Vicedom must have obtained the Latin term from Karl Hartenstein's conference report in *Mission zwischen Gestern und Morgan*, because the phrase does not occur in the printed Willingen documents, only the idea (1972,6).

4. Rosin states that consideration of the thought, "God has a mission," does not take away from the sovereignty of God, "God himself—in Christ, through the Holy Spirit, with the participation of the Church—is totally engaged and involved in a world where he rules in 'judgment and redemption' " (1972,18).

5. John V. Taylor somewhat prophetically noted the danger in the misuse of *missio Dei* when he stated, "There is a real danger lest the blanket phrase *missio Dei*, which is meant to establish the divine initiative is used so vaguely that it includes the whole action of God throughout time and space, as though, if he chose, God might have accomplished the renewal of man without Jesus Christ" (Rosin 1972,34).

6. Rosin mentions that this "illusion" is the case with conciliar discussions on mission, and he says this in terms of the problematic activity of God in mission. He states concerning the CWME conference at Mexico City: "The discussion raised a theological issue which remained unresolved. Debate returned again and again to the relationship between God's action in and through the Church and everything God is doing in the world apparently independently of the Christian community. Can a distinction be drawn between God's *providential action* and God's *redeeming action*? If the restoration and reconcilliation [*sic*] of human life is being achieved by the action of God through secular agencies, what is the place and significance of faith? If the Church is to be wholly involved in the world and its history what is the true nature of its separateness?" (1972,26; italics mine).

Chapter 7 The Pentecostal and the Kingdom of God

1. Various terms are used for the Kingdom: "God's rule and reign," "a dynamic power at work," "the nature of God's present activity," "God's redemptive working in history," "God's supernatural breaking into history in the person of Jesus," "a new realm of blessing foretold by the prophets," Jesus himself or His words, and the messengers of the gospel themselves (Ladd 1974,139,142,167-168,171-172,189,204-205,256).

2. The pneumatological hiatus is conspicuous when Ladd treats "The Ethics of the Kingdom" in chapter 12. The subjects of righteousness apart from Law, the ethical demands of the reign of God, sanctification, and the inner spiritual life and renewal are treated under the Kingdom theme without even mentioning the enablement of the Holy Spirit. The third person of the Trinity

appears to be intentionally avoided in his book when he deals with biblical texts articulating the ministry of the Holy Spirit (Ladd 1974,298). Is this an example of a latent christomonism in evangelical theology?

3. Acts 1:3,6-8; 8:12; 14:22; 19:8; 20:24-25; 28:23,31.

4. Montague states, "What is important [in the Acts 1:1-8 passage] is the present world mission of the church impelled by the Holy Spirit. . . . In Acts the fact that the Kingdom has begun is manifested on earth by the activity of the Spirit" (1976,273).

5. Boer states further, "If we ask, what is the 'meaning' of the Spirit, we must answer: it consists in this that he is the Gift of speaking about the mighty acts of God" (1961,103). Boer refers to Peter's quotation of Joel's prophecy in his sermon to indicate what this gift of speaking means for the church, "This is what was spoken by the prophet Joel: 'In the last days God says, I will pour out my Spirit on all people. Your sons and daughters will *prophesy* . . .'" (Acts 2:16-17; italics mine).

6. Boer states concerning these two forms of witness: "The difference between the two types of speaking can perhaps best be so described: *The speaking with other tongues dramatically demonstrated the witnessing character of the Church; Peter's sermon set the pattern through which that witnessing character finds normal and continuing expression* (1961,103).

7. Following the summary description of the primitive church in Acts 2:42-47 (where both *A* and *B* signs are mentioned), Montague notes that Luke's first recorded event is the healing of the cripple at the beautiful gate (Acts 3:1-10). He states concerning this event: "This cure is important not only in that it gives Peter another opportunity to preach Jesus Christ (3:11-26) but also because it is a sign typical of the messianic age (Isa 35:3,6) and moreover typical of the new life of the resurrection already experienced here and now (4:2). Significantly, though the Holy Spirit is not expressly mentioned in the Speech, Jesus is portrayed as the prophet raised up and acting through the apostles (3:22,26). The man is healed *in the name of Jesus Christ* (3:6,16). It seems to be a consistent pattern for the Acts that while the charismatic gifts of tongues and prophecy are attributed to the Holy Spirit . . . cures and exorcisms are attributed to the name of Jesus . . . " (1976,289).

8. At the Melbourne meeting of the World Council of Churches' CWME, Joaquim Beato stated: "Pentecostalism today is, without any doubt, the most dynamic Protestant group, and it has experienced such growth. In spite of signs of 'aging' in some of their groups, it is the only group with close ties with the poor and the working classes, and it is the one which has absorbed the cultural characteristics of the lower classes. It does not seem to me, however, that this fact is considered by the Pentecostals as of value

in itself, nor that it is the result of a conscious strategy" (1980,95).

9. Only a view of the poor as synonymous with the true, elect people of God, in an extreme calvinistic sense, would avoid the absurdity (See Ridderbos 1962,192). But even that view emphasizes the spiritual nature of the relationship between God and His people, "The special relation to God that was first applied to the totality of Israel is now restricted (and extended) to those who respond to the preaching of the Kingdom with faith and repentance..." (Ridderbos 1962,198).

10. The crucial passages concerning the poor in the New Testament are linked with the Kingdom theme. The Luke 4:18-19 passage quoted above is somewhat typical in that it contains the characteristic twofold sign of the Kingdom in the new age: the preaching of the gospel and the charismatic signs of the Spirit. The parallel passage in Matthew 4:12-17 and the reference in Luke 4:43 specifically mention the preaching of the "good news of the kingdom of God." The mention of the poor at the beginning of the ministry of Jesus in the Synoptic Gospels comes at a crucial point in salvation history. The reference to "the poor" as the recipients of the gospel is a sign of the messianic age, because it refers to the universalization of salvation in the new age (Luke 7:22; cf. Matt 11:11-13).

11. Luke 14 is instructive for telling the difference between "socioeconomic poor" references and "salvation history poor" references." In Luke 14:1-14, the socioeconomic poor as an economic class are in view (14:13). But even in this case Jesus uses the poor to illustrate the importance of humility in the kingdom of God (14:7-11). The passage, however, is a clear reference to the Christian duty to the socioeconomic poor. But the second reference to the poor in Luke 14:15-24 is entirely different in its thrust and meaning. The parable of the Great Banquet in the second passage refers to the "salvation history poor." It is occasioned by the statement, "Blessed is the man who will eat at the feast in the kingdom of God" (14:15). The reference to the poor here is connected with the kingdom of God. The point of the parable is not the socioeconomic status of those who finally attend the banquet. Rather, it is that *the poor respond to the invitation*, others who were invited did not respond (Luke 14:21-24). The opening up of the banquet to all, regardless of class, is emphasized (14:23). The parable is like the parable of the vineyard and the tenants (Mark 12:1-11) in that it alludes to the general Jewish rejection of the Kingdom which is the occasion of offering the Kingdom to the Gentiles. The parable illustrates the universalization of the gospel and the responsiveness of the poor.

12. Also the Pharisees are contrasted with the common people in Luke. The common people were responsive to the gospel, but the

Pharisees and experts of the Law were typical of Israel's rejection of the Kingdom: "I tell you, among those born of women there is no one greater than John; yet the one who is least in the kingdom of God is greater than he. (All the people, even the tax collectors, when they heard Jesus' words, acknowledged that God's way was right, because they had been baptized by John. But the Pharisees and experts in the law rejected God's purpose for themselves, because they had not been baptized by John)" (Luke 7:28-30). The salvation history transition is evident in the above passage, as well as the "principle of the poor"—the necessity of repentance and faith. The Pharisees are also consistently condemned because of their suppression of the knowledge of God, for being obstacles in the widening of God's purpose to the "common man" (Luke 11:37-52; 14:1-14; 20:45-47).

13. Speaking of the Cappadocians Bray states: "To them it was clear that the work of each person was the common work of all three, without however detracting from the specific aspects attributed to each one. Thus, it was the Son, not the Father nor the Spirit, who suffered in a human body on the cross . . . and the Spirit not the Father nor the Son who descended on the Apostles at Pentecost . . . the fullness of God was present and active in both great typical works in a way which the human mind can perceive yet never fully understand" (1980,58).

14. In their rejection of "church-centrism," conciliar theologies state that God is not primarily related to the world by means of the church. Rather, they state that God's primary relationship is to the world; it is the focus of God's plan (Hoekstra 1979,75). The Church is only instrumental in God's plan; it is defined as function not essence. It is this view, that the church is not in essence any different from the world, to which the Frankfurt Declaration addressed itself, "*We therefore oppose* the view that the church, as the fellowship of Jesus, is simply a part of the world. The contrast between the church and the world is not merely a distinction in function and in knowledge of salvation; rather, it is an essential difference in nature" (McGavran 1972,291).

15. Jenkins expresses this radically different view of *missio Dei* by saying, "The mission is the actvity of God, not the conversion of men to belief or the recruiting of men to the ranks of the saved . . . but the living out in the world of the life of God which is the life of love and in which the church lives" (Johnston 1978,88).

16. This missionary role of the Spirit can be observed elsewhere in the New Testament (especially in the "trinitarian" passages concerning the divine Paraclete: John 14:16,26; 15:26; 16:7; and chapter 17). But the story of the new creation of the Spirit, the church, and its mission in the first century is central in revealing the

continuing role of the Spirit. Allen speaks of the cruciality of the Acts in this regard: "In the Acts it [the missionary role of the Spirit] is the one prominent feature. It is asserted, it is taken for granted, from the first page to the last . . . it is necessary to any true apprehension of the Holy Spirit and his work that we should understand it and realize it . . . if we ignore it . . . we lose sight of the perfection of the Spirit. Our view is necessarily one-sided, our understanding of the past is robbed of its true foundations, *our conception of our present duty is incomplete*, and our hope for the future is rendered doubtful and indistinct" (1960,21; italics mine).

17. The Holy Spirit is also Lord (2 Cor 3:17). As initiator, motivator, and superintendent of mission He is the Lord of the Harvest (Matt 9:37-38). The word "harvest" is often used in the Bible to express spiritual readiness (John 4:35; Matt 9:37-38). Making men and women ready to receive the gospel is the work of the Spirit (John 16:8). Sending laborers into the harvest is also the work of the Spirit (Acts 13:2,4; Matt 9:38). The Holy Spirit is the inner motivation and dynamic of the church's mission. It is His harvest, He is its Lord. This missionary role of the Spirit is clearest in the Acts where we read of His motivating, empowering, and supervising the mission of the early church (Acts 8:29; 13:2,4; 15:28; 16:6,7,10; 20:28).

18. "When the Counselor [Paraclete] comes, whom I will send to you from the Father, the Spirit of truth who goes out from the Father, he will testify about me . . . " (John 15:26).

19. Oscar Cullmann explains the theological context of the universalizing ministry of the Spirit in terms of salvation history. He sees God's redemptive focus to be contracting and expanding in salvation history according to the principle of election and representation. God begins the redemptive purpose in creation and it expands to mankind, contracts to Abram, expands to Israel, contracts to the remnant, and finally contracts to the faithful Servant of the Lord—Messiah. Christ's Incarnation is the midpoint of salvation history. From the midpoint there is an expanding movement in the redemptive purpose of God. The previous movement from creation to midpoint (creation—mankind—Israel —remnant—Messiah) is primarily conceived as a *contracting* movement in salvation history. On the other side of the midpoint, (Messiah—apostles—church—mankind) there is an *expanding* movement in salvation history. Christ is the midpoint of a "bow tie-like" progression in the movement of salvation history (Cullmann 1964,78). It is in this expanding movement of salvation history, in the Age of the Spirit, that the Holy Spirit has a prominent role and work. A chief work of the Spirit in "the time between the times" is the universal witness of the gospel.

20. However, beyond the Acts the Epistles also show the Holy Spirit to be the agent who universalizes mission. The Spirit has a primary role in accomplishing what Paul speaks of as the "mystery," the eschatological union of Christ with Israel and the Gentiles in His Body, the universal church (Rom 11:25,26; 16:25,26; Eph 1:9,10; 1:3-6,8-11; 5:32; Col 1:26-27; 1 Tim 3:16). The mystery is spoken of in eschatological and universal terms. The concept of mystery has three emphases which condition it in nearly all of its expressions: its eschatological setting, its Christ-centeredness, and its universalistic reference (Boer 1961,153). Pentecost is of significance for the "mystery" because through the Spirit's work all are baptized into one Body, whether Jew or Greek (1 Cor 12:13; Eph 2:18,22). At Pentecost the revelation of the mystery first took place. The Spirit reveals this mystery to God's apostles, prophets, and saints (Eph 3:5; Col 1:26), and enables them to proclaim it (Eph 3:8-9; 6:19; Col 1:29; 4:3).

BIBLIOGRAPHY

Books

ALLEN, Roland
    1960 *The Ministry of the Spirit*. Grand Rapids, Wm. B.
    Eerdmans Publishing Company.

ANDERSEN, Wilhelm
    1955 *Towards a Theology of Mission: A Study of the*
    Encounter between the Missionary Enterprise and the Church
    and Its Theology. London, SCM Press.

ANDERSON, Gerald H., ed.
    1961 *The Theology of the Christian Mission*. London, SCM
    Press LTD.

ATTER, Gordon
    1962 *The Third Force*. Peterborough, The College Press.

BARR, James
    1978 *Fundamentalism*. Philadelphia, The Westminster Press.

BARRETT, David B.
    1968 *Schism and Renewal in Africa*. Nairobi, Oxford
    University Press.

BARTLEMAN, Frank
    1980 *Azusa Street*. Plainfield, Logos International.

BASSHAM, Roger C.
    1979 *Mission Theology 1948-1975 Years of Worldwide*
    Creative Tension Ecumenical, Evangelical, and Roman
    Catholic. Pasadena, William Carey Library.

BAVINCK, J.H.
    1960 *Introduction to the Science of Missions*. Grand Rapids,
    Baker Book House.

BERKOUWER, G.C.
    1952 *The Providence of God: Studies in Dogmatics*. Grand
    Rapids, Wm. B. Eerdmans Publishing Company.
    1975 *Holy Scripture: Studies in Dogmatics*. Grand Rapids,

Wm. B. Eerdmans Publishing Company.

1977 *A Half Century of Theology: Movements and Motives.*
Grand Rapids, Wm. B. Eerdmans Publishing Company.

BLAUW, Johannes
1962 *The Missionary Nature of the Church: A Survey of the Biblical Theology of Mission.* London, McGraw-Hill Book Company, Inc.

BLOCH-HOELL, Nils
1964 *The Pentecostal Movement: Its Origin Development and Distinctive Character.* Oslo, Universitetforlaget.

BLOESCH, D.G.
1973 *The Evangelical Renaissance.* Grand Rapids, Wm. B. Eerdmans Publishing Company.

BOER, Harry
1961 *Pentecost and Missions.* Grand Rapids, Wm. B. Eerdmans Publishing Company.

BOSCH, David J.
1975 *Theology of Mission: Missiology and Science of Religion (B.Th).* Pretoria, University of South Africa.
1980 *Witness to the World: The Christian Mission in Theological Perspective.* London, Marshall, Morgan & Scott.

BRAY, Gerald Lewis
1980 "The Patristic Dogma," in *One God in Trinity*, eds. Peter Toon and James D. Spiceland. Westchester, Cornerstone Books.

BRIGHT, John
1953 *The Kingdom of God: The Biblical Concept and Its Meaning for the Church.* New York, Abingdon Press.

BROMILEY, Geoffrey
1958 "Church Doctrine of Inspiration," in *Revelation and the Bible*, ed. Carl F.H. Henry. Grand Rapids, Baker Book House.

BRUMBACK, Carl
1961 *Suddenly . . . From Heaven: A History of the Assemblies of God.* Springfield, Gospel Publishing House.

BRUNER, Frederick Dale
1970 *A Theology of the Holy Spirit: The Pentecostal Experience and the New Testament Witness.* Grand Rapids, Wm. B. Eerdmans Publishing Company.

CHRISTENSON, Larry
1975 "Pentecostalism's Forgotten Forerunner," in *Aspects of Pentecostal-Charismatic Origins*, ed. Vinson Synan. Plainfield, Logos.

CONN, Harvie M., ed.
1976 *Theological Perspectives on Church Growth.* Nutley,

Presbyterian and Reformed Publishing Co.

CULLMANN, Oscar

1964 *Christ and Time: The Primitive Christian Conception of Time and History.* Translated from the German by Floyd V. Filson. Philadelphia, The Westminster Press.

CWME

1980 "Section Reports," in *Your Kingdom Come: Missions Perspectives Report on the World Conference on Mission and Evangelism, Melbourne, Australia 12-25 May 1980.* Geneva, CWME WCC.

DAYTON, Donald W.

1976 *Discovering the Evangelical Heritage.* Grand Rapids, Wm. B. Eerdmans Publishing Company.

DAYTON, Edward R., and FRASER, David A.

1980 *Planning Strategies for World Evangelization.* Grand Rapids, Wm. B. Eerdmans Publishing Company.

DUNN, J.D.G.

1970 *Baptism in the Holy Spirit.* London, SCM Press.

FAUPEL, David W.

1972 *The American Pentecostal Movement: A Bibliographical Essay.* Franklin Springs, The Society for Pentecostal Studies.

FEE, Gordon

1976 "Hermeneutics and Historical Precedent—A Major Problem in Pentecostal Hermeneutics," in *Perspectives on the New Pentecostalism,* ed. Russell P. Spittler. Grand Rapids, Baker Book House.

FILSON, Floyd

1950 *The New Testament Against Its Environment.* London, SCM Press LTD.

FRODSHAM, Stanley H.

1946 *With Signs Following: The Story of the Pentecostal Revival in the Twentieth Century.* Springfield, Gospel Publishing House.

GAUSE, R. Hollis

1976 "Issues in Pentecostalism," in *Perspectives on the New Pentecostalism,* ed. Russell P. Spittler. Grand Rapids, Baker Book House.

GAXIOLA, J.

1970 *La Serpiente Y La Paloma.* Pasadena, William Carey Library.

GEE, Donald

1949 *The Pentecostal Movement.* London, Elim Publishing Company.

GORDON, A.J.

1964 *The Ministry of the Spirit*. Minneapolis, Bethany Fellowship Inc.

GRASSI, Joseph

1978 *The Secret of the Apostle Paul*. New York, Orbis Books.

GREEN, Michael

1975 *I Believe in the Holy Spirit*. Grand Rapids, Wm. B. Eerdmans Publishing Company.

GREENWAY, Roger S.

1976 "Winnable People," in *Theological Perspectives on Church Growth*, ed. Harvie M. Conn, Nutley, Presbyterian and Reformed Publishing Company.

HESSELGRAVE, David J.

1978 *Dynamic Religious Movements: Case Studies of Rapidly Growing Religious Movements Around the World*. Grand Rapids, Baker Book House.

HESSELGRAVE, David J., ed.

1978a *Theology and Mission: Papers Given at Trinity Consultation No.1*. Grand Rapids, Baker Book House.

HODGES, Melvin L.

1957 *Build My Church*. Springfield, Gospel Publishing House.

1977 *A Theology of the Church and Its Mission*. Springfield, Gospel Publishing House.

1977a "A Pentecostal's View of Mission Strategy," in *The Conciliar-Evangelical Debate: The Crucial Documents 1964-1976*, ed. Donald McGavran. South Pasadena, William Carey Library.

HOEKENDIJK, J.C.

1977 "The Call to Evangelism," in *The Conciliar-Evangelical Debate: The Crucial Documents 1964-1976*, ed. Donald McGavran. South Pasadena, William Carey Library.

HOEKSTRA, Harvey T.

1979 *The World Council of Churches and the Demise of Evangelism*. Wheaton, Tyndale House Publications, Inc.

HOLLENWEGER, W.J.

1972 *The Pentecostals: The Charismatic Movement in the Churches*. Minneapolis, Augsburg.

HOLY BIBLE

New International Version. Grand Rapids, Zondervan Bible Publishers. 1978.

HORTON, Robin

1979 "Ritual Man in Africa," in *Reader in Comparative Religion*, eds. William A. Lessa and Evon Z. Vogt. New York, Harper & Row Publishers.

HUMMEL, Charles E.
1978 *Fire in the Fireplace: Contemporary Charismatic Renewal*. Downers Grove, InterVarsity Press.

INCH, Morris A.
1978 *The Evangelical Challenge*. Philadelphia, The Westminster Press.

JOHNSTON, Arthur P.
1978 *The Battle for World Evangelism*. Wheaton, Tyndale House Publishers, Inc.

KÄSEMANN, Ernst
1980 "The Eschatological Royal Reign of God," in *Your Kingdom Come: Missions Perspectives Report on the World Conference on Mission and Evangelism, Melbourne, Australia 12-25 May 1980*, Geneva, CWME WCC.

KANE, J. Herbert
1974 *Christian Missions in Biblical Perspective*. Grand Rapids, Baker Book House.
1981 *The Christian World Mission: Today and Tomorrow*. Grand Rapids, Baker Book House.

KAUFFMANN, Yehezkel
1972 *The Religion of Israel*. New York, Schocken Books.

KRAEMER, Hendrik
1961 "Syncretism as a Theological Problem for Missions," in *The Theology of the Christian Mission*, ed. Gerald H. Anderson. London, SCM Press LTD.

KRAFT, Charles H.
1979 *Christianity in Culture: A Study in Dynamic Biblical Theologizing in Cross-Cultural Perspective*. Maryknoll, Orbis Books.

LADD, George Eldon
1974 *The Presence of the Future: The Eschatology of Biblical Realism*. Grand Rapids, Wm. B. Eerdmans Publishing Company.

LATOURETTE, Kenneth Scott
1967 *A History of the Expansion of Christianity: Three Centuries of Advance Vol. 3*. Grand Rapids, Zondervan Publishing Company.

LINDSELL, Harold
1949 *An Evangelical Theology of Mission*. Grand Rapids, Zondervan Publishing House.

LINTON, Ralph
1979 "Nativistic Movements," in *Reader in Comparative Religion: An Anthropological Approach*, eds. William A. Lessa and Evon Z. Vogt. New York, Harper & Row Publishers.

MacDONALD, William G.
1964 *Glossolalia in the New Testament*. Springfield, Gospel Publishing House.

McDONNELL, Kilian
1976 "Classical Pentecostal/Roman Catholic Dialogue: Hopes and Possibilities," in *Perspectives on the New Pentecostalism*, ed. Russell P. Spittler. Grand Rapids, Baker Book House.
1980 *Presence, Power, Praise: Documents on the Charismatic Renewal, Vol. III*. Collegeville, The Liturgical Press.

McGAVRAN, Donald A., ed.
1977 *The Conciliar-Evangelical Debate: The Crucial Documents 1964-1976*. South Pasadena, William Carey Library.

McGAVRAN, Donald A.; HUEGEL, John; TAYLER, Jack
1963 *Church Growth in Mexico*. Grand Rapids, Wm. B. Eerdmans Publishing Company.

McINTIRE, C.T., ed.
1977 *God, History and Historians: An Anthology of Modern Christian Views of History*. New York, Oxford University Press.

McNEILL, John T., ed.
1960 *Calvin: Institutes of the Christian Religion, Vol. XX*. Translated and Indexed by Ford Lewis Battles, Philadelphia, The Westminster Press.

McQUILKIN, J. Robertson
1973 *How Biblical is the Church Growth Movement?* Chicago, Moody Press.

MARGULL, Hans-Jochen
1960 "The Awakening of Protestant Missions," in *History's Lessons for Tomorrow's Mission: Milestones in the History of Missionary Thinking*. Geneva, World Student Christian Federation.

MARTY, Martin
1975 "Pentecostalism in the Context of American Piety and Practice," in *Aspects of Pentecostal-Charismatic Origins*, ed. Vinson Synan. Plainfield, Logos International.

MENZIES, William W.
1971 *Anointed to Serve: The Story of the Assemblies of God*. Springfield, Gospel Publishing House.
1975 "The Non-Wesleyan Origins of the Pentecostal Movement," in *Aspects of Pentecostal-Charismatic Origins*, ed. Vinson Synan. Plainfield, Logos International.
1979 "The Holy Spirit in Christian Theology," in *Perspec-*

tives in Evangelical Theology, ed. Kenneth Kantzer. Grand Rapids, Baker Book House.

MONTAGUE, George T.
1976 *The Holy Spirit: Growth of a Biblical Tradition*. New York, Paulist Press.

MONTGOMERY, Jim
n.d. (1967) *New Testament Fire in the Philippines*. Manila, FEBC Marshburn Press.

NABABAN, Soritua
1980 "Your Kingdom Come," in *Your Kingdom Come: Missions Perspectives Report on the World Conference on Mission and Evangelism, Melbourne, Australia 12-25 May 1980*, Geneva CWME, WCC.

NEEDLEMAN, Jacob, and BAKER, George, eds.
1978 *Understanding the New Religions*. New York, Seabury Press.

NEILL, Stephen
1964 *A History of Christian Mission*. Middlesex, Hazell Watson & Viney LTD.

NEWBIGIN, Lesslie
1954 *The Household of God*. New York, Friendship Press.

OOSTERWAL, Gottfried
1973 *Modern Messianic Movements*. Elkhart, Institute of Mennonite Studies.

OOSTHUIZEN, G.C.
1968 *Post-Christianity in Africa: A Theological and Anthropological Study*. Grand Rapids, Wm. B. Eerdmans Publishing Company.

PALMER, Donald C.
1974 *Explosion of People Evangelism*. Chicago, Moody Press.

PEEL, J.D.Y.
1968 *Aladura: A Religious Movement Among the Yoruba*. London, Oxford University Press.

PETERS, George W.
1972 *A Biblical Theology of Missions*. Chicago, Moody Press
1973 *Indonesian Revival: Focus on Timor*. Grand Rapids, Zondervan Publishing House.

PIEPKORN, Arthur Carl
1979 *Profiles in Belief: The Religious Bodies of the United States and Canada, Vol. II Holiness and Pentecostal*. San Francisco, Harper & Row, Publishers, Inc.

PINNOCK, Clark H.
1976 "The New Pentecostalism: Reflections of an Evangelical Observer," in *Perspectives on the New Pentecostalism*,

ed. Russell P. Spittler. Grand Rapids, Baker Book House.

QUEBEDEAUX, Richard
1974 *The Young Evangelicals*. New York, Harper & Row Publishers.
1978 *The Worldly Evangelicals*. San Francisco, Harper & Row Publishers.

RAMM, Bernard
1959 *The Witness of the Spirit: An Essay on the Contemporary Relevance of the Internal Witness of the Holy Spirit*. Grand Rapids, Wm. B. Eerdmans Publishing Company.
1961 *Special Revelation and the Word of God*. Grand Rapids, Wm. B. Eerdmans Publishing Company.
1973 *The Evangelical Heritage*. Waco, Word Books, Publishers.
1977 "Is 'Scripture Alone' the Essence of Christianity?" in *Biblical Authority*, ed. Jack Rogers. Waco, Word Books, Publishers.

RANAGHAN, Kevin and Dorthy
1969 *Catholic Pentecostals*. New York, Paulist Press.

READ, William
1965 *New Patterns of Church Growth in Brazil*. Grand Rapids, Wm. B. Eerdmans Publishing Company.

READ, William, MONTERROSO, V.M., and JOHNSON, H.A.
1969 *Latin American Church Growth*. Grand Rapids, Wm. B. Eerdmans Publishing Company.

RIDDERBOS, Herman
1962 *The Coming of the Kingdom*. Philadelphia, Presbyterian and Reformed Publishing Company.

ROGERS, Jack
1966 *Scripture in the Westminster Confession: A Problem of Historical Interpretation for American Presbyterianism*. N.V. Kampen, J. H. Kok.

ROGERS, Jack, ed.
1977 *Biblical Authority*. Waco, Word Books, Publishers.

ROGERS, Jack B., and McKIM, Donald K.
1979 *The Authority and Interpretation of the Bible*. San Francisco, Harper & Row Publishers.

SHENK, Wilbert R., ed.
1980 *Mission Focus: Current Issues*. Scottdale, Herald Press.

SIDER, Ronald J.
1977 *Rich Christians in an Age of Hunger: A Biblical Study*. Downers Grove, Inter-Varsity Press.

SMART, James D.
1979 *The Past, Present and Future of Biblical Theology*. Philadelphia, The Westminster Press.

SMITH, Ebbie C.
1970 *God's Miracles: Indonesian Church Growth*. Pasadena, William Carey Library.

SPICELAND, James D.
1980 "Process Theology," in *One God in Trinity: An analysis of the primary dogma of Christianity*, eds. Peter Toon and James D. Spiceland. Weschester, Cornerstones Books.

STOTT, John R.W., and COOTE, Robert, eds.
1980 *Down to Earth: Studies in Christianity and Culture*. Grand Rapids, Wm. B. Eerdmans Publishing Company.

SUNDKLER, B.G.M.
1961 *Bantu Prophets in South Africa*. London, Oxford University Press.

SYNAN, Vinson
1971 *The Holiness-Pentecostal Movement in the United States*. Grand Rapids, Wm. B. Eerdmans Publishing Company.
1980 "Frank Bartleman and Azusa Street," in *Azusa Street*. Plainfield, Logos International.

TAYLOR, John V.
1969 "Selfhood: Presence or Persona?" in *The Church Crossing Frontiers*, eds. Peter Beyerhaus and Carl F. Hallencrentz. Upsala, Almquist & Wiksells.

THIELICKE, Helmut
1974 *The Evangelical Faith Vol. 1*. Grand Rapids, Wm. B. Eerdmans Publishing Company.

VERKUYL, J.
1978 *Contemporary Missiology: An Introduction*. Grand Rapids, Wm. B. Eerdmans Publishing Company.

VICEDOM, Georg F.
1965 *The Mission of God: An Introduction to a Theology of Mission*. Translated by Gilbert A. Thiele and Dennis Hilgendorf. St. Louis, Concordia Publishing House.

WAGNER, C. Peter
1971 *Frontiers in Missionary Strategy*. Chicago, Moody Press.
1973 *Look Out! The Pentecostals Are Coming*. Carol Stream, Creation House.
1981 *Church Growth and the Whole Gospel: A Biblical Mandate*. San Francisco, Harper & Row, Publishers.

WAGNER, C. Peter, and DAYTON, Edward R., eds.
1978 *Unreached Peoples '79*. Elgin, David C. Cook Publishing Company.

WALLACE, A.F.C.

1979 "Revitalization Movements," in *Reader in Comparative Religion*, eds. William A. Lessa and Evon Z. Vogt. New York, Harper & Row Publishers.
WARREN, Max
1976 *I Believe in the Great Commission*. Grand Rapids, Wm. B. Eerdmans Publishing Company.
WEBBER, Robert, and BLOESCH, Donald eds.
1978 *The Orthodox Evangelicals*. Nashville, Thomas Nelson Inc., Publishers.

Encyclopedias

BARRETT, David B.
1979 "African Christianity," in *Encyclopedic Dictionary of Religion*, eds. Paul Devin Meagher, Thomas C. O'Brien, and Consuelo M. Aherne. Washington D. C., Corpus Publications.
BARRETT, David B., ed.
1982 *World Christian Encyclopedia: A comparative study of churches and religions in the modern world AD 1900-2000*. Nairobi, Oxford University Press.
McCLINTOCK, John Rev. the, and STRONG, James, s.t.d.
1880 *Cyclopedia of Biblical, Theological, and Ecclesiastical Literature Vol. ix-RH-ST*. Grand Rapids, Baker Book House.

Articles

HODGES, Melvin L.
1970 "My Spirit Upon all Flesh." *Paraclete* Vol. 4, No. 4:3-6.
HOLLENWEGER, W.J.
1980 "Charismatic Renewal in the Third World: Implications for Mission." *Occasional Bulletin* Vol. 4, No. 2:68-74.
HURST, D.V.
1968 "The Evidence Points to the Evidence." *Paraclete* Vol. 2, No. 1:22-30.
KANTZER, Kenneth
1980 "The Charismatics Among Us." *Christianity Today* (Feb. 22, 1980) Vol. XXIV., No. 4:24-29.
LOEWEN, Jacob A.
1976 "Mission Churches, Independent Churches, and Felt Needs in Africa." *Missiology* 4:405-525.
MACOMBER, Donald E.
1958 "The Concept of the Kingdom of God in the Preaching

of the Apostles." *Gordon Review* 4:72-76.

MARSHALL, I. Howard
1977 "Preaching the Kingdom of God." *Expository Times* Vol. 89, 1:211-214.

NEWBIGIN, Lesslie
1960 "From 'Mission' to 'Missions.' " *Christianity Today* (Aug. 1, 1960), p. 23.

NIKLAUS, Robert L.
1982 "Brazil: Pentecostal Invasion." *Evangelical Missions Quarterly* Vol. 18, No. 2:117-118.

RECKER, Robert
1977 "The Concept of the *Missio Dei* and Instruction in Mission at Calvin Seminary." *Calvin Theological Journal* Vol. 2, No. 2:181-198.

SENGWE, Ngoni
1981 "Identity Crisis in the African Church." *Evangelical Missions Quarterly* Vol. 17, No. 2:91-99.

SHENK, Wilbert R.
1979 "Church Growth and God's Kingdom." *Mission Focus* Vol. 7, No. 2:21-26.

TURNER, Harold W.
1963 "African Prophet Movements." *Hibbert Journal* Vol. 62, No. 242:122-116.

Van DUSEN, Henry P.
1955 "Caribbean Holiday." *Christian Century* 72 (Aug. 17. 1955), pp. 946-947.
1958 "The Third Force in Christendom." *Life* (9 June 1958), pp. 113-124.

WASDEL, David
1980 "HUP: A Defense Against Anxiety." *Global Church Growth Bulletin* January/February, pp. 1-3.

WOODWARD, Kenneth L.
1982 "The Split-Up Evangelicals." *Newsweek* (April 26, 1982), pp. 88-91.

Unpublished Reports

CHANT, Barry
1981 "Australian Pentecostalism...." Unley, Australia, House of Tabor, no date, pp. 1-3.

DIVISION OF FOREIGN MISSIONS
1981 "Official Statistics Assemblies of God." Springfield, Division of Foreign Missions, pp. 1-8.

PADILLA, C. Rene
1977 "The Unity of the Church and the Homogeneous Unit

Principle.'' Pasadena, Pasadena HUP Consultations, pp. 1-14.

AVERY, Allen Wade Jr.

1969 "African Independency: A Study of the Phenomenon of Independency and the Lessons to be Learned from it for Greater Church Growth in Africa.'' Master's Thesis, School of World Mission Fuller Theological Seminary, Pasadena, California.

BRANNER, John K.

1975 "Roland Allen, Donald McGavran and Church Growth.'' Th.M. Thesis, School of World Mission Fuller Theological Seminary, Pasadena, California.

CONN, Harvie M.

1977 "The Homogeneous Unit Principle: Some Background Perspectives.'' Unpublished manuscript, Westminster Theological Seminary, Philadelphia, Pennsylvania.

HODGES, Melvin L.

1974 "MSS 535 Pentecostal Movement in Missions.'' Unpublished mimeographed class notes, Assemblies of God Graduate School, Springfield, Missouri.

MENZIES, William W.

1978 "A Taxonomy of Pentecostal-Charismatic Theologies.'' Unpublished address given Nov. 30, 1978 at the Annual meeting of the Society for Pentecostal Studies.

POMERVILLE, Paul A.

1980 "A Case Study in the Contextualization of Theology: A Critique of the Reformed View of Scripture in the Post-Reformation Period.'' Master's Thesis, Seattle Pacific University, Seattle, Washington.

ROSIN, H. H.

1972 "'Missio Dei': an examination of the origin, contents and function of the term in Protestant missiological discussion.'' Unpublished paper from the Interuniversitair Instituut voor Missiologie en Oecumenica Afdeling Missiologie, Leiden Nederland.

SANDIDGE, Jerry L.

1976 "The Origin and Development of the Catholic Charismatic Movement in Belgium.'' Unpublished Master's Thesis, Leuven, Katholieke Universiteit te Leuven, Belgie.

WATNEY, Paul

1982 "Positive Missiological Assessment of an African Independent Church.'' Ph.D. dissertation proposal for the School of World Mission Fuller Theological Seminary, Pasadena, California.

Correspondence/Interviews

DURASOFF, Steve
  1982 Missionary Evangelist to Eastern Europe. Correspondence February 18, 1982.
HARRISON, David
  1981 Assemblies of God Missionary to Brazil. Interview, April 25, 1981.
SELEKY, Trinidad E.
  1982 Far East Advanced School of Theology, Manila Philippines. Correspondence March 2, 1982.

INDEX

208